SOCIOLOGICAL STUDIES IN ROMAN CATHOLICISM

Historical and Contemporary Perspectives

SOCIOLOGICAL STUDIES IN ROMAN CATHOLICISM

Historical and Contemporary Perspectives

Edited by:

Roger O'Toole

Studies in Religion and Society
Volume 24
The Edwin Mellen Press
Lewiston/ Lampeter/ Queenston

Library of Congress Cataloging-in-Publication Data

BX
1753
.S635
1989

Sociological studies in Roman Catholicism : historical and
   contemporary perspectives / edited by Roger O'Toole.
      p.   cm. -- (Studies in religion and society ; vol. 24)
      Includes bibliographical references.
      Contents: The evolution of Roman Catholicism in Quebec / Peter
Beyer -- Italian Catholicism / Michael P. Carroll -- Nineteenth
-century Irish Catholicism, farmers' ideology, and national religion
/ Eugene Hynes -- Containing the luciferine spark : the Catholic
Church and recent movements for social change in the Republic of
Ireland / John A. Hannigan -- Refugees from the national myth : the
English Catholic odyssey / Roger O'Toole -- The quandary of dissent
on the Catholic right / William D. Dinges -- Keepers of the faith:
lay militants, abortion, and the battle for Canadian Catholicism /
Michael W. Cuneo -- Liberation theology as social science / W.E.
Hewitt
      ISBN   0-88946-850-8
      1. Sociology, Christian (Catholic)   2. Catholic Church--History.
3. Catholic Church--History--1965-   I. O'Toole, Roger, 1942- .
II.   Series : Studies in religion and society (New York, N.Y.) ;   v.
24.
BX1753.S635   1990
306.6'82--dc20   89-37719
                                                                          CIP

This is volume 24 in the continuing series
Studies in Religion and Society
Volume 24 ISBN 0-88946-850-8
SRS Series ISBN 0-88946-863-X

A CIP catalog record for this book
is available from the British Library.

      The Edwin Mellen Press   The Edwin Mellen Press
            Box 450   Box 67
         Lewiston, NY   Queenston, Ontario
         USA 14092   CANADA L0S 1L0

                        The Edwin Mellen Press, Ltd.
                         Lampeter, Dyfed, Wales,
                        UNITED KINGDOM SA48 7DY

                  Printed in the United States of America

Contents

Contributors

Peter Beyer is Assistant Professor of Religious Studies at St. Michael's College, University of Toronto. His publications include a translation of Niklas Luhmann's *Religious Dogmatics and the Evolution of Societies* and articles on French-Canadian religion in such journals as *Studies in Religion/Sciences Religieuses* and *Sociological Analysis*. He is currently writing a book on religion and globalism.

Michael P. Carroll is Professor of Sociology at the University of Western Ontario. He is the author of *The Cult of the Virgin Mary* and numerous scholarly articles on the topics of myth, religion and popular Catholicism. His second book, which deals with a variety of Catholic devotions, will be published soon.

Michael W. Cuneo is Assistant Professor of Sociology at Fordham University and has just completed a year as Killam Postdoctoral Fellow in the Department of Comparative Religion at Dalhousie University. His articles have appeared in such journals as *Studies in Religion/Sciences Religieuses* and *Pro Mundi Vita*, and he is the editor (together with Anthony J. Blasi) of *Issues in the Sociology of Religion: A Bibliography*. His book *Catholics Against the Church* is scheduled for publication this year.

William D. Dinges is Associate Professor in the Department of Religion and Religious Education at the Catholic University of America. His articles have been published in such journals as *Sociological Analysis*, *America* and *Commonweal*. He is currently engaged in research on a broad range of dissident Catholic movements and is involved in the American Academy of Arts and Science project on Fundamentalism.

John A. Hannigan is Associate Professor of Sociology at the University of Toronto, Scarborough Campus. His articles on social movements have appeared in such journals as *Social Problems*, *Sociological Quarterly* and *Review of Religious Research*. His current research focuses on the relationship between social movement theory and the sociology of religion.

W. E. Hewitt is Assistant Professor of Sociology at the University of Western Ontario, having recently held a similar appointment at the University of Lethbridge. His articles have appeared in such places as *Sociological Analysis, Journal for the Scientific Study of Religion, Journal of Church and State* and *Journal of Latin American Studies.* At present, he is concluding a book on Basic Christian Communities in Brazil.

Eugene Hynes is Associate Professor of Sociology at G.M.I. Engineering and Management Institute. His articles have appeared in journals such as *Sociological Quarterly, Societas* and *Sociological Perspectives.* His current research interests range from world-systems analyses of religion and family to the use of humour in teaching sociology.

Roger O'Toole is Professor in the Department of Sociology and the Centre for Religious Studies at the University of Toronto. He is the author of *The Precipitous Path* and *Religion: Classic Sociological Approaches,* and is a former editor of *Sociological Analysis.* He recently edited *Philosophy, History and Social Action* (with Sidney Hook and William L. O'Neill) and is currently investigating various aspects of Canadian religion.

Introduction

The links between Catholicism and sociology are more complex than might be supposed in the conventional wisdom of their respective practitioners. As a creation of the Enlightenment, sociology is traditionally perceived as party to that subsequent demystification and disruption of the world so immediately and unsparingly anathematized by the papacy. In the increasingly polarized intellectual context of the nineteenth century, Roman Catholicism and scientific sociology faced each other as mortal enemies in a conflict intensified rather than mitigated by the admiration of authoritarian sociologists for the machinery of authoritarian theocracy. If sociology was, as Thomas Huxley maintained, "Catholicism without Christianity," it was a heresy which neither gave nor expected quarter in its war with the Holy See, the forces of unreason, and all defenders of an outmoded social order. The battle lines seemed irrevocably drawn and compromise appeared unthinkable as the warfare between science and theology escalated toward a cataclysmic finale which never occurred.[1]

If the Vatican's facility in forging concordats with its rivals is legendary, so too is the more general genius of the Catholic Church for coexistence with, and co-optation of, its enemies. A wary truce, rooted partly in increasing mutual respect for intellectual boundaries and scholarly jurisdictions led, in the present century, to a growing appreciation of sociology in Catholic circles and its increasing utilization in the interests of the Church. Both in Europe and America, ecclesiastical educators and administrators attuned to the intellectual currents of the age astutely ignored positivistic pedigree and proclaimed the potential benefits of sociological research for an organization struggling to cope with the onslaughts of secularization. Practitioners of "religious sociology" exhibited little difficulty in combining a "value-free" stance in scholarly research with the firmest value-commitment in the employment of their findings. Unashamedly enlisting the theoretical and methodological sophistication of contemporary social science in the service of their sacred cause, they became, intellectually and organizationally, a readily identifiable presence within the sociological world. Focussing attention on Catholic institutions and organizations, primarily in the context of local diocesan or parish communities, their

---

1 See Robert R. Palmer, *Catholics and Unbelievers in Eighteenth-Century France*, Princeton: Princeton University Press, 1939 and Frank Manuel, *The Prophets of Paris*, New York: Basic Books, 1962.

work offered valuable insights into the changing attitudes and behaviour of Catholic clergy and laity in the years preceding and immediately following the Second Vatican Council. It is questionable whether the contribution of "religious sociology" through the detailed documentation of Catholic life in the mid-twentieth century was ever sufficiently appreciated or effectively exploited by those ecclesiastical authorities under whose auspices research was undertaken. Nonetheless, in conducting these investigations Catholic sociologists wrote a distinct chapter in the history of the sociology of religion.[2]

If Catholicism was quick to appreciate the merits of sociology, however, such appreciation was far from mutual. Sociological lack of interest in Catholicism was, in one sense, merely a specific manifestation of a general perception that investigation of religion in the twentieth century represented, at best, a form of research into endangered species and, at worst, a kind of rescue archaeology. If commitment to a vague secularization thesis inspired by the Enlightenment was characteristic of general sociology, the subdisciplinary sociology of religion soon developed a decidedly Protestant focus. From the legacy of Weber and Troeltsch, which stimulated "mainstream" scholarship in this field, emerged a primary preoccupation with matters whose significance lay essentially in the context of Protestant Christianity.[3] It is evident, in retrospect, that much of this work, such as its central concern with the dynamics of sectarianism, had greater relevance for Catholicism than was immediately apparent. Nonetheless, research into Catholicism remained the monopoly of Catholic "religious sociologists" seemingly uninterested in placing the analysis of their religion in a broader sociological setting. Parochial, often in more than one sense of the term, the competent undertakings of "religious sociology" were calculated neither to shake the theoretical or methodological foundations of orthodox sociology nor to imbue secular sociologists with an irresistible impulse to come to

---

2 On European "religious sociology" (*sociologie religieuse*) see Gabriel Le Bras, *Etudes de Sociologie Religieuse* (2 vols.), Paris: Presses Universitaires de France, 1955–56 and Fernand Boulard, *An Introduction to Religious Sociology: Pioneer Work in France* (trans. M. J. Jackson), London: Darton, Longman & Todd, 1960. The best general sources for examples of American "Catholic Sociology" are the volumes of the *American Catholic Sociological Review*. The contributions of the Jesuit sociologist, Joseph H. Fichter are especially notable. For useful perspectives on his work see J. H. Fichter, *One-Man Research: Reminiscences of a Catholic Sociologist*, New York: John Wiley, 1973 and J. K. Hadden and T. E. Long (eds.), *Religion and Religiosity in America: Studies in Honour of Joseph H. Fichter*, New York: Crossroad, 1983, pp. 1–14.

3 The literatures surrounding the topics of the "Protestant Ethic" and "Church and Sect" are the most obvious examples, with Max Weber and Ernst Troeltsch having laid the foundations in both cases. For useful summaries see Michael Hill, *A Sociology of Religion*, London: Heinemann, 1973, pp. 47–139 and Roland Robertson, *The Sociological Interpretation of Religion*, New York: Schocken Books, 1970, pp. 113–149.

grips with the socio-historical significance of Catholicism.[4]

In recent decades, sociologists have explored many blind alleys and advanced many lost causes. Sociologists of religion, in particular, have generated a rich literature on topics of questionable sociological significance in their attempts to document the new, the exotic and the marginal at the expense of the familiar, the dull and the mainline.[5] The general case for sensitive study of *mainline* religion even (and perhaps especially) in a period of decline may, naturally, be applied to Catholicism in many instances. However, it seems indisputable that the Roman Catholic Church, past and present, asserts a unique claim to sociological attention in its own right. This is so, not simply because "everything has happened" to an organization surviving recognizably over two millennia, but because it is *not* merely a piece of living history garbed in baroque grandeur and conveniently cloistered in its own sacred space. If the scholar who seeks to comprehend the political, economic and ideological forces shaping the modern world cannot ignore the currently dynamic manifestations of Catholicism in Poland or Latin America, the sociological theorist does well to ponder the fate of Catholicism in the last quarter-century as a provocative paradigm of contemporary social and cultural change.[6]

Fortunately, an increasing awareness of the potential long and short-term profits to be gained from investment in the study of Catholicism is evident in sociological circles.[7] Yet, if such a perception is to be translated with greater frequency

---

4 Of course there were honourable exceptions; the work of Thomas F. O'Dea or Werner Stark could hardly be described as parochial. See, for example, T. F. O'Dea, *Sociology and the Study of Religion: Theory, Research Interpretation*, New York: Basic Books, 1970 and W. Stark, *The Sociology of Religion* (5 vols.), London: Routledge & Kegan Paul, 1960–65. O'Dea was astute in perceiving the utility of the concept of sectarianism in Catholic settings (see pp. 23–38).

5 A number of scholars have suggested, for example, that the social significance of so-called "New Religious Movements" has been exaggerated by some sociologists.

6 See, for example, Bernice Martin, *A Sociology of Contemporary Cultural Change*, Oxford: Basil Blackwell, 1981; Peter Hebblethwaite, *The Runaway Church*, New York: Seabury Press, 1975; and (in fiction) David Lodge, *How Far Can You Go?* London: Martin Secker & Warburg, 1980.

7 See, for example, Bill McSweeney, *Roman Catholicism: the Search for Relevance*, Oxford: Basil Blackwell, 1980; Lester R. Kurtz, *The Politics of Heresy*, Berkeley: University of California Press, 1986; Thomas A. Kselman, *Miracles and Prophecies in Nineteenth-Century France*, New Brunswick, N.J.: Rutgers University Press, 1983; John A. Coleman, *The Evolution of Dutch Catholicism, 1958–1974*, Berkeley: University of California Press, 1978; Daniel H. Levine, *Religion and Politics in Latin America*, Princeton: Princeton University Press, 1981; Jean-Guy Vaillancourt, *Papal Power*, Berkeley: University of California Press, 1980; and David I. Kertzer, *Comrades and Christians*, Cambridge: Cambridge University Press, 1980. For a number of European examples consult the References in Karel Dobbelaere, "Some Trends in European Sociology of Religion: the

into fruitful scholarly research, two preliminary presuppositions require constant invocation. The first involves rejection of an inappropriate monolithic stereotype and a recognition of the *varieties* of Catholicism discernible in contemporary and historical contexts. The second constitutes a denial that a genuine sociology of Catholicism, of significance to the academic discipline as a whole, can flourish or even survive in the confines of a "religious sociology." In suggesting the necessity of studying *catholicisms* rather than Catholicism, the former extends an insight of the French sociologist Desroche who suggests that it may be more appropriate to refer to a *sociology of religions* rather than the Sociology of Religion.[8] The latter suggests, colloquially, that if war is too important to be left to generals and religion too important to be left to churches, then the study of Catholicism is too important to be confined to Catholics. In the case of either presupposition, it is clear that a sociology of catholics replaces Catholic Sociology.

A new sociology of Catholicism is in the making. Attuned to the historical and comparative diversity of Catholic experiences, its practitioners and advocates have an opportunity both of drawing upon, and contributing to, other areas of sociology in an enterprise which is catholic in the broadest sense of the term.[9]

Although its authors investigate Catholicism in the diverse contexts of French and English Canada, Italy, Switzerland, the United States, Latin America and the British Isles, this collection is in no sense intended as a geographical survey.[10] It merely represents a sampling of the kinds of scholarship which can be undertaken in this field under the inspiration of a variety of sociological perspectives. Its contents are meant to be provocative rather than definitive, insightful rather than exhaustive.

In his examination of Catholicism in French Canada, Peter Beyer makes creative use of the contemporary German neo-functionalist theorist Niklas Luhmann. By tracing the evolution of Quebec in Luhmannian terms, he explores a crucial paradox in a novel manner. Asserting that (like Weber's Puritans)[11] Ultramontane

---

Secularization Debate," *Sociological Analysis*, Vol. 48, No. 2, Summer 1987, pp. 133–137.

8 Henri Desroche, *Jacob and the Angel: An Essay in Sociologies of Religion* (trans. J. K. Savacool), Amherst: University of Massachusetts Press, 1973. (Originally published as *Sociologies Religieuses*, Paris, 1968). A *double* pluralism of *sociologies of religions* seems even more appropriate.

9 A theoretically and methodologically broad-minded approach would, in particular, draw upon and contribute to the fields of Social Movements, Collective Behaviour, Political Sociology and Social Change.

10 For such a survey see Thomas M. Gannon, S. J. (ed.), *World Catholicism in Transition*, New York: Macmillan Publishing Company, 1988. The recent appearance of this collection is further evidence of an increasing interest in Catholicism among sociologists. The classic geographical survey is Hans Mol (ed.), *Western Religion: A Country by Country Sociological Enquiry*, The Hague: Mouton, 1972.

11 See Max Weber, *The Protestant Ethic and the Spirit of Capitalism* (trans. T. Parsons),

churchmen knew not what they did in the long run, he perceives the unintended and unanticipated consequences of their efforts to construct a sacred social order as political transformation and ecclesiastical erosion. There is supreme irony in Beyer's suggestion that by laying the foundations of modernity, the church became the chief architect of its own irrelevance and, consequently, his arguments should elicit interest far beyond the rarefied realm of macrosociological theory.

By grappling with the so-called "Italian Problem" Michael P. Carroll considers the nature of resistance to the "Romanizing" process of rationalization and homogenization characteristic of Catholicism from the mid-nineteenth to the mid-twentieth century. By "digging deeper" than superficial folk-religious manifestations, Carroll penetrates various layers of belief and practice to reveal a distinct tradition of "direct and unmediated contact with the sacred." In his view, this version of Catholicism inspires an impulse to innovation which inevitably and inexorably repels religious routinization.

For Carroll, the roots of "creative instability" may only be uncovered by digging deep into the social and psychological conditions of ordinary life. Appropriately enough, in a study of Irish farmers' ideology and national religious consciousness, Eugene Hynes shares this down-to-earth stance. Struggling to link ecclesiastical policies and institutions to the "activities of ordinary believers in their various local contexts," he stresses, like Carroll, "the active rather than passive stance of ordinary people in creating their own cultural and religious understandings."[12] If Italians offered the chief obstacle to Romanization in the nineteenth century, the Irish became more Roman than Rome. In examining the reasons for this, Hynes echoes themes from Beyer's and Carroll's research while setting the stage for subsequent chapters by John Hannigan and myself.

Hynes regards current theories based on a "folk-canonical" dichotomy and on the notion of a "devotional revolution" orchestrated from above as inadequate and misleading. Explanation of success in preaching from the top, he insists, requires acute understanding of the audience at the bottom. In his opinion, Romanization of the Irish population was promoted by the compatibility of interests between clergy and tenant farmers, a convergence central also to the forging of an indissoluble bond between Catholicism and national identity. With sensitivity, he portrays tenant farmers embracing the new authoritarianism of the Vatican while selecting and combining doctrinal beliefs in accordance with their everyday experiences and interests. Hynes thus accords this socioeconomic group a uniquely active role in the creation of an Ultramontane clergy, a submissive laity, and an emotive vision of an independent "Holy Ireland" which persists to our own day.

The tenacity of this vision is admirably indicated in John Hannigan's treatment

---

London: George Allen and Unwin, 1930.

12 For another version of this viewpoint see Otto Maduro, "Is Religion Revolutionary?" *The New England Sociologist*, Vol. 5, No. 1, 1984, pp. 129–130.

of recent political events in the Irish Republic. Focussing upon recent challenges to Church moral monopoly in the sphere of state legislation, his investigation of a "catholic ideological *bloc*" echoes or anticipates themes addressed by Beyer, Carroll, Hynes and Cuneo. Rather than interpreting the political victories of this *bloc* simply as unmitigated clerical triumphs, Hannigan stresses the significance of independent grass-roots movements of laity, discerning in their initiatives evidence of fragmentation in a once monolithic Catholic presence. In espousing a *dialectical* theory of Catholic adaptation to secularization, Hannigan explicitly asserts his dissatisfaction with the *evolutionary* model adopted by Beyer. By comparing the specific inquiries of Beyer and Hannigan, therefore, readers may also assess the respective merits of the general theoretical approaches which they advocate.

Sketching a transition from a small, indigenous, rural, upper-class sect to a populous, proletarian, urban church, my own discussion of English Catholicism overlaps the contents of earlier chapters in a number of ways. Indicating the traditionally diabolical role assigned to "popery" within British national mythology, it depicts the hoary marginality of the English Catholic community as exacerbated by mass intrusion of Irish immigrants during the second half of the nineteenth century. In a manner which recalls Hynes' argument, a historically crucial elective affinity is posited between a defiant, emerging minority and the siege-mentality which characterized English Ultramontanism for over a century.

If Ultramontane ideology was generated and sustained in an atmosphere of crisis, the same is undoubtedly true of the Catholic Traditionalist movement analyzed perceptively by William D. Dinges. Focussing attention upon the schismatic Archbishop Lefebvre, Dinges explores the central paradox of Traditionalism. By explicating the manner in which profound dissent is legitimated within the movement, he demonstrates how members come to view themselves as "more Catholic than the Pope." Utilizing sociological literature in the fields of Collective Behaviour and Social Movements, he not only clarifies the nature of conservative revolt within contemporary Catholicism, but also "sheds light on the dynamics of sectarianism, on the sociology of dissent, on . . . the acquisition and maintenance of unconventional belief systems and on the construction of social movement ideologies." Not the least of Dinges' contributions is his cogent reminder that sectarianism, schism and fundamentalism are by no means restricted to Protestants or the devotees of New Religious Movements.

Michael W. Cuneo needs no such reminder; his study of "pro-life" militants admirably complements Dinges' insights while making its own distinctive contribution to the understanding of religious dissent. In an investigation which parallels Hannigan's in a number of respects, Cuneo emphasizes the danger of sociologically stereotyping so-called Catholic Conservatism. Rightly rejecting conventional wisdom, he regards abortion as a divisive rather than unifying issue within Canadian Catholicism and portrays anti-abortion militants as sworn enemies rather than puppets of the ecclesiastical hierarchy. The movement described by Cuneo is no clerically-dominated, submissive body of the Simple Faithful pining for the Tridentine Mass, it is a "conventicle of lay dissent" whose participants view themselves as "a holy elect called to rescue the Canadian church from spiritual lassitude and, ultimately, from absorption in the melting-pot of secular humanism."

In contrast to Dinges and Cuneo, W. E. Hewitt analyzes what is probably the best-known contemporary form of "radical" or "progressive" Catholicism. Disturbed that "Liberation Theology" is often treated too reverently and uncritically, he approaches its social-scientific claims with considerable scepticism. Doubtful of its vaunted indigenous character and viewing its prime inspirational source as foreign-educated intellectuals rather than the wretched-of-the-earth, he criticizes its fragile foundations in neo-Marxist dependency theory and class analysis. Unconvinced that the "Preferential Option for the Poor" is a genuine product of the poor themselves, Hewitt is also incredulous of the role of "Basic Christian Communities" as principal carriers of Latin American revolutionary fervour. Although unlikely to please Liberationists, Hewitt's carefully documented research deserves close scrutiny as a rare effort at sociological rather than theological appraisal of their views. It also merits the attention of anyone seriously interested in current trends in Catholicism.

From the foregoing description, it may be anticipated that the contributions to this book are original, probing, controversial and even iconoclastic. It may also be correctly inferred that intellectually the volume as a whole amounts to much more than the sum of its parts. This collection is by no means preoccupied with either the labyrinthine paths of Vatican diplomacy or the sacred politics of ecclesiastical bureaucracies, although both are pertinent to many of its chapters. Concerned as much with revolt as with authority, with laity as much as clergy, it underlines the active role of ordinary Catholic believers in selecting and shaping religious doctrine and ritual according to their individual and social needs. Consequently, the collective depiction of Catholicism which emerges in this volume is in no sense monolithic. Exploring catholicisms rather than Catholicism, its authors would endorse Antonio Gramsci's observation:

> Every religion, even Catholicism (indeed Catholicism more than any, precisely because of its efforts to retain a "surface" unity and avoid splintering into national churches and social stratifications), is in reality a multiplicity of distinct and often contradictory religions: there is one Catholicism for the peasants, one for the *petits-bourgeois* and town workers, one for women, and one for intellectuals which is itself variegated and disconnected.[13]

---

13 Antonio Gramsci, *Selections from the Prison Notebooks* (ed. and trans. Q. Hoare and G. Nowell Smith), New York: International Publishers, 1971, p. 420. For a recent acknowledgement of Catholic pluralism see Mark A. Noll, "The Eclipse of Old Hostilities *between* and the Potential for New Strife *among* Catholics and Protestants Since Vatican II" in Robert N. Bellah and Frederick E. Greenspahn, *Uncivil Religion: Interreligious*

It is to be hoped that many such past and present "sundry Catholicisms" will be the targets of future sociological investigations. The present volume indicates how rewarding such research may be.

Roger O'Toole

Hostility in America, New York: Crossroad Publishing Company, 1987, p. 92.

1.

The Evolution of Roman Catholicism in Quebec:
A Luhmannian Neo-Functionalist Interpretation

Peter Beyer

The history of Roman Catholicism since the French Revolution has primarily involved a reluctant and gradual coming-to-terms with Western modernity. More often than not, this struggle manifested itself in a persistent reactionary stand provoked by a perceived loss of power and influence among the church's organizational hierarchy. This aggressively defensive posture took on various forms—from the effort to reestablish the old order, to the attempt to preserve the political independence of the papal states as a vital remnant in the flood of apostasy, to a more accommodating policy of "social Catholicism" promulgated by Pope Leo XIII in the eighteen nineties.[1] This last strategy enjoined Catholics to become involved in modern structures, often by erecting institutions that ran parallel to and competed with those controlled by secular forces, especially governments and socialist organizations. Such institutions, from Catholic schools and hospitals to Catholic political parties and Catholic labour unions, were designed to reassert the influence of the church in secular life, to "re-Christianize" society, or at least to minimize the participation of the faithful in secular and state-controlled institutions. If a Catholic social order could not be reestablished in a country as a whole, then a form of protection and isolation from the corrupting influences of the modern and secular world was to be constructed for

---

1 Leo's encyclical, *Rerum Novarum*, of course stands out as the key manifestation of this switch in strategy. While his emphasis on land as the source of wealth, on social hierarchy as the foundation of order, and on moral decline as the principal problem of modernity shows that he still sees proper social order in premodern terms, Leo's recommendation of worker's unions as crucial for addressing the plight of the urban industrial worker points the way for the organizational and ideological response that his successors developed into social Catholicism. For analyses of the papal response, see Camp, 1969; Dorr, 1983; Vaillancourt, 1980.

the flock of the faithful.[2]

Since World War II, but especially since Vatican II, the social Catholicism strategy has been seriously undermined in many areas of the world.[3] Since the papacy of John XXIII, the Catholic social "teaching" that informed the strategy has taken a new, less isolating direction. Many of the institutions that this teaching spawned have disappeared; others, such as schools and hospitals, have changed so that now relatively little distinguishes them from their secular counterparts. The church as a whole is in a state of transition, the end result of which cannot be foreseen with any clarity at the moment. The response to the modern world has entered a new phase. The question then becomes, what brought about the decline of the social Catholicism phase? Why has it not persisted?

It is not my purpose here to give a global answer to this question since such an answer would vary greatly from place to place. Rather, I approach the general question by looking at a specific example, that of Quebec. I present a sociological analysis of the role of Catholicism in Quebec during the nineteenth and twentieth centuries on the basis of concepts derived from Luhmannian neo-functionalist sociological theory. I offer an hypothesis that not only assigns a critical role to Roman Catholicism in the history of Quebec—something which is obvious—but also suggests how this role was crucial for the modernization of Quebec during recent decades. My hypothesis can be formulated as follows: Roman Catholicism in Quebec has had the critical role, *first*, of establishing an exclusivistic "national identity" whose aim was to discourage the modernization of Quebec society, and, *second*, of (unintentionally perhaps) helping to lay the foundations on which a modern society has been erected. In the second enterprise, the role of social Catholicism is demonstrated to be of particular importance. Not only did modernization result in the decline of social Catholicism in Quebec, but social Catholicism also had a not insignificant role in bringing about this modernization and hence carried within it the seeds of its own decline.

It is possible that the analysis may shed light on the role and fate of social Catholicism in other Catholic countries and regions such as Spain or Belgium (cf., for instance, Dobbelaere, 1988; Orensanz, 1988); but my argument does not assume such generalization. Roman Catholicism is monolithic only in the eyes of some of its staunchest defenders and opponents. A proper appreciation of its complexity requires studies that take into account the uniqueness of each of its local manifestations. The present study should be regarded as one such contribution.

To students of modern, especially ethnic, nationalism, aspects of my hypothesis may sound at least vaguely familiar. Indeed, there are some important and inten-

---

2 David Martin (1978) has analyzed the overall response of the Catholic church under the title of "reactive organicism." My argument in this chapter essentially confirms Martin's analysis but sets it in a broader theoretical context.

3 See Gannon, 1988 for numerous examples, especially from Europe.

tional similarities with the work of others such as Ernest Gellner (1964:147ff; 1983.) and Patricia Mayo (1974).[4] Encapsulated within it, for instance, are the notions of uneven development, cultural boundaries, and threatened loss of communal identity. However, these concepts are set in a quite different theoretical framework, one that analyzes the complex process of modernization in terms of a fundamental change in the basic structure of society. Before turning to a concrete examination of the Quebec of the past and of the present, therefore, it is necessary to outline this framework since, to a large degree, it is on the theoretical level that my contribution must be assessed.

The Theoretical Framework

The Luhmannian perspective sees society as the encompassing social system of all those communicative acts that can be meaningfully related to one another (cf. Luhmann, 1982:73f.) This broad definition quickly leads to the question of the internal structural differentiation of societal systems; for, beyond a very simple level, the complexity of such a system makes it almost inevitable that groups of such acts will form into subsystems: not everyone can communicate with everyone about everything. This differentiation can proceed along at least three lines: segmentary, stratified, and functional.[5] Segmentary differentiation divides society into roughly equal subsystems, with little interdependence: tribes, clans, or villages in simpler societies being examples. A dominance of stratified differentiation is found in more complex societies. Here subsystem differentiation is according to strata, unequal in terms of power and influence, but interdependent. Functional differentiation is the dominant form in modern society. Communicative acts are divided according to what function they fulfill, whether economic, political, religious, familial, or several others (cf. Luhmann, 1982a:229–254). In Luhmannian theory, *dominance of functional subsystem differentiation is what makes modern society modern.* The frequently discussed characteristics of modernity, such as heightened individualism, industrialism, urbanization, secularization (however conceived), the importance of bureaucracy and technology, and many more, are consequences of this fundamental socio-structural feature.

Theoretically, dominance of each of the three forms of differentiation corresponds to increasing levels of inner-societal complexity: dominance of segmentary differentiation is found in the least complex societies, dominance of the stratified form in more complex societies, and dominance of functional differentiation in an even

---

4 For discussion and critique of these and similar positions, see Smith, 1981:43ff; and See, 1986:6–17.

5 For a somewhat parallel division and periodization into pre-agrarian, agrarian, and industrial societies, see Gellner, 1983:5–38. Although Gellner uses evidently economic categories, he does recognize, with Luhmann, that stratification characterizes agrarian societies more fundamentally than it does either pre-agrarian or industrial societies.

more complex society. Empirically, however, increase in societal complexity and hence eventual switch to functional differentiation is by no means inevitable. While the model is evolutionary, it is not thereby teleological.

Historically, only one society, that of Western Europe, has undergone an endogenous transition from dominance of stratified to functional differentiation (cf. Elias, 1978; 1982; Luhmann, 1980–81). This fact is of importance in the current context given that today's world society has developed from Western European society outward, depriving all other hitherto territorial societies of the historical opportunity to develop in completely autonomous directions. This is the case not only for non-Western societies in the Third World, but also for those regions and populations in the West that were not part of the dominant core of modernization but remained peripheral to it for various reasons. Quebec society was one such region and Roman Catholicism played a vital role in reinforcing its peripheral status.

To further elaborate this Luhmannian perspective, we must look at some of the implications of dominance of functional subsystem formation in modern society. In contrast to Parsons, Luhmann rejects an analytic four-function paradigm in favour of a theory that sees the historical development of various functional spheres for the economy, politics, science, education, religion, and others (cf. Parsons, 1971; Luhmann, 1982). These systems did not develop equally or at the same time. Particularly the first three just mentioned have been the dominant ones, with others—subsystems for education and health—developing comparatively late, and still others—for religion and the family—developing comparatively slowly. This uneven development of subsystems (not to be confused with the uneven development of regions) does not, however, lead to an inherent structural inequality among the systems that would make modern society primarily economic, political, or scientific and only derivatively religious or familial.

One of the critical consequences of a dominance of functional differentiation is that individuals can no longer be identified primarily with one subsystem, as was possible in stratified or segmentarily differentiated societies of the past. Access to function can therefore no longer be mediated through membership in a particular group. Since all functions are required by all persons, pressure develops for inclusion of all members of the society in the benefits of all the subsystems. The obverse of this pressure for inclusion is a sharp increase in the independence of the individual *vis-à-vis* the dominant social systems, an independence that manifests itself in the increased establishment of exclusive identities for individuals. This exclusivity results from the great increase in the number of possible life circumstances that is occasioned by releasing individuals from such holistic identification with one societal subsystem.

The seemingly paradoxical simultaneity of inclusion and exclusion leads to a double pluralism: the pluralism that results from the pressure to include (and in this sense, legitimize) a plurality of exclusive worldviews, and the pluralism that is a reflection of the diverse perspectives of the principal functional subsystems of society. These pluralisms can and do overlap in that individuals identify themselves with one or some of the alternative societal system perspectives much more than others, associations that lead, for instance, to a sharp increase in the role of "careers" in personal identity. In addition, and of critical importance in the present context, such overlapping can manifest itself at the level of the group.

The perceived identity of a group, its motivation for solidarity, can be and often is expressed with reference to the perspective of one or more of the functional subsystems. In particular, in those instances where the group is mobilized for the fuller inclusion of its members, its self-conception is likely to be primarily in terms of specific subsystemic criteria, whether economic (class), religious, familial (sex or descent), or political (region). Such identification need not be restricted to one system and often is not, as in the case of ethnic identifications. Furthermore, the motivational identification of the group needs to be distinguished from the type of action taken to further its aims. Thus, an ethnic group may choose political action but need not; it can also pursue its goals through economic means. The ethnic group may also simply develop its specificity, so much the better if religious identity overlaps. However, since the political system is concerned primarily with making collectively binding decisions, political action can be expected to be the dominant mode in the modern world, regardless of self-conception.[6]

Seen globally, imperialist expansion, especially of the core regions of Western society, has brought more than capitalism and the bureaucratic state to the peripheral and non-Western regions: it has moreover brought these in a form shaped by the religious, familial, and other cultural characteristics specific to the development of modernity in the core. Modernization in these areas has therefore implied the threat of *wholesale change in all areas of these societies at once*, without the luxury of establishing continuity between the new structures and local traditions. This point is critical for an understanding of Quebec history at least until the middle of this century. What it implies is that the elaboration of modern society as a society with a dominance of functional differentiation is not simply a matter of core development followed by diffusion or conquest. It involves a complex and far from

---

6 Scholars such as A.D. Smith (1981; 1986) argue that ethnicity is in fact a category of identification quite independent of others, notably economic and political, and not a combination as I am claiming. Not only does such an argument confuse group identity and group culture with functional systems of action and their cultural manifestations, it also does not go far enough if it remains at this level. Precisely because it stresses real or imagined group-cultural continuity, ethnicity provides an ideal platform for the selective appropriation (see below) and mobilization for inclusion that I am discussing. Under conditions of modernity, however, such appropriation and mobilization will channel itself along functional, usually political, lines and not along segmentary or stratified communal lines as in past societies. Smith himself recognizes this difference implicitly in his distinction between ethnicism and nationalism. See Smith, 1986:esp. 50–58; 153ff.

inevitable process of appropriation of modern structures by various regions with their own societal traditions. Such appropriation has occurred and is still occurring in the Western core regions. It requires time, continuity, and the opportunity to experiment with various transitional arrangements such as, for instance, *laissez-faire* bourgeois capitalism in Western Europe or party-led dictatorships of the proletariat in the Soviet Union or China.[7] Like the latter two, regions that are marginal to the dominant trend or colonialized by its core regions can be expected to respond in ways that reflect the dominance of functional differentiation. In addition to being styled as a battle between regions and cultural traditions, such conflicts can also be expected to manifest the primacy of functionally differentiated structures in various ways. Accordingly, whereas some regional movements will stress economic growth or political independence, others will produce religious movements as a response to the basic problem. Which possibility occurs in a given region or at a given time in the same region will depend on the historical context. In any case, while in the long run such movements may have as a practical result the fuller inclusion of these regions in world society, the short and medium run effect will be to set up a kind of communicative barrier that allows the selective appropriation under discussion.

These abstract and theoretical formulations will now be applied to the role of Roman Catholicism in Quebec. It is shown that, for specific historical reasons, Quebec became a marginalized region of Western society; that it gave rise to a political movement whose failure made room for a religiously dominated response to the challenge of modernity; and that this religious response, while more or less institutionalized in Quebec for about a century, eventually helped to create the foundations for a rapid appropriation of modernity with all its implications. In proceeding to this more concrete discussion, it must be borne in mind that the central role of Roman Catholicism in the entire process points to the dominance of *function*. While Quebec until 1960 may appear to have been a place where reaction, anti-modernism, and traditionalism reigned, the prevalence of functionally specific interpretations by Quebeckers themselves of their own identity reflects the primacy of functional differentiation in the larger society in which Quebec is but one region.[8] The prevalence of Roman Catholic religion in the identity of Quebeckers made possible cultural

---

7 Styling these forms as transitional may give the appearance that teleological developmentalism has been reintroduced shortly after it has been denied. There are at least two ways in which this is not the case. First, the "developed" West is considered to be in as transitional a stage as the rest of the world and is therefore not paradigmatic. Second, the degree of uniformity among the different regions of world society after these transitional stages is not prejudged. The resultant differences may be greater or as important as the similarities.

8 A note of theoretical caution and clarification is warranted here. Strictly speaking, the word identity conceals a critical difference: outside Quebec, Quebeckers used the functionally specific characteristic of religion (of which the French language was considered to be a feature) to differentiate themselves from others; inside Quebec, religion in the

consolidation and continuity in the process of modernization. When, in the post-World War II era, it became increasingly evident to many Quebeckers—including a number of bishops and priests—that the various characteristics of modernity, such as industrialism and urbanization, were solidly established and acceptable features of *French-Canadian* society, Roman Catholic religion could be rapidly divested of its role as integrating buffer between Quebec culture and alien modernism. After 1960, the face of Quebec society changed rapidly and began to show all the typical characteristics of modern Western society. The accompanying changes in the Roman Catholic church were equally dramatic.

From Religious Revival to Quiet Revolution

The French colony in North America that came under British rule in 1763 was in many respects a child of the *ancien régime*. The attempt to implant in the New World the traditional stratified structures of the old was reflected in the seigneurial system of land tenure, the Gallican solution to the problem of church and state, and the congruence of influence with rank. Nevertheless, the very different conditions in North America, including geography and climate, chronic underpopulation, and military insecurity, combined with the undermining of these same structures in France to make of New France more of a policy ideal than an institutional reality. When most of the members of the French upper classes emigrated after the conquest, the remaining French population had few institutions left beyond their farms, their families, and their church. By the middle of the next century, these became the foundation of a religio-national mythic complex that dominated the French-Canadian cultural identity until well into the twentieth century. The logic of this development and its aftermath in terms of the theoretical model just outlined are the subject of what follows.

On its conquest of New France in 1760, the British government decided to allow retention of the characteristic features of this society rather than force adoption of British political, legal, economic, and cultural institutions. Of critical importance here is that the colonial regime allowed the toleration of the Roman Catholic church in its new colony several decades before Catholic emancipation in Great Britain itself.[9] As one of the few institutions (along with the seigneurial regime and the

form of the Catholic church attempted to set critical limits to independent, functional communication and hence acted as an integrator of Quebec society. The differentiation and the integration are two aspects of the same phenomenon and not contradictory notions of the function of religion as the generator of *either* social conflict *or* cohesion. Luhmannian theory, for essentially heuristic reasons, emphasizes differentiation. The problem of integrative identity is treated as one of self-descriptions or ideologies. Therefore, whenever, in this chapter, I speak of French-Canadian identity, I am referring to an ideological self-conception, one which may diverge from the actual socio-structural features of French-Canadian society.

9 For a more detailed discussion, see Roger O'Toole, "Refugees from the National Myth:

family) not immediately decimated by the exodus of the French colonial elite, the church held the promise of assuring the loyalty of the King's new subjects despite the growth of democratic and revolutionary agitation in the old colonies to the south. Indigenous land tenure, laws, customs, and religion were to be maintained in return for the active discouragement among the farmer *habitants* of liberal and democratic ideas.

The strategy was successful but not entirely so. A combination of circumstances led to the creation of new institutions and new elites which eventually led to abortive rebellions in 1837–38.

To begin with, representative political institutions were not part of the original British colonial plan. Yet legislative assemblies were created in 1791 after loyalists fleeing the American revolution and British soldiers retiring after this conflict settled primarily in the frontier areas of the new northern colony and immediately demanded political rights such as were present in Britain and the former colonies to the south. The Constitutional Act of 1791 not only conceded such rights, but also split the colony into Upper Canada (now Ontario) and Lower Canada (now Quebec), giving the French subjects a colony in which the old policy of toleration was to continue, though with the incorporation of representative political institutions.[10]

The toleration of the Catholic church, moreover, included the classical colleges run by the clergy. Here the clergy trained a new, indigenous French-Canadian lay elite for whom Quebec would be the sole native sphere of influence. Much like twentieth-century intelligentsia in the Third World (cf. Smith, 1981:108ff.), this group of doctors, lawyers, notaries, small merchants, and others, came to see themselves as the representatives of a French-Canadian nation, distinct from the English-speaking nations around it. They founded an ethnic nationalist movement (the *patriote* movement) that skilfully and ambivalently identified itself in terms of both the *traditional* old French colonial structures, such as seigneurial land tenure and Catholicism, and the *modern* ideals of political freedom and democracy (cf. Ouellet, 1964). Through the Lower Canadian legislative assembly, this elite tried not only to wrest political control from the colonial regime, but also to extricate the embryonic educational system (to which it largely owed its own existence) away from clergy control. Culminating in the disastrous *patriote* rebellions of 1837–38, the movement failed on both fronts. The reasons for the rebellions and their failure are multiple, but certain key ideological features of the *patriote* movement are instructive for understanding the subsequent role of Catholicism in the history of Quebec. They must, therefore, be examined here.[11]

One of the more revealing factors was the *patriote* attitude to the economy. The development of a bourgeois economic system was proceeding apace in Canada as

---

The English Catholic Odyssey," in this volume.

10 A good overview of this period in Quebec's history is to be found in Neatby, 1966.

11 For a good overview of this period in Quebec's history, see Ouellet, 1980.

a whole; but French-Canadians, and above all the lay elite, were very poorly represented among its leaders and prime beneficiaries. On the contrary, economically, the *patriote* elite had its base in the "semi-feudal" agricultural economy which it defined as an important element of what it styled as the French-Canadian nation. This sector of the overall Quebec economy was in serious decline during this time, a fact which in no small way contributed to the eventual rebellions. The vital and growing sectors of the economy (lumber, shipbuilding, etc.) were in the hands of Anglophones with French speakers as only residual beneficiaries.

The *patriotes* responded to this imbalance in *functional* terms: they defined the problem politically. The English had more *economic* power only because they had more *political* power! Hence a political solution through confrontational tactics in the legislative assembly and ultimately through rebellion was seen as the way to solve the economic problems. The irony and critical aspect of this attitude is that the meaningful inclusion of particularly the elite French-Canadians in the benefits of the economic system was eliminated by the very definition of the situation espoused by the *patriotes*. The French-Canadian nation was regarded as an agricultural nation by tradition, and merchant capitalism, with its requirements for different laws and land tenure, different attitudes to money and social change, contradicted the communal identity of that nation. Capitalism, like the English language and Protestant religion, was a characteristic of an alien, Anglo-Saxon identity. Yet the *patriotes* and their supporters did not fail to claim the benefits of this capitalism as their patrimony, reflecting the modern face of their nationalism which sought inclusion of French-Canadians in the benefits of the devoloping world society, primarily through political action. The political view of economic problems accurately reflected the political nationalism preached by the *patriotes*. In seeking to benefit from capitalist enterprises while regarding them as alien to the national identity, their movement expressed its commitment to a doctrine of political primacy.

Rather than simply exhibiting cultural or social myopia, however, this position clearly reflected the nature of Quebec at that time. The classical colleges did not prepare their graduates for the capitalist business world: their prime purpose was to educate priests and pious lay people. They stressed the continuity of a closed symbolic system dedicated to the preservation and perfection of a traditional religious heritage. The orientation of a capitalist economic system, with its locus of decision-making in an open, indeterminate future and its greater discontinuity with traditional social forms, was hardly compatible with such an educational ideology. Moreover, these economic forms were *de facto* in the hands of the British bourgeoisie; and attempted entrance into this world entailed the risk of profound changes in just those social structures and cultural correlates which were most distinctively French-Canadian. By contrast, representative political structures, while definitely Anglo-Saxon in character, were vehicles which the *patriotes* were educationally qualified to utilize and appropriate in the perceived interests of the French-Canadian nation. The political road to cultural continuity in the process of modernization was favoured by the situation.

Thus, even though the *patriote* movement evidently exhibited ambiguities, it was, in terms of the theoretical model presented here, an understandable response in its historical context.' French Canada had been effectively cut off from European French developments by the British conquest and the French Revolution. Distinctly French-Canadian institutions were isolated and underdeveloped. It had in effect become a marginalized region in a rapidly modernizing Western world. The *patriotes* sought to counter this marginalization in continuity with their cultural traditions as they saw them; and they did this by pursuing an expressly political course of action. Unfortunately for them, the British colonial policy that was instrumental in making such cultural continuity possible was instituted, as we have seen, expressly to counter political independence movements such as those of the *patriotes* and the Americans to the south. The colonial regime was ruthless in suppressing the uprising, thus eliminating the *patriotes* as representatives of French-Canadianism.[12]

The *patriotes* were, however, not alone in their claim to represent French-Canadianism. Alongside the lay elite, the classical colleges also gradually produced a clerical elite, as was their prime purpose. Far from being immune to the attractions of nationalism, this latter group developed its own vision of the nation, albeit more slowly and cautiously.

With the British conquest, the Roman Catholic church in French-Canada was cut off almost completely from developments in both the Gallican church and Rome. In the decades thereafter, while the church's organizational structures remained intact and even grew at the parish level, the number of priests declined drastically because the church was not allowed to import priests from France or its colonies. Only as the colleges began to produce indigenous priests did this situation reverse, turning decisively in the church's favour only in the 1830s, the decade in which the *patriote* movement reached its denouement.

Beside internal dissension, military ineptitude and uncertain support among sectors of the farmer *habitants*, one of the important reasons for the dismal failure of the rebellions was the virtually unanimous opposition of the Catholic clergy (cf. Chabot, 1975). This opposition was effective not only because the clergy now had more voices, but also because it had managed, during the preceding decades, to avoid identification as a willing collaborator of the colonial regime. Not least among those responsible for this distancing was the first bishop of Montreal, Jean-Jacques Lartigue, the principal architect of the fundamental tenets of subsequent French-

---

12 Ironically enough, British colonial policy was changing rapidly and, had the *patriotes* managed to keep their agitation within the walls of the Lower Canadian legislative assembly, they may have won substantial autonomy within the next decade or two, as did the united Canadian colony in 1849 with the granting of responsible government. See Monet, 1969.

Canadian religio-cultural nationalism and a first cousin to Louis Joseph Papineau, the *patriote* leader.[13]

Lartigue's nationalism was similar to the *patriote* version with a few crucial differences. First and foremost, Lartigue, together with the dominant portion of the Roman Catholic church of the time, distrusted democratic institutions, and certainly was not in the least attracted to economic liberalism. He and his clerical *confreres* were ultramontanists in the conservative sense that this term acquired after the condemnation of Lamennais.[14] Second, and connected with this, he considered the church to be the central institution of the French-Canadian nation. Accordingly, he had no difficulty in seeing the situation of his nation in North America in terms of a French Catholic society surrounded and opposed by Anglo-Saxon Protestant societies. For Lartigue, not only was economic liberalism characteristic of the latter and not the former, so was political liberalism. Lartigue's option tended toward a congruence between two perceived dichotomies: English/French and liberal/conservative. What distinguished the French-Canadian nation from the English-Canadian and American nations surrounding it was analogous to what set the Roman church in Europe against the development of modern structures there (cf. Beyer, 1985).

In the 1830s, therefore, there existed in Quebec two opposed versions of French-Canadian nationalism: the somewhat ambiguous, but ultimately liberal political nationalism represented by the *patriotes*, and a rapidly developing religious nationalism led by the Montreal bishops. While the former disapproved of the conservative attitude of the clergy, they were not demonstrably anti-clerical because they too saw Roman Catholicism and the church as a vital aspect of the nation. The latter, however, saw in the political liberalism of the former an enemy to be fought, for the good of the church and the health of the nation (cf. Eid, 1978:esp.65–162).

The *patriotes* were defeated in 1838 and their form of nationalism faded with that defeat. The clergy, however, were just coming into their own. Their numbers were increasing. In the wake of Catholic emancipation in Britain and the significant role the clergy played in opposing the rebellions, the colonial government no longer

---

13 There is a certain enticing symbolic significance to the fact that, not only were these two cousins, but a third first cousin of both of them, Denis-Benjamin Viger, became a leading figure among the conservative French-Canadian laity, a growing group whose role in the subsequent institutionalization of the clerical religio-nationalist option was critical.

14 In the first half of the nineteenth century, Félicité de Lamennais led a French Catholic movement that looked "beyond the mountains" to Rome and the papacy for leadership in the battle against the restoration of the old order in Western European society. In 1832, Pope Gregory XVI condemned Lamennais and the entire liberal movement in the church. Thereafter, "ultramontanism" came to signify a conservative and reactionary attitude more in tune with the tendencies of the nineteenth-century papacy. For a brief but informative account, see Vidler, 1971: chapter 6.

felt it necessary to control Roman Catholicism in Quebec. The vital organizational link with Rome could be reestablished and used to strengthen the Quebec church. Moreover, in 1840, much of Quebec was witness to a religious revival led by the Catholic clergy and helped along by conservative and Catholic revivalist preachers from Europe (cf. Rousseau, 1986). The situation presented an opportunity for the clerical option for the nation to consolidate itself.

The clerical vision did not attempt a return to *ancien régime* social structures. The elaborated class structure for this was missing in Canada and the forces of a dominance of functional differentiation were already too well developed in the Western society of which Quebec was nevertheless a part. The clerical strategy must therefore be seen in functional systemic terms. From this perspective, Quebec religio-nationalism sought to maintain the distinction between French-Canadian society and the English-speaking societies around it by making the religious system the dominant system within Quebec. The developing educational, scientific, familial, artistic, and health systems were to be subordinated to it. Human action associated with these systems was to be judged to a great extent by religious criteria which in turn were determined by religious professionals, the Roman Catholic clergy.[15] Accordingly, in the decades after 1840, all French education in Quebec gradually came under the control of the Catholic clergy (cf. Lajeunesse, 1971); religiously based cultural associations like temperance leagues (an expression of the "social Catholicism" of the time) and pious confraternities were encouraged while liberal literary clubs were persistently and to a large extent successfully combatted (cf. Bernard, 1971:153ff). The family was hailed as the indispensable building block of society and the nation: large families were a sign of God's favour to the parents and the nation.

Perhaps most importantly, the economic system was functionally divided into subsistence farming that was proper to French-Canadians and business or industrial pursuits, activity that was alien and ultimately contrary to religion. Subsistence farming and colonization of the hinterland were activities increasingly recommended and blessed by religion as conducive to individual and national salvation. Business and industrial pursuits, while usually not condemned outright, were deemed dangerous to the extent that they detracted from the agricultural life so conducive to the maintenance of religious identity. Throughout the century between 1840 and 1940, the holders of this vision saw industrialization (along with its concomitant urbanization) as a threat to the faith and therefore to the identity of the French-Canadian (cf. Brunet, 1964; Levitt, 1973 for the by no means most extreme example of Henri Bourassa).

The policy toward the political system was to treat it with the suspicion deserving of something alien. Between 1840 and 1867, under the Union government, there

---

15 For a Parsonian version of this kind of "dedifferentiation," albeit in a different context, see Lechner, 1985.

were no centralized political institutions proper to Quebec alone. After Confederation, the more powerful federal government was under the control of the English speakers. On the provincial level, Quebeckers again had a government of their own, one with restricted powers, to be sure; but one that controlled the vital areas of natural resources, education, and social legislation. However, in a relatively short space of time, this government was controlled by liberals who were constantly and vigorously opposed by the clerical elite and its lay allies, especially regarding anything remotely resembling social legislation (cf. Dupont, 1972; Vigod, 1986). In a decidedly attenuated form, the clerical, religio-nationalist ideology became ingrained among the influential in late nineteenth- and early twentieth-century Quebec, even the supposedly liberal politicians who controlled the state apparatus. In areas that it felt were vital to the identity and health of the nation, including colonization of the agricultural hinterland, the church and its lay supporters could almost always mount a sufficiently strong opposition to halt or postpone changes regarded as secularist or modernist.

In sum then, under the guidance of the clergy and its lay allies, the most typical manifestations of developing modern structures—differentiated bourgeois economic activity and the powerful and centralizing modern political state—were neutralized to a significant degree; and other societal subsystems were subordinated to religion in the name of a religiously defined ethnic identity.

The institutionalization of this identity did not put a halt to modernization (especially urbanization and industrialization) in Quebec. Nevertheless, it did allow a kind of relative communicative isolation of Quebec society. By communicative isolation, I mean more than simply the control of what books are read and what ideas are espoused in public. Communication includes the use of what Luhmann (1982a:255ff.) calls "media of communication" such as money, power, truth, and faith. Isolation then refers to the attempt to limit the growth of some of these media, in the Quebec case, principally money and political power. By contrast, the proliferation of the religious medium of faith was encouraged.

An analogy between this and the corresponding situation of the Catholic Church in Europe would not be an unwarranted distortion.[16] The religio-national strategy that institutionalized itself in Quebec during the nineteenth century created and preserved the French-Canadian *ethnie* in a way which paralleled the resistance of the Roman Catholic church in Europe against the modernization of Western society. As the church in Rome struggled to "preserve its identity," so the Quebec religio-national

---

16 The more extreme Quebec ultramontane position, as represented, for instance, by Bishops L.F. Laflèche and Ignace Bourget, could in this case be seen as comparable to the hardline attitude of Pius IX and the Syllabus of Errors. Leo XIII's more open attitude to the problems of the modern world had no strict parallel in the Quebec of his time; but by the time of Pius XI, Quebec clerical attitudes were by and large again in tune with those of the reigning pontiff.

view adopted a similar path in opposing change and sanctifying tradition. Even the liberal members of the elite sounded a lot like their traditionalist adversaries when called upon to defend the nation against outside challenges, usually emanating from English Canada. In other words, even when held with some degree of insincerity, traditionalist attitudes had become so inseparable from the identity of Quebec, that to question them was tantamount to apostasy (cf. Vigod, 1986). This was the negative face of clerical nationalism.

On the positive side, the religio-national movement created, over a century, a unique legacy in precisely those domains of social action that it most favoured. Instead of developing a bourgeois capitalist economy and a centralized liberal-democratic state, Quebec developed its own religious, familial, artistic, and educational character under the aegis of an ultramontane Roman Catholicism. By 1840, French Canada had built on what institutions it did possess to give its population—and especially its elites—a solid locus of personal identity and therefore potential group solidarity which they might maintain and develop.

In the century after 1840, this positive development continued. The central importance of the church ensured that there was no shortage of clerical personnel of both sexes to run parishes, schools, hospitals, leisure activities (cf. Bellefleur, 1986), and other "social welfare" agencies. The literary and artistic culture of Quebec blossomed in numerous newspapers, journals, and literary works. Ecclesiastical art and architecture developed a recognizable style and tradition of its own; while popular culture solidified into a unique repertoire of distinct customs and traditions. More and more, as the century proceeded, the church became a dominant force in the everyday lives of Quebeckers, both urban and rural, elite and common. In these circumstances, Quebec faced the nevertheless inevitable encroachment of modernity. Such encroachment occurred when, despite the attempt to isolate French-Canadian society through the nurturing of different language, religion, and culture, the conservative elite failed to prevent capitalist industrialism and strong, centralized political institutions from becoming an integral part of Quebec society.

The industrialization of Quebec began in the late nineteenth century and reached full speed in the first half of the twentieth. It was, by and large, controlled by English-Canadian, British, and American interests, though, to be sure, many French Quebeckers welcomed the resultant revived economy. Especially for sons and daughters of the large French-Canadian rural families, it meant the possibility of staying in Quebec rather than having to emigrate to New England because of the lack of opportunity at home. The Quebec government, for its part, cooperated with the process, particularly when the Liberals were in power (from 1897–1944 with the exception of three years) (cf. Vigod, 1986). But the control still maintained by the religio-nationalist conservative elite over educational and cultural institutions ensured that the "nation" was not identified with the process. It was something that "happened" in French Quebec and to French Canadians; but most of the French-

Canadian elite witnessed it from the margins and often expressed their unease with its consequences.

Concomitant with industrialization was gradual, then rapid urbanization. The ideal of the farming and colonizing life in small villages was definitively undermined by this process, its realization becoming less and less of a possibility for Quebeckers. Clinging to a conception of social order and a moral code correlated with a land-based economy, the church adjusted to the fact that its flock was increasingly urban and industrial only with difficulty and complaint. Much as the Catholic church in Europe developed its "social teaching" slowly and reluctantly in response to similar circumstances, so the Quebec church fought a long rearguard action in its own territory.

Thus, until World War II, Quebec religious and lay elites remained critical of encroaching modernity: industrial wealth was viewed as essentially ephemeral and the Great Depression was characterized as only the worst symptom of this weakness. Colonization, in their opinion, presented the sole, secure alternative to industrialism. Similarly, movements for women's rights and compulsory free education were portrayed as foreign (i.e., Anglo-Saxon and Protestant) ideas that undermined the traditional family that comprised the basic building block of Quebec society. Government action respecting the sacrosanct areas of the family and morals (e.g., public charities, liquor laws, old age pensions) was tenaciously fought if it did not conform with religious priorities (for various examples, with nuances and contradictions, cf. Bélanger, 1974; Dumont, et al., 1974; 1978).

In the present, theoretical context, the spread of an industrial economy in Quebec raises the question of whether the clerico-national strategy was really the sort of filter for a selective appropriation of modernity that I am claiming it was. After all, it can be argued that this defensive religious nationalism was really only an elite ideology bearing little relation to social reality in Quebec and resulting in the powerlessness of the French-Canadian elite and in the progressive proletarianization of the urban masses. While these outcomes cannot be denied, they look at the matter too exclusively from the point of view of the economic system. A central aspect of the thesis I am presenting is that the inclusion of a marginal area into the developing global society involves more than economic development, political centralization, and technico-scientific advance. "Cultural" continuity is also at issue, particularly in those areas, such as Quebec, where certain key economic, political, and scientific features of modernity were not or are not a part of the indigenous culture. To appropriate these features means to find a way of being French-Canadian *and* a capitalist, French-Canadian *and* a liberal or social democrat; or, what amounts to the same, of being Roman Catholic *and* modern. Again, the struggle of Quebeckers and the struggle of the Roman church in Europe to "preserve their identities" in the process of profound change are parallel. What makes them parallel is the focus of both identities on the religious system of modern society.

Therefore, beside the negative response of the Quebec clerico-national elite to industrialization and urbanization, one must also look at the positive and creative side. As this modernizing process was occurring, Quebeckers created new institutions inspired by the social Catholicism that had, from the beginning of the twentieth century, arisen in Europe for similar reasons.[17] Catholic trade unions would ensure that the industrial environment in which an increasing percentage of the people found themselves would not destroy the religio-cultural priorities on which the moral health of the nation depended. Supporting organizations such as the *Ecole sociale populaire*,[18] with its espousal of "corporatism,"[19] would ensure that the workers and their families would not be seduced by alternative interpretations of their socioecomomic situation, especially those deemed socialist. Agricultural colonization of new areas in the Canadian Shield continued to be promoted as the chief solution to the social problems associated with an industrial and urban environment. Catholic Action groups, especially for the working-class youth, would evangelize the various industrial and urban milieux under the watchful eye of the episcopal hierarchy and in response to the call of the popes (cf. Hamelin, 1984; Hamelin and Gagnon, 1984). Social Catholicism also inspired new political movements. Above all the *Action Libérale Nationale* of the mid-1930s sought a Quebec government that would limit the power of large foreign industrial and financial concerns, as well as instituting other social and political reforms. After allying itself with the Quebec Conservatives to form the *Union Nationale*, it came to power in 1936 only to have

---

17 There is, of course, some similarity between what happened in Quebec and the phenomenon called "pillarization" in the Benelux countries (see Moberg, 1961; Martin, 1978; Coleman, 1979; Dobbelaere, 1987). The critical difference, however, is the Quebec association with nationalism which makes it perhaps more comparable to the history of Ireland or Poland.

18 Founded in 1911, the *Ecole sociale populaire* was a multi-functional organization dedicated to guiding the application of Catholic social teaching in Quebec. Among other activities, it published newspapers and journals, trained lay leaders, organized retreats, mini-courses (esp. *Semaines sociales*), and other educational activities. Especially in the nineteen twenties and 'thirties, it saw itself as providing an explicit alternative to what it perceived as communist and socialist threats, often, as with the Commonwealth Cooperative Federation (the forerunner of the current New Democratic Party), emanating from English Canada. Cf. Bélanger, 1974:307–328.

19 This term refers to that vision of societal organization that sought a solution to the economic class divisions and isolating individualism of modern Western society in "corporations" that would include all the members of each industry or profession in one organization. These corporations would have legal status between the individual and the state; and include both management and labour. This "third way" between communism and capitalism was particularly promoted by Pius XI and thus, at least until after World War II, was an official part of Catholic social teaching and hence a common goal of social Catholic ideologues.

its programme abandoned as the old political ways continued,[20] but now with an even more conservative attitude to social questions such as the role of unions (cf. Quinn, 1979).

None of these responses, of course, broke in any decisive way with the traditional religio-national strategy. Nonetheless, especially as regards the Catholic trade unions and the *Union Nationale*, the conservative and traditionalist upholders of this strategy were becoming increasingly involved in an institutional and practical way in precisely those societal subsystems that had previously been avoided, considered suspect, and looked upon as somehow alien to true French-Canadian identity. Critical in the current context is that they did this on the basis of the system which they considered the most central to this identity, the religious. The vital role of social Catholicism in all this cannot be overestimated. Here, in effect, was an indigenous,[21] trusted way of responding to increasingly dominant modern structures; one in complete continuity with the national self-conception. Admittedly, what has been mentioned thus far can be seen as an attempt to *incorporate*—and the philosophy of corporatism expresses it well—the new economic and political pressures into the existing religio-cultural ideology. Yet from another angle, the political and economic derivations from social Catholicism that institutionalized themselves in Quebec provided the solid beginnings of a way of being a true Catholic French-Canadian without necessarily holding a traditional conception of these vital areas of social life.

The key factor in this reversal was the immersion of the traditional ideology in the modern structures. Movements such as *Action Libérale Nationale* and organizations such as Catholic trade unions and Catholic Action groups had the approval of the traditional elite, including of course most of the Catholic hierarchy. They also exposed Quebeckers imbued with the religio-national vision to the exigencies and ideals of the modern structures. Catholic trade unions were founded with the full approval of the bishops to counter the divisive and conflictual attitude of the international unions. However, rather than being able to reestablish harmony and unity between workers and management on the basis of Catholic social teaching, the appalling working conditions of their members forced the Catholic unions to act in consonance with conflictual class divisions within the economic system or lose their members to the religiously neutral (and therefore suspect) international unions. Especially after World War II, the Catholic unions became more militant, often with

---

20 The old ways were those that the Liberals had pursued: full cooperation with foreign-controlled industry, and a great reluctance to enact social legislation. Cf. Vigod, 1986; Quinn, 1979.

21 Given the European origin of social Catholicism in general, the indigenous character of this tradition in Quebec may seem questionable. Its key role in traditional Quebec identity, however, allows any movement spawned by Roman Catholicism to be perceived as indigenous since it flows from that society's very nature.

the full approval of the clerical advisors appointed to guide them. A characteristic example was the Asbestos Strike of 1949 (cf. Trudeau, 1974), a bitter and some-times violent affair that saw the advisors (chaplains) and even several bishops join the battle on the side of the workers. Shortly after this event, the Quebec bishops issued a joint pastoral letter in which they acknowledged that Quebec society was irrevocably industrial and urban, a fact that few of them had granted before.

An analogous "radicalization" occurred within the Catholic Action groups. These were founded in the nineteen thirties on the Belgian and French models as a method of involving lay Catholics in the reappropriation of their respective milieux for the church and Catholicism. Chief among them were youth groups for the worker and student milieux (JOC, *Jeunesse Ouvrière Catholique*; JEC, *Jeunesse Etudiante Catholique*). These had some success among clerical workers and students in the classical colleges, but did not succeed in penetrating the industrial workplace or ei-ther of the two French-speaking universities. Unlike in other Catholic countries of Europe and Latin America, Catholic Action in Quebec had no significant socialist or communist threat to counter, despite official fears to the contrary. Without a clear enemy to give them cohesion and purpose, Catholic Action militants resorted to fighting among themselves and with their clerical directors and the bishops over the control and activity of their organizations. Although Catholic Action accom-plished little as regards its original purpose, it did act as the training ground for a number of future lay leaders who played a signficant role in the secularized Quebec society of the nineteen sixties and seventies.[22] As with the Catholic unions, the church's attempt to respond to the problems and pressures of modern structures in Quebec eventually led more to the questioning of the traditional ideology than to its reinforcement and revitalization.

As the examples of *Action Libérale Nationale*, the Catholic unions, and Catholic Action show, the attempt by the Roman Catholic church in Quebec to maintain its cultural hegemony did not prevent Quebec society from becoming increasingly modern. The demands, especially of the political and economic systems, could not be met with responses that took the religious system as their principal point of departure. Almost invariably, social Catholicism in Quebec spawned organiza-tions that merely talked about Quebec's problems, disappeared in the attempt to put ideology into practice, or took on the functional priorities of the milieux that they were intended to capture for the traditional religiously dominated vision. In the

---

22 To mention but a few names: Pierre Juneau has been head of the Canadian Radio and Television Commission and Air Canada; Gérard Pelletier came to Ottawa in the nine-teen sixties with Pierre Trudeau and Jean Marchand (a Catholic union leader during the Asbestos Strike) and was a federal cabinet minister and later Canadian ambassador to France; Camille Laurin was a Parti Québécois cabinet minister under René Lévesque; Claude Ryan was editor of the influential Montreal daily, *Le Devoir*, and leader to the opposition Liberal Party in Quebec during Lévesque's tenure.

process, social Catholicism in Quebec provided a significant transitional path between this traditional identity and the modern, expressly political nationalism of the nineteen sixties and 'seventies with its emphasis on a strong centralized state, democratic socialist or capitalist economic structures, secularized and uniform education and health facilities, an independent and thriving artistic community, a pluralistic religious system, and individualistic personal identities.

To be sure, such unintended consequences of Catholic social action were complemented by expressly counter-traditional forces within Quebec Catholicism. "Pioneer ideologies" (Bélanger, 1977) of the nineteen thirties and 'forties began to break with traditional nationalism. Inspired by the left-wing Catholic thought of Europeans like Emmanuel Mounier and Jacques Maritain, "neo-nationalists" (Behiels, 1985:20–60) like André Laurendeau of the Montreal daily, *Le Devoir*, and Robert Charbonneau of the revue, *La Relève*, defended a new Catholicism that maintained its critique of modern capitalism and individualism while rejecting the defensive and isolationist view of traditional French-Canadian Catholicism. Such developments among the young Quebec intelligentsia prepared the ground for more definitive breaks with religio-nationalism. In the 1950s, periodicals such as *Cité Libre* and *Parti Pris* presented an inter-national and politico-national alternative respectively. Here too, a vision of Catholicism intended to maintain religion's relevance in the face of modernizing structures played the unintended role of midwife to its own secularized replacements.

Within the church-controlled educational system, there were equally significant developments. Here the Dominicans played a critical role, in particular Georges-Henri Lévesque, a professor at Laval University in Quebec City. In the nineteen thirties, Lévesque established Quebec's first French school of social science there with the purpose of training students in empirical, research-oriented social science. Although he staunchly defended the church's social teaching and viewed the school as an application of it, Lévesque nevertheless institutionalized a distinction between the religiously grounded teaching and the quite independent realm of scientific research. His students, while remaining good Catholics, were to become and did indeed become good social scientists as well. Lévesque's critics among the traditional elite opposed him precisely because his efforts implied what, in Luhmannian terms, is the functional differentiation of religion and science. And indeed, under Lévesque's successors and former students, the school of social science was transformed into a purely secular institution that practiced social science instead of applying the church's social teaching. Again, social Catholicism had produced an institution that, rather than reasserting the influence of Catholicism in Quebec society, undermined that influence instead.

Lévesque's role, moreover, was not limited to developments at Laval University. The Dominican leader was also active in the cooperative movement in Quebec. As another major plank in the Catholic social platform, cooperatives of various kinds were founded by the Catholic church in Quebec to buffer French-Canadians from the harshness and insecurity of the market and to embody Catholic social principles in their economic activity. Here again, in the immediate post-war period, Lévesque and the Dominicans advocated the "de-confessionalization" of the cooperatives, arguing expressly that keeping them Catholic would make them less efficient economically *and* potentially damaging to the influence of the church when they failed (cf. Hamelin, 1984:91–96). While the subject of much controversy in Quebec at the time, the Dominican attitude to cooperatives eventually prevailed.

The shift in Quebec identity in the post-war period was, of course, not just a consequence of developments within the religious system. Within the artistic system, for example, Paul-Emile Borduas withdrew the visual arts from the domination of church and farm, and, with a number of other artists, published *Le Refus global*, a manifesto rejecting the traditional Quebec view of the arts in favour of international artistic culture. In the world of drama, playwrights such as Gratien Gélinas pointed to the disparity between the sacred ideology and the profane motivations that really directed the actions of most Quebeckers. At the same time, the French language network of the Canadian Broadcasting Corporation, *Radio Canada*, not only brought cultural communication from the outside, but more importantly provided an entirely new arena in which Quebec writers and artists could flourish on a hitherto unprecedented scale (cf. Trofimenkoff, 1982:282ff).

Throughout the century, the educational system had been expanding, making it increasingly difficult for the church to finance its operation and fill its teaching vacancies with clerics and members of religious orders. The church was most solidly entrenched here, more solidly than in any other major institution in the province. Yet the introduction of compulsory education to age 14 by the Liberal government during the Second World War signalled the changing place of education in Quebec society. With increasing difficulty could the church claim the schools as primarily an extension of its moral mission. The Catholic schools were *de facto* virtually the only French-speaking schools. If French Quebeckers were to be given that general education necessary for full participation in a modern industrial society, the school system had to do more than acculturate its charges to the traditional Catholic worldview. The establishment of a Ministry of Education in 1964, a political decision that had been fought successfully on previous occasions, meant that the Catholic church no longer had the final word on many aspects of education, reflecting the increased range and complexity of the educational task.

The political system was witness to analogous developments. It was the *Union Nationale*, in power for the entire post-war period up to 1960, that extended its influence into such areas as the church had previously serviced. This was not done for ideological reasons, but because the size of these institutions now exceeded the capacities of the church, and because this was the only way of preventing federal authorities from increasing their influence in these areas as they had done elsewhere in Canada. The *Union Nationale* government, under its leader Maurice Duplessis, was highly traditional in its methods and outlook; and during another era would undoubtedly have embraced the religio-national ideology. Yet, in seeking to defend its traditional vision of Quebec society, it found itself, of necessity, contributing to the building of an unprecedented, modern state apparatus in Quebec. All that remained was for the growing anti-traditional forces to take over the government after Duplessis' death.

While these developments in other functional spheres of Quebec society were important aspects of the change that occurred in Quebec society in the post-war period, they do not diminish the role of social Catholicism in the process. The functional sphere around which Quebec's "national identity" had been constructed in the past now provided a way for Quebeckers to modernize in continuity with that past identity. The leaders of Quebec's "Quiet Revolution," the name given to the period of rapid change after 1960, did not have to be anti-clerical and anti-Catholic to institute their program. Many of them were products of social Catholicism and saw no radical contradiction between their efforts and the position of the church. Within the church, some, such as the Dominicans through their review, *Communauté Chrétienne* (cf. Poirier, 1981), encouraged change. Others, notably the Quebec epis-copate, while generally reluctant, recognized that the church and the new lay elite could coexist on friendly and, by and large, cooperative terms. Unlike in many countries in Europe and Latin America, secularization and modernization in Quebec did not bring with it significant anti-clericalism. The combination of Quebec's tradi-tional religio-national identity and social Catholicism were instrumental in allowing this to happen (cf. Baum, 1986/87).

Since the advent of the Quiet Revolution in 1960, the role of Roman Catholicism in Quebec society has changed dramatically. The church has lost its central role in the definition and maintenance of French-Canadian identity. In what to many was a reversal of the *patriote* defeat of the nineteenth century, Quebeckers of the nineteen sixties and 'seventies increasingly espoused a political nationalism that offered Quebeckers a political and secular salvation where before they had assumed that the ultimate goals of life and nation were religious. Reflecting this loss of centrality, the church of the nineteen sixties considered itself a church in crisis. The number of priests and members of religious orders declined dramatically (cf. Hamelin, 1984:II,269ff). Religious practice among Catholic Quebeckers showed similar tendencies. In 1965, for instance, almost ninety percent of Quebec Catholics attended mass regularly; by 1985, this figure had dropped to less than forty percent (Bibby, 1987:20).

Following the decline in the dominant church, new groups and old ones formerly marginal or confined to the English-speaking population have entered the religious scene. Evangelical Protestantism, New Religious Movements (the so-called "cults"), and human potential groups have all attracted the attention of French Quebeckers, even though in absolute numbers these tendencies are quite small. A new variety has come to characterize religious life.

This variety is, moreover, also very evident within the Catholic church itself. From French-Canadian "marriage encounter" groups to Catholic pentecostalisin, from politically oriented "basic ecclesial communities" to feminist theology, from conservative Catholic parents' associations to liberal bishops, the number of new developments in the Quebec church seems endless.[23] Certainly, in the traditional church, there existed a variety of organizations and activities, but these were under the control of the episcopacy and, without exception, expressive of a consistent and even monolithic ideology. Today the organizational and ideological pluralism of Catholicism is not only consistent with the diversity of a modern, secularized society, but is also significantly less subject to the clear control of the episcopal hierarchy.

Again, as was the case in the past, developments in Quebec Catholicism reflect and parallel those in the worldwide church. Since Vatican II, Roman Catholicism has undergone dramatic changes in most parts of the globe. While the manifestations of these changes in Quebec bear the stamp of the unique context there, they are nevertheless entirely consistent with what is happening worldwide. From Catholic Action groups that have become sociopolitical action groups to women's movements within the church; from charismatic renewal to traditionalist groups that yearn for the "good old days"; these and many more are witness to the fact that the church has changed and is changing—in Quebec as elsewhere.

Conclusion

As David Martin has pointed out, the case of Quebec has numerous partial parallels in the Catholic world, parallels with Flanders in Belgium and the Basque country in Spain, parallels with Poland and Ireland (Martin, 1988:13f). The path to industrialization and modernization it shares to a large degree with the former; the strong traditional religious identity with the latter. Although in its details the story of Quebec Catholicism is unique, in its general pattern it serves to illustrate aspects of a wider phenomenon within Catholicism and within global society.

---

23 Unfortunately, there exist relatively few detailed studies on many of these developments. For a general overview, see Hamelin, 1984:356ff. Some indication of the variety and degree of religious involvement by Quebeckers in the Catholic church of today can be found in Dumont, et al., 1982; and Bissonette, et al., 1982. Catholic family movements like "Marriage Encounter" are discussed in Caron, et al., 1985. Various aspects of the changed situation for Catholicism in Quebec, including the role of religion in education, the family, and psychological well-being are analyzed in the contributions to Desrosier, 1986. On the Catholic charismatic movement, see Chagnon, 1979; Zylberberg and Montminy, 1984; on Catholic sociopolitical movements, see Vaillancourt, 1984; on women's movements within the church, Lacelle, 1984.

This modern global society first developed its key structural characteristic, a dominance of functional subsystem formation, in Western society, predominantly in North-Western Europe and North America. The spread of this characteristic to the rest of the world and to peripheral areas of the core regions has been uneven and incomplete. It has presented the peripheral regions with the prospect or reality of very rapid and discontinuous social change. It has also excluded many of these regions and their inhabitants from the full benefits of the modern structures, leaving them only with the not insignificant costs. In areas where it is dominant, Roman Catholicism has frequently attempted to act as a buffer to such change, very often with the express intention of preventing it or even restoring the supposedly sounder social order of the traditional past. For approximately a century, Catholicism successfully played this role in the once peripheral region of Quebec.

What this chapter has demonstrated is that the success of the Roman church in filling this role in Quebec and the eventual rapid modernization of this society after the Second World War are both connected with the centrality of function in modern circumstances. Catholicism was able to act as the guarantor of Quebec identity, as the integrator of that society during the century before the war, because it allowed a solution to the problem of cultural and structural continuity in terms of function. The cost, of course, was the relative exclusion of Quebec from the power and wealth of modernity. When the rapid development of especially the economic, political, and scientific-technological systems in North America threatened to inundate (i.e., assimilate) French-Canadian culture during the first half of the nineteenth century, Roman Catholic religion provided the self-conception for Quebeckers to resist this cultural extinction successfully. When, in the late nineteenth and twentieth centuries, the industrialization of Quebec meant the relative exclusion of Quebeckers from the benefits of modernity while not sparing them the costs,[24] Roman Catholicism played an important role in providing for the greater inclusion of Quebeckers without sacrificing cultural distinctiveness. In particular, the institutions of social Catholicism allowed many Quebeckers, especially the traditional elite, to enter the functional spheres from which they were relatively excluded without ceasing to be French-Canadian. When the functional priorities of these spheres eventually impinged themselves on these institutions as well, the transition had to a large degree been successfully accomplished. Reflecting this transition, Catholicism in Quebec, as elsewhere, changed dramatically as its old role became redundant. Since the Quiet Revolution, Quebec Catholicism has developed in new and varied directions, attempting to deal with a functional independence that it had not experienced before.

---

24 To give but two outstanding examples, at the beginning of our century, Montreal was perhaps the unhealthiest city in North America for working-class people. Housing conditions, education, and public health were all woefully inadequate (cf. Copp, 1974). In addition, as late as 1961, the average income of French-Canadians in Quebec was among the lowest of all ethnic groups in that province (cf. Gagnon, 1969).

Cut adrift in a secularized Quebec partly and unintentionally of its own making, the Roman Catholic church is faced with new and unaccustomed choices that are reshaping it for an indeterminate future.

LIST OF WORKS CITED

Baum, Gregory. 1986/87. "Catholicism and Secularization in Québec." *Cross Currents* 36: 436–458.

Behiels, Michael D. 1985. *Prelude to Quebec's Quiet Revolution: Liberalism versus Neo-nationalism 1945–1960.* Kingston/Montreal: McGill-Queen's University Press.

Bélanger, André-J. 1974. *L'Apolitisme des idéologies québécoises: Le grand tournant de 1934–1936.* Quebec City: Presses de l'Université Laval.

——————. 1977. *Ruptures et constantes: Quatre idéologies en éclatement: La Relève, la JEC, Cité Libre, Parti Pris.* Montreal: Hurtubise HMH.

Bellefleur, Michel. 1986. *L'Eglise et le loisir au Québec avant la Révolution Tranquille.* Quebec City: Presses de l'Université du Québec.

Bernard, Jean-Paul. 1971. *Les Rouges: Libéralisme, nationalisme et anticléricalisme au milieu du XIXe siècle.* Montreal: Presses de l'Université du Québec.

Beyer, Peter. 1985. "The Mission of Quebec Ultramontanism: A Luhmannian Perspective." *Sociological Analysis* 46:37–48.

Bibby, Reginald W. 1987. *Fragmented Gods: The Poverty and Potential of Religion in Canada.* Toronto: Irwin.

Bissonnette, Jean-Guy, et al. 1982. *Situation et avenir du catholicisme québécois. Tome I: Milieux et témoignages.* Montreal: Leméac.

Brunet, Michel. 1964. "Trois dominantes de la pensée canadienne-française: l'agriculturisme, l'anti-étatisme et le messianisme" in his *La présence anglaise et les Canadiens: Etudes sur l'histoire et la pensée des deux Canadas.* Montreal: Beauchemin.

Camp, Richard L. 1969. *The Papal Ideology of Social Reform: A Study in Historical Development 1878–1967.* Leiden: E.J. Brill.

Caron, Anita, et al. 1985. *La famille québécoise: Institution en mutation?* Montreal: Fides.

Chabot, Richard. 1975. *Le curé de campagne et la contestation locale au Québec (de 1791 aux troubles de 1837–38).* Montreal: Hurtubise HMH.

Chagnon, Roland. 1979. *Les charismatiques au Québec.* Montreal: Québec/Amérique.

Coleman, John A. 1979. *The Evolution of Dutch Catholicism.* Berkeley: University of California.

Copp, Terry. 1974. *The Anatomy of Poverty: The Condition of the Working Class in Montreal 1897–1929.* Toronto: McClelland & Stewart.

Desrosiers, Yvon, ed. 1986. *Religion et culture au Québec. Figures contemporaines du sacré.* Montreal: Fides.

Dobbelaere, Karel. 1987. "Some Trends in European Sociology of Religion: The Secularization Debate," *Sociological Analysis* 48:107–137.

——————. 1988. "Secularization, Pillarization, Religious Involvement, and Religious Change in the Low Countries," pp. 80–115 in Thomas M. Gannon, ed., *World Catholicism in Transition.* New York: Macmillan.

Dorr, Donal. 1983. *Option for the Poor: A Hundred Years of Vatican Social Teaching.* New York: Orbis.

Dumont, Fernand, et. al. 1973. *Idéologies au Canada Français 1900–1929.* Quebec City: Presses de l'Université Laval.

——————, et. al. 1978. *Idéologies au Canada Français 1930–1939.* Quebec City: Presses de l'Université Laval.

——————, et. al. 1982. *Situation et avenir du catholicisme québécois. Tome II: Entre le temple et l'exil.* Montreal: Leméac.

Dupont, Antonin. 1972. *Les relations entre l'Eglise et l'Etat sous Louis-Alexandre Taschereau 1920–1936.* Montreal: Guérin.

Eid, Nadia F. 1978. *Le clergé et le pouvoir politique au Québec: Une analyse de l'idéologie ultramontaine au milieu du XIXe siècle.* Montreal: Hurtubise HMH.

Elias, Norbert. 1978. *The History of Manners: The Civilizing Process. Volume I.* Edmund Jephcott, trans. New York: Pantheon.

——————. 1982. *Power and Civility: The Civilizing Process Volume II.* Edmund Jephcott, trans. New York: Pantheon.

Gagnon, Lysiane. 1969. "Les conclusions du Rapport B.B.: De Durham à Laurendeau-Dunton: Variations sur le thème de *la dualité canadienne,*" pp. 233–252 in Robert Comeau, ed., *Economie Québécoise.* Montreal: Université du Québec à Montréal.

Gannon, Thomas M., ed., 1988. *World Catholicism in Transition.* New York: Macmillan.

Gellner, Ernest. 1964. *Thought and Change.* London: Weidenfeld and Nicolson.

——————. 1983. *Nations and Nationalism.* London: Basil Blackwell.

Hamelin, Jean. 1984. *Histoire du catholicisme québécois: Le XXe siècle. Tome 2: De 1940 à nos jours.* Nive Voisine, ed. Montreal: Boréal Express.

—————— and Nicole Gagnon. 1984. *Histoire du catholicisme québécois: Le XXe siècle. Tome 1: 1898–1940.* Nive Voisine, ed. Montreal: Boréal Express.

Lacelle, Elisabeth J. 1984. "Le mouvement des femmes dans le christianisme récent. D'une Eglise éclatée à une foi en éclatement," pp. 207–234 in Jean-Paul Rouleau and Jacques Zylberberg, eds., *Les mouvements religieux aujourd'hui: Théoriques et pratiques.* Les Cahiers de recherches en sciences de la religion, Volume 5. Montreal: Bellarmin.

Lajeunesse, Marcel. 1971. "L'évêque Bourget et l'instruction publique au Bas-Canada, (1840-1846)," pp. 41–58 in Marcel Lajeunesse, ed. *L'éducation au Québec (19e – 20e siècles).* Montreal: Boréal Express.

Lechner, Frank J. 1985. "Modernity and Its Discontents." pp. 157–176 in Jeffrey Alexander, ed., *Neofunctionalism.* Beverley Hills: Sage.

Levitt, Joseph. 1973. "Henri Bourassa: The Catholic Social Order and Canada's Mission." pp. 193–222 in Fernand Dumont, et al., *Idéologies au Canada Français 1900–1929.* Quebec City: Presses de l'Université Laval.

Luhmann, Niklas. 1980–81. *Gesellschaftsstruktur und Semantik: Studien zur Wissenssoziologie der modernen Gesellschaft.* 2 vols. Frankfurt/M: Suhrkamp.

——————. 1982. *The Differentiation of Society,* trans. Stephen Holmes and Charles Larmore. New York: Columbia UP.

Martin, David. 1978. *A General Theory of Secularization.* New York: Harper & Row.

——————. 1988. "Catholicism in Transition," pp. 3–35 in Thomas M. Gannon, ed.,

World Catholicism in Transition. New York: Macmillan.

Mayo, Patricia. 1974. *The Roots of Identity: Three Nationalist Movements in Contemporary European Politics.* London: Allen Lane.

Moberg, David O. 1961. "Religion and Society in the Netherlands and in America," *American Quarterly* 13:172–178.

Monet, Jacques. 1969. *The Last Cannon Shot: A Study of French-Canadian Nationalism, 1837–1950.* Toronto: University of Toronto.

Neatby, Hilda. 1966. *Quebec: The Revolutionary Age, 1760–1791.* Canadian Centenary Series. Toronto: McClelland & Stewart.

Orensanz, Aurelio. 1988. "Spanish Catholicism in Transition," pp. 133–146 in Thomas M. Gannon, ed., *World Catholicism in Transition.* New York: Macmillan.

Ouellet, Fernand. 1964. "Le nationalisme canadien-français: De ses origines à l'insurrection de 1837." *Canadian Historical Review* 45:277–292.

───────. 1980. *Lower Canada 1791–1840: Social Change and Nationalism.* Trans. Patricia Claxton. Canadian Centenary Series. Toronto: McClelland & Stewart.

Parsons, Talcott. 1971. *The System of Modern Societies.* Englewood Cliffs, NJ: Prentice-Hall.

Poirier, Marcel. 1981. "Une réforme inachevé: La Revue *Communauté Chrétienne,* 1962–1972," pp. 299–324 in Fernand Dumont, et al., *Idéologies au Canada Français 1940–1976. Vol. III: Les Partis politiques—L'Eglise.* Quebec City: Presses de l'Université Laval.

Quinn, Herbert F. 1979. *The Union Nationale: Quebec Nationalism from Duplessis to Lévesque.* Rev. ed. Toronto: University of Toronto Press.

Rousseau, Louis. 1986. "A l'origine d'une société maintenant perdue: le réveil religieux montréalais de 1840," pp. 71–92 in Yvon Desrosiers, ed., *Religion et culture au Québec. Figures contemporaines du sacré.* Montreal: Fides.

See, Katherine O'Sullivan. 1986. *First World Nationalisms: Class and Ethnic Politics in Northern Ireland and Quebec.* Chicago: University of Chicago Press.

Smith, Anthony D. 1981. *The Ethnic Revival.* Cambridge: Cambridge Univ. Press.

───────. 1986. *The Ethnic Origins of Nations.* London: Basil Blackwell.

Trofimenkoff, Susan Mann. 1982. *The Dream of Nation: A Social and Intellectual History of Quebec.* Toronto: Macmillan.

Trudeau, Pierre Elliott, et al. 1974. *The Asbestos Strike.* Toronto: James Lewis & Samuel.

Vaillancourt, Jean-Guy. 1980. *Papal Power: A Study of Vatican Control over Lay Catholic Elites.* Berkeley: University of California.

───────. 1984. "Les groupes socio-politiques dans le catholicisme québécois contemporain," pp. 261–282 in Jean-Paul Rouleau and Jacques Zylberberg, eds., *Les mouvements religieux aujourd'hui: Théoriques et pratiques.* Les Cahiers de recherches en sciences de la religion, Volume 5. Montreal: Bellarmin.

Vidler, Alec R. 1971. *The Church in an Age of Revolution: 1789 to the Present Day.* Harmondsworth: Penguin.

Vigod, Bernard L. 1986. *Quebec before Duplessis: The Political Career of Louis-Alexandre Taschereau.* Montreal and Kingston: McGill-Queen's University Press.

Zylberberg, Jacques, and Jean-Paul Montminy. 1984. "Soumission charismatique: Thanatologie d'un mouvement sacral," pp. 283–298 in Jean-Paul Rouleau and Jacques Zylberberg, eds., *Les mouvements religieux aujourd'hui: Théoriques et pratiques.* Les Cahiers de recherches en sciences de la religion, Volume 5. Montreal: Bellarmin.

2.

Italian Catholicism:
Making Direct Contact with the Sacred

Michael P. Carroll

Writing in 1897, Durkheim could say that "All variation is abhorrent to Catholic thought."[1] I suspect that a great many people, scholars and non-scholars alike, still think of the pre-Vatican II Catholic Church in the same terms. What is generally overlooked is that the doctrinal and devotional homogeneity that we associate with the pre-Vatican II Catholic Church was itself a relatively recent phenomenon. Indeed, it was only in the middle of the 19th century that Church authorities began a systematic and fairly intense campaign to standardize and homogenize Catholicism. This campaign, usually called "romanization," was a natural complement to the ul-tramontanist campaign to strengthen the authority of the Pope over the Universal Church.[2]

At one level, romanization meant that Church authorities, notably including the Pope himself and the Curia, greatly intensified the promulgation of "universalistic" Catholic devotions, that is, devotions which were not tied to specific geographical settings and which could be practiced by any Catholic anywhere in the world. Sometimes this meant a renewed emphasis upon devotions that had had some degree of popular support for centuries, like, for example, the devotions associated with the Rosary, the Brown Scapular of Our Lady of Mount Carmel, the Forty Hours, the Sacred Heart of Jesus, the Immaculate Conception, and so on. In other cases, it meant promulgating new devotions. The most well-known case here involved

---

1 Emile Durkheim, *Suicide*, New York, The Free Press, 1951, p. 158.

2 For an overview of the romanization and ultramontanist campaigns of the 19th century, see J. Derek Holmes, *The Triumph of the Holy See*, London, Burns and Oates, 1978; R. Aubert, J. Beckmann, P. J. Corish, and R. Lill, *The Church in the Age of Liberalism*, New York, Crossroad Publishing, 1981; Ann Taves, *The Household of Faith*, Notre Dame, Indiana, University of Notre Dame Press, 1986.

devotion to Our Lady of Lourdes, who was quickly cut loose from her French origins and made an object of devotion throughout the Catholic world.

Less often noted by modern commentators, but just as important, romanization also mean promulgating a standardized set of criteria for defining what constituted a "good Catholic." The literature of the period makes it quite clear that a "good Catholic" was now defined to be someone who attended mass on a regular basis (read: every Sunday and on "Holy Days of Obligation"); who received the Sacraments regularly (read: regular Confession and Communion); who knew his or her catechism; who respected the authority of the clergy, and above all, of the Pope; who saw his or her local church as the center of religious activity; and who was willing to contribute to the financial support of the local church.

Though it might now seem obvious that a "good Catholic" would be defined in these terms, the fact is that these criteria were at odds with the practice of Catholicism that prevailed, or at least that had prevailed, in many areas of the Catholic world. For instance, it is now clear that Catholic practice in pre-Famine Ireland would not have matched the romanized ideal. On the contrary, in the pre-Famine period attendance at weekly mass was very low, and Catholic religious life was centered not upon the local church but rather upon pilgrimages and gatherings ("patterns") associated with various springs and ruins.[3]

Still, in the face of the romanization campaign, post-Famine Irish Catholics abandoned most of the old forms and became one of the most romanized of all Catholic groups. Far more interesting are those variants of Catholicism which were not only at odds with the romanized ideal, but which *persisted* despite the romanizing reforms. In trying to isolate the most "un-roman" of all the variants of Catholicism, we can avail ourselves of what amounts to a naturally-occurring experiment in the United States.

The Italian Problem

As a result of successive waves of immigration from Europe, the United States became home to a number of quite different "Catholicisms." There was of course the Catholicism of Spanish-speaking Catholics in the Southwest, and the Catholicism of French-speaking Catholics in the northeast. Then there were the various Catholicisms brought by immigrants from Ireland, Germany, Poland, Italy and other areas of Europe.[4] Faced with this situation, the hierarchy of the American Catholic

---

3 For a detailed discussion of Catholicism in pre-Famine Ireland, and how it differed from later forms of Irish Catholicism, see John Brady and Patrick J. Corish, "The Church under the Penal Code," in *A History of Irish Catholicism: Volume II, Part 2*, Dublin, Gil and Macmillan, 1971; S. J. Connolly, *Priests and People in Pre-Famine Ireland: 1780–1845*, Dublin, Gil and Macmillan, 1982; Emmet Larkin, "The Devotional Revolution in Ireland, 1850–1875," *American Historical Review*, 77, June, 1972, pp. 625–652.

4 For an overview of the various Catholicisms that coexisted in the United States, see Jay

Church eagerly embraced the reforms of the romanizers as a way of bringing unity to this diversity. The fact that the U.S. hierarchy at the turn of this century was dominated by Irish Catholics, that is, by men from the most romanized of all Catholic groups, only made this process easier.

But it quickly became apparent that certain "Catholicisms" were more easily romanized than others, and virtually everyone in the U.S. hierarchy agreed that the most difficult case involved the *Italians*. Indeed, there were any number of articles by American Catholic commentators in the first half of this century which talk quite openly, if indelicately, of the "Italian problem" in the American Catholic Church.[5]

The "Italian problem" involved far more than simply a desire to maintain an Old World cultural identity in a New World context. As early as the 1890s for instance the American hierarchy had been willing to allow the establishment of "national churches," that is, churches designed to serve the need of particular ethnic communities rather than all those Catholics living within a particular parish. Such national parishes were even allowed to use the language of the ethnic communities involved rather than English in the conduct of religious services. Nevertheless, figures from the beginning of this century indicate that although Italian Catholics outnumbered Polish Catholics, Polish Catholics were about twice as likely as Italian Catholics to found "national parishes" and about *three* times as likely to establish churches which used only a foreign language (that is, a language other English).[6] Polish Catholics, in other words, seemed far more concerned about maintaining their ethnic identity than Italian Catholics. Yet for most Catholic commentators, the Italians, not the Poles, were still "the problem."

It seems that there was something about the very nature of Italian Catholicism (in contrast, say, to Polish Catholicism, German Catholicism, etc.) that was radically inconsistent with the new romanized ideal. What?

The Nature of Italian Catholicism

Studies of the folk religion found in Italian and Italian-American communities in-

---

P. Dolan, *The American Catholic Experience*, Garden City, New York, Image Books, 1987.

5 See for instance Albert Bandini, "Concerning the Italian Problem," *The Ecclesiastical Review*, 62, March, 1920, pp. 278–285; John Tolino, "The Church in America and the Italian Problem," *The Ecclesiastical Review*, 100, January, 1933, pp. 22–32; Henry J. Browne, "The 'Italian Problem' in the Catholic Church of the United States 1880–1900," United States Catholic Historical Society, *Historical Records and Studies*, 35, 1946, pp. 46–72. For more recent discussions of the "Italian problem" see Rudolph J. Vecoli, "Prelates and Peasants: Italian Immigrants and the Church," *Journal of Social History*, 2, 1969, pp. 217–268; Edward C. Stibili, "The Italian St. Raphael Society," *U.S. Catholic Historian*, 6, 1987, pp. 301–314.

6 See Richard M. Linkh, *American Catholicism and European Immigrants (1900–1924)*, Staten Island, N.Y., Center for Migration Studies, 1975, pp. 108–109.

variably begin by making the same point: Italian folk religion is an admixture of two quite different sets of elements.[7] On the one hand, there are those obviously "Catholic" elements which are to some degree approved by Church authorities, at least at the local level. Included here would be the various beliefs and practices associated with the cult of the saints and the cult of the Madonna. On the other hand, there are all those elements variously labelled "pagan," "non-Christian," or "occult." The most important beliefs and practices here are those associated with the Evil Eye and with witches. This is not to deny that some of these "occult" elements may invoke Catholic imagery. On the contrary, one of the most common charms used to ward off the Evil Eye in South Italian communities is a folded copy of the "One True Letter of Jesus Christ," and candles or other objects blessed in church on the feast of St. Blaise are often used as a remedy for sore throats. The point is rather that these occult elements did not receive the approval of Church authorities and the local clergy played no official role in promulgating such beliefs and practices.

When confronting this mix of elements it is easy for commentators to become seduced by what seems "exotic" to the modern mind and to give the occult elements in Italian folk religion a disproportionate amount of attention. In some popular commentaries, for example, an emphasis upon the occult completely dominates the discussion of Italian folk religion, as in one early article which described it simply as a "religion of lucky pieces, witches and the evil eye."[8] Even in many of the scholarly studies cited above more attention is given to the "occult" elements in Italian folk religion than to anything else. It might be argued that these occult elements are given more attention, not because observers find them more exotic, but because they are in some sense "more important." Perhaps, but I have yet to see any arguments or evidence in support of that hypothesis.

What is clear is that to the romanizers in the U.S. Catholic Church earlier in this century, these occult elements were *not* the most important stumbling block in the

---

7 For some accounts of folk religion in Italian communities in both Italy and the United States, see Edward Banfield, *The Moral Basis of A Backward Society*, Glencoe, Ill., The Free Press, 1958, pp. 129–145; Carla Bianco, *The Two Rosetos*, Bloomington, Indiana University Press, 1974, pp. 84–106; Jan Brogger, *Montevarese*, Bergen, Oslo, Universitetforlaget, 1971; Charlotte Chapman, *Milocca: A Sicilian Village*, Cambridge, Mass., Schenkman, 1971, pp. 158–207; A. L. Maraspini, *The Study of an Italian Village*, Paris, Mouton, 1968, pp. 221–255; Sydel Silverman, *Three Bells of Civilization: The Life of an Italian Hill Town*, New York, Columbia University Press, 1975, pp. 149–177; Williams, Phyllis, *South Italian Folkways in Europe and America*, New York, Russell and Russell, 1969, pp. 135–159. For other studies, see Silvano M. Tomasi and Edward C. Stibili, *Italian Americans and Religion: An Annotated Bibliography*, New York, Center for Migration Studies, 1978.

8 Anonymous, "Religion of Lucky Pieces, Witches and the Evil Eye," *World Outlook*, 3, October, 1917, pp. 24–25.

romanization of Italian Catholics. Strange as it may seem, Catholic commentators who discussed the "Italian problem" in the United States paid little attention to the beliefs and practices surrounding the Evil Eye, witches, etc. They (unlike journalists and later social scientists) focused almost entirely upon the *Catholic* elements in Italian folk religion. There was something about these *Catholic* elements, they felt, that was at odds with romanization.

True Piety

Of all the literature dealing with the Italian problem in the United States, the most revealing is almost certainly the series of letters published in the Jesuit magazine *America* in the closing months of 1914. These letters should be required reading for anyone who sees the pre-Vatican II Catholic clergy as presenting a common front on Church-related matters. It all started innocently enough. In the October 17, 1914 issue of *America*, Joseph M. Sorrentino, himself a Jesuit, sought to reassure American Catholics that "religious conditions in Italy are infinitely better than many people are inclined to think," despite the strained relations between the Italian government and the Holy See.

Sorrentino's letter was a catalyst which released a torrent of criticism, mainly from Catholic priests, on the deplorable condition of Catholicism among Italians in both Italy and the United States. A few other priests tried to defend Italian Catholics, and in all something like 29 letters on this subject were published until the editor of *America* brought the debate to an end with an editorial on December 19, 1914. That editorial, incidentally, summarized the debate by indicating that indeed "there is an Italian problem."

Reading over these letters as a group, it is clear that the same charges were levelled at Italian Catholics over and over again: they don't attend Mass on a weekly basis; they don't know the catechism; they don't contribute to the support of their parish church; they don't make Confession and receive Holy Communion on a regular basis. The image of "good Catholic" that lies behind these criticisms is easily recognizable as the image defined by the criteria being promulgated by the romanizers. But even the severest critic could not quite say that Italian Catholics were "non-religious." They were religious all right, but they practiced the wrong *kind* of Catholicism.

The following comments, however negative, can still provide us with a glimpse of those aspects of Italian Catholicism that most bothered the romanizers:[9]

> ... piety does not consist in processions or carrying lighted candles, prostrations before a statue of the Madonna, in processions in honor of patron saints of villages. . . . (October 31, p. 66)
> ... it would appear that this environment which kills the essentials of Catholicity in

9 All of the following extracts are taken from *America*, Volume 12, on the dates indicated.

the Italian immigrant seems rather favorable to the growth of the incidentals, such as processions, festas , etc . . . (November 21, p. 145)

I entered a big Italian church in a big city [and saw many devotees] but to my surprise and . . . my disgust, their devotion consisted in lighting candles, prostrating themselves before statues, going from shrine to shrine, from side altar to side altar, side-tracking altogether the main altar wherein reposed the Saviour of men. . . . (December 19, p. 244)

Even remarks by those sympathetic to Italian Catholics are useful in pinpointing the unique features of Italian Catholicism. Thus to the charge that Italian Catholics do not attend Mass regularly, Bishop E. M. Dunne (who had worked in a large South Italian parish in Chicago) pointed out that on certain days Italian-American Catholics did flock to their churches:

My experience has been to see the church crowded on the feasts of SS. Peter and Paul, Nativity of St. John the Baptist, SS. Vitus, Roch, Lucy, Sebastian and all the feasts of the Blessed Virgin just the same as on Sunday. (November 21, p. 144)

All the saints named by Bishop Dunne are recognizable as saints whose cults are widely popular through southern Italy. Another priest, commenting upon the "simple and beautiful faith" of a group of Italian immigrants he met on a steamer tells us:

They showed me with pride their rosaries and related to me with glowing vivacity their devotional experiences at the Shrine of St. Anthony, whither they had gone in pilgrimage before leaving for America. (Nov. 28, 1914, p. 169)

In a later letter, Sorrentino himself focused upon the same elements in Italian Catholicism that most appalled his critics, giving these elements a more positive cast:

As to statues, processions, heavy candles, emotionalism. etc. . . . I know as well as [my opponents] that religion does not consist in such exterior practices; often however they are a sign of the faith abiding in the heart and, moreover, are a real help in drawing people nearer to God. (December 5, p. 194)

It seems, in short, that all camps were in agreement upon the "distinctive" features of Italian Catholicism: it was a type of Catholicism dominated by festas, processions, statues, devotions to Madonnas and saints, emotionalism and pilgrimages. Later investigations have fleshed out these distinctive features in greater detail.

The festa, in particular, has attracted the attention of later scholars. In its simplest terms, the festa was a public celebration in honor of some particular Madonna or saint, and it was usually linked to official Catholicism in three ways. First, the celebration often (though by no means always) took place on the occasion of the feast day which the Church had established for the saint or Madonna in question. Second, some portion of the celebration involved attendance at a ceremony, usually a Mass, held in the local church and presided over by a priest. Finally, some portion of the proceeds raised by the festa went towards the support of the local church (though my sense is that this was not nearly as common in Italy as it became in the festa organized by Italians in North America).

But it must be emphasized that the *central* events in the festa were the processions and other activities which took place outside the local church and which were usually organized by lay associations. Moreover, it was expected that the festa would provide the occasion for a wide variety of non-religious activities—including drinking—whose purpose was quite clearly to foster sociability.

Festas are described in virtually all the monographs cited above. One of the best descriptive accounts of the typical festa held in North America can be found, perhaps surprisingly, in Tolino's 1938 polemic against Italian Catholicism.[10] Vecoli also provides a good account of the characteristics of the "ideal" festa in both North America and Italy.[11] More recently still, Orsi has provided a fairly detailed description of the festa in honor of the Madonna del Carmine which dominated social life in Italian Harlem in New York earlier this century.[12] Sciorra gives a brief account of six different festas, some of which have been revived in recent years, celebrated by Italian-Americans in Brooklyn.[13] Incidentally, the one Brooklyn festa which dominates all others is in honor of St. Paulinus of Nola (a town near Naples). This festa involves building a "tower" that is 65 ft. in height and weighs 3,000 pounds. This tower *and* a band are then set upon a platform that is carried aloft through the town by 125 men. As impressive as all this is, it is still only a pale reflection of the celebration in Nola itself, which involves building *eight* towers of the sort just described, each of which is carried by about 120 men. Surprisingly, although the Nola festa is one of the most impressive festas still being celebrated in Italy, it has received virtually no attention from English-speaking scholars.[14]

Apart from the festa, another feature of Italian Catholicism that has attracted considerable scholarly attention is the "logic" of the cult of the saints. Saints, first and foremost, are supernatural beings who can be induced—by vows, the promise of votive offerings, even threats—to grant favors to individual supplicants. While

---

10 John Tolino, "Solving the Italian Problem," *The Ecclesiastical Review*, 99, September, 1938, pp. 254–255.

11 Rudolph J. Vecoli, "Cult and Occult In Italian-American Culture: The Persistence of a Religious Heritage," in R. M. Miller and T. D. Marzik (eds), *Immigrants and Religion in Urban America*, Philadelphia, Temple University Press, 1977, pp. 30–32.

12 Robert Orsi, *The Madonna of 115th Street*, New Haven, Yale University Press, 1985.

13 Joseph Sciorra, "Religious Processions in Italian Williamsburg," *The Drama Review*, 29, Fall, 1985, pp. 65–81.

14 A few pictures of the Nola festa appear in I. Sheldon Posen and Joseph Sciorra, "Brooklyn's Dancing Tower," *Natural History*, 92, June, 1983, pp. 30–37, but the text is mainly concerned with its Brooklyn counterpart. For an Italian language account of the Nola festa, see Franco Mangarella, *La Festa Infelice*, Napoli, Istituto Anselmi, 1973.

the official doctrine of the Church is that saints can only "intercede" with God on behalf of supplicants, the folk belief is clearly that saints themselves have the power to grant requests.

Not all saints are equally powerful in all regards. On the contrary, the cult of the saints is characterized by an extensive division of labor. Thus in Milocca, the Sicilian village studied by Chapman, St. Rosalia was more likely to be invoked in the face of perceived dangers from thunder and lightning; St. Zaccaharia was particularly adept at curing the inflammations of the breast which develop in nursing women; St. Prizzita could best secure for you a foreknowledge of approaching death; St. Calogero cured hernias; St. Onofrio healed burns; St. Vito offered protection against dogs; and so on.[15]

This is not to say that beliefs surrounding the cult of the saints are homogeneous throughout Italy. On the contrary, although some saints do indeed have a wide popularity throughout Italy (St. Rocco and St. Rita of Cascia come to mind), in other cases saints which are important in some regions might be missing entirely from others. Even within the same village, there can be disagreements over particular issues. In the Apulian village studied by Maraspini, for example, there were disagreements about which saints were most deserving of veneration and which were best at curing certain ailments.[16]

What is common throughout Italy then is only that in any given location a variety of different saints will be venerated and will as a group be characterized by a fairly extensive division of labor.

Cross-cutting these beliefs about saintly specialization is the belief that individuals have a stronger claim on the powers of their "patron" saint than on other saints. Generally, a "patron" saint is a saint considered to have a special relationship with some social category. The historical causes by which such relationships come to be established are many and varied. The most important patron saints, for example, are those associated with a particular village (or city), and these may have become patron saints because they were born in that village; because they had lived there for a long time; because their relics have resided there for centuries and have been particularly efficacious in warding off disaster, etc. But patron saints can also be associated with occupations, and broadly defined social categories, and the same saint can be patron for different groups in different places. In the Milocca, for example, St. Joseph was regarded most of all as patron saint of the poor,[17] while in the central Italian town of Montecastello, he was patron saint of artisans.[18] Finally, a patronal relationship can be formed with individuals as well as groups, so that Italian Catholics often regard the saint after whom they are named to be their patron

---

15 Chapman, op. cit., pp. 178–186.

16 Maraspini, op. cit., p. 227.

17 Chapman, op. cit., pp. 176–178.

18 Silverman, op. cit., p. 156.

saint. If someone has been given a name that corresponds to no known saint, the existence of a saint by that name might even be inferred simply by virtue of the fact that the name exists.[19]

Anyone who takes the time to read through the descriptive material dealing with the festas and devotions associated with Italian Catholicism in both Italy and North America will quickly realize that it is a type of Catholicism shaped by preferences and values quite different from those that underlay the romanized ideal. It becomes clear, for instance, that Italian Catholicism is a type of Catholicism in which: devotion to saints and the Madonna is central; devotions which depend upon the active participation of the entire community are to be preferred over those devotions (like the mass) where the clergy leads a basically passive congregation; the local church should be given a role to play in the conduct of religious devotions, but not the central role; attendance at church is "seasonal," that is, on the occasion of certain specific feast days, rather than weekly; the church is seen as a place for socializing with other members of the community and not primarily as a center for celebrating mass, and so on.

But there is more.

Digging Deeper

As already indicated, the romanizers of the early 20th century did not feel that the "Italian problem" derived most of all from the occult practices which Italian immigrants had brought with them from Italy. The problem lay rather in the type of Catholicism which they practiced. In seeking to isolate the "objectionable" features of this Catholicism, they focused upon its most obvious manifestations, notably the various festas in honor of the Madonna and the saints, and the various beliefs surrounding the cult of the saints.

Later scholarly investigators, once they get past the Evil Eye and witches, have tended to focus on these same obvious manifestations. These later investigators, of course, have not approached these folk devotions with the same negative outlook as the early romanizers. If anything, in fact, recent scholars have probably been more prone to romanticize these devotions. In describing the festa in honour of Our Lady of Mount Carmel in New York, for instance, Orsi gravitates towards populist imagery (as when he calls the festa a "theology of the streets"), and his detailed description of the food, community organization and general merrymaking which characterized the festa clearly creates the impression that the festa made a positive and important contribution to the well-being of the Italian community in Harlem.[20]

But I now want to argue that in focusing upon the festas and the cult of the saints both the romanizers and the romanticizers have overlooked some non-obvious

---

19 Chapman, op. cit., p. 186.
20 Orsi, op. cit.

features of Italian Catholicism that were just as important as anything else in understanding why Italian Catholicism resisted romanization.

Many Madonnas

One of the general features that has always distinguished Catholicism in general from Protestantism is the emphasis that Catholics place upon veneration of the Virgin Mary. Indeed, elsewhere I have argued that from the perspective of outside observers, Catholic/Protestant differences over the Virgin Mary are at least as important as any of the other differences between these two religious traditions.[21] Devotion to Mary has always been especially strong in Italy, but this alone does not sharply distinguish Italian Catholicism from other varieties of Catholicism. What is most unique about Marian devotion in Italy is the tendency to "splinter" such devotion into a range of devotions, each of which is separate and complete in itself. This is done mainly by venerating Mary under some unique title and devising a distinct set of devotions to her under that title.

For instance, limiting ourselves simply to the separate Madonnas mentioned in Besuti's brief overview of Marian shrines in Italy,[22] we find that Mary is venerated as the Madonna di Crea; the Madonna di Tirano; the Madonna della Ghianda; the Madonna dell'Olmo; the Madonna di Lonigo; the Madonna del Borgo; the Madonna dei Miracoli; the Madonna della Stella; the Madonna delle Grazie; S. Maria della Consolazione; the Madonna di S. Maria in Trastevere; the Madonna della Quercia; the Madonna delle Vittorie; the Madonna della Catena; the Madonna delle Lacrime; the Madonna del Carmine; the Madonna del Paradiso—and this by no means exhausts the list of Italian Madonnas. Moreover, the simple fact of two Madonnas in different parts of the country sharing the same title is not in itself evidence of a historical link between the two. It seems likely, for instance, that at least some of the very many Madonnas throughout Italy who are called "Madonna dei Miracoli" developed independently of one another, and the same thing is likely true of the many Madonnas called "Madonna delle Grazie" and "Madonna dell'Olmo" ("Madonna of the Elm").

In trying to make sense of this panorama of Madonnas, it is easy to draw a conclusion that severely distorts the nature of the Mary cult in Italy. For instance, it is abundantly clear that within Italy itself the veneration of some particular Madonna varies from region to region. Furthermore, studies of Italian-American communities in the United States make it clear that groups of Italian immigrants often formed themselves into regional societies that were organized around some Madonna who was especially popular in the region from which they had come.

---

21 See Michael P. Carroll, *The Cult of the Virgin Mary*, Princeton, Princeton University Press, 1986.

22 G. M. Besuti, "Santuari, apparazioni, culto locale, ex voto—Rassegna bibliografica," *Marianum*, 105, 1972, pp. 52–77.

From all this it would be easy to conclude that Marian devotion in Italy consists mainly in venerating Mary under some particular title that just happens to be popular in your village. Such a conclusion would be misleading, since it overlooks the fact that in most regions of Italy, several different Madonnas are venerated *simultaneously*, and considered to be at least somewhat distinct. In the village near Rome studied by Silverman, there were important community-wide ceremonies organized around at least two different Madonnas, the Madonna Addolorata and the Madonna dei Portenti.[23] In Milocca, the two most important festas were organized around the Madonna Immacolata and the Madonna Addolorata, but there was some devotion also to the Madonna del Carmine, the Madonna Assunta, the Madonna di Trapani, and the Madonna del Monte Racalmuto.[24] In the Lucanian village studied by Banfield, five separate Madonnas were the focus of cultic activity: (1) the Madonna di Pompei, (2) the Madonna del Carmine, (3) the Madonna della Pace, (4) the Madonna Assunta, and (5) the Madonna Addolorata.[25]

Furthermore, this tendency to splinter the image of Mary seems to have been a part of Italian Catholicism for quite some time. In his study of popular religion in Florence during the 15th century, for instance, Trexler makes it clear that the most important Florentine Madonna was the Madonna di Impruneta. But he also makes it clear that there were several other Madonnas venerated in Florence and that *each* of these Madonnas was invested with psychic power, with sensate qualities, and with "individuality and animism."[26]

Banfield also provides some information on how Italian Catholics perceive the relationship between the various Madonnas. Thus, when an ex-seminarian tried to explain to a woman of the village that there was really only one Madonna, the woman replied: "You studied with the priests for eight years and you haven't even learned the differences between the Madonnas?" It is difficult to imagine a remark that more clearly indicates the psychological reality of the splintering process.[27]

In short, Italian Catholics don't simply venerate "Mary" under some particular title. They venerate simultaneously a *range* of "Marys," each designated by a separate title, each of whom is venerated at a different time in the year (since different Madonnas have different feast days) and each of whom is addressed using at least slightly different prayers. Though there is no denying that all these Marys are perceived to be linked in some way, this should not blind us to the fact that they are to a large extent considered to be separate and distinct.

This tendency to "splinter" devotion to Mary is worth focusing upon if only

---

23 Silverman, op. cit., pp. 150–154.

24 Chapman, op. cit., pp. 172–173.

25 Banfield, op. cit., p. 131.

26 Richard C. Trexler, *Public Life in Renaissance Florence*, New York: Academic Press, 1980, pp. 62–73.

27 Banfield, op. cit., p. 131n.

because it represents an intensification of a feature of Catholicism generally that itself is often overlooked. In the case of Mary, for instance, the Church has replicated the Italian pattern on a smaller scale by promoting universalistic devotions to Mary under a number of separate titles, viz., Our Lady of LaSalette, the Immaculate Conception, Our Lady of Lourdes, Our Lady of Fatima, etc. A similar pattern is evident in Christocentric devotions promoted by the Church. Thus in Beringer's list of indulgenced devotions[28] we find separate devotions to the Holy Name of Jesus; Jesus as the Infant of Prague; the Sacred Heart of Jesus; the Five Wounds of Jesus; the Precious Blood of Jesus; the Seven Words of Jesus on the Cross; Jesus in the Blessed Sacrament, etc. This tendency to splinter the image of Christ into several different "aspects," and to make each aspect the object of a separate and distinct religious devotion that conveys spiritual benefits in and of itself, is absent from the Protestant tradition.

The fact that the splintering of religious devotions in Italian Catholicism seems more extensive (than in Catholicism generally) and more focused on Mary exclusively (as opposed to both Mary and Christ) means only that Italian Catholicism bears much the same structural relationship to Catholicism generally as Catholicism generally bears to Protestantism.

Direct Contact with the Sacred

The idea that human beings should have a direct relationship with God, that is, a relationship unmediated by institutional structures, will strike many readers as a prototypically "Protestant" view. Similarly, the view that God has ordained that the institutional Church should mediate between the human and the divine will strike many as a prototypically "Catholic" view. While such views do reflect some very real differences between Catholics and Protestants, they overlook the fact that there has long been a tradition within Catholicism centered around individuals who are supposed to have established *direct* and *unmediated* contact with the sacred. Moreover, despite the fact that such individuals seem to undercut the *raison d'être* of Church, they have seen themselves to be good Catholics, and have often been made the objects of veneration by Church authorities. For instance, although Protestants often talk of having "a personal relationship with Jesus Christ," I know of few Protestants who claim to have seen and heard Jesus Christ during the course of an earthly apparition. By contrast, the number of Catholics over the centuries who claim to have heard, seen and talked to Christ during an apparition easily runs into the hundreds. If we expand our notion of the "sacred" to include all the supernatural beings venerated by Catholics, notably including the Virgin Mary and the saints, then the number of Catholics who have experienced apparitions of these beings runs into the thousands.

---

28 R. P. Beringer, *Les Indulgences, Leur Nature et Leur Usage*, Tomes I and II, Paris, P. Lethielleux, 1925.

What I now want to establish is that this Catholic tradition involving "direct and unmediated contact with the sacred" is far more firmly entrenched in Italian Catholicism than in any other Catholic tradition, and that this as much as anything else has created the "Italian problem."

Apparitions, Stigmatization, Incorruptibility

I know of no readily available sample of apparitions involving Christ or the saints. Apparitions of the Virgin Mary, however, have been well-studied. Elsewhere, I have presented two separate samples of Marian apparitions.[29] The first sample includes 50 Marian apparitions which were all experienced sometime between 1100 and 1900 and which have received some degree of approbation from the Church. The second sample is quite different: it includes 105 Marian apparitions, all experienced by a single person, all of which occurred in the period 1927–1971, and *none* of which were recognized by Church authorities. The geographical distribution of the apparitions in each sample is presented in Table 1.

Table 1

Geographical Distribution of Marian Apparitions

	50 Marian Apparitions Recognized by the Church, 1100–1900	105 Marian Apparitions *Not* Recognized by the Church, 1927–1971
Italy	30%	41%
France	22%	9%
Germany/Austria	10%	12%
Spain	8%	–
British Isles	8%	–
Poland	2%	2%
All other European locations	6%	18%
All non-European locations	14%	18%
	100% (N = 50)	100% (N = 105)

29 See Carroll, op. cit., pp. 129–132. These two samples were derived from information presented in William Walsh, *The Apparitions and Shrines of Heaven's Bright Queen*, Four Volumes, New York, Cary-Stafford, 1904; Bernard Billet, "Le fait des apparitions non reconnues par l'Eglise," in B. Billet et al., *Vraies et fausses apparitions dans l'Eglise*, Paris, Editions P. Lethielleux, 1973, pp. 5–54.

Even though there is no overlap between the two samples, the geographical pattern is virtually the same: in both cases, Italy accounts for far more Marian apparitions than any other national group.

But apparitions are not the only ways in which Catholics have directly experienced the sacred; some have developed the *stigmata*. In its most precise sense, the "the stigmata" refers to the five wounds inflicted upon Christ during his Crucifixion (the nail wounds in each of hand and foot, the spear wound in the side), and a "stigmatic" is thus someone who develops these five wounds. Somewhat more loosely, the term "stigmatic" has routinely been applied to someone who develops *any* of the wounds inflicted upon Christ during the Crucifixion, so that some stigmatics have developed only the "spear" wound, some only the punctures produced by the Crown of Thorns, etc. The first stigmatic is supposed to have been St. Francis of Assisi, who reportedly received his stigmata on Mount La Verna in 1224 (two years before his death) during the course of an apparition. Over the intervening centuries, hundreds of other Catholics have claimed to have developed the stigmata as the result of divine intervention.[30]

The Church's view towards stigmatization has always been ambivalent. In only two cases, for example, involving St. Francis himself and St. Catherine of Siena (d. 1380), has the Church stated clearly that the stigmata experienced by these individuals was of supernatural origin. On the other hand, by affirming the supernatural origin of the stigmata in these two cases, the legitimacy of all other claims to stigmatization is enhanced to some degree. More importantly, a great many stigmatics have been canonized, or at least beatified, which means that the Church has given permission to the faithful to make these individuals the object of cultic devotion.

The most comprehensive single listing of stigmatics (in the broad sense of the term) is still the one published in 1894 by Imbert-Gourbeyre.[31] A classification of these stigmatics by geographical location is given in the first half of Table 2. As in the case of apparitions, this appears to be a phenomenon that is clearly associated with Italian Catholicism. Fully 40% of all stigmatics have been Italian, and no other national group even comes close to this percentage.

There is one final indicator that can be used to assess a cultural emphasis upon "direct access to the sacred" in the Catholic world, and it concerns *incorruption*. "Incorruption" refers to the belief that as a result of divine intervention the corpses of certain holy persons are sometimes exempted from the natural processes of decay and

---

30 For some speculation on the psychological processes that lead to stigmatization, see Michael P. Carroll, "Heaven-Sent Wounds: A Kleinian View of the Stigmata in the Catholic Mystical Tradition," *The Journal of Psychoanalytic Anthropology*, 10, Winter, 1987, pp. 17–38.

31 Antoine Imbert-Gourbeyre, *La Stigmatisation, L'Extase Divine, et Les Miracles de Lourdes, Tome I: Les Faits*, Paris, Clermont-Ferrand, 1894, pp. xxi–xli.

Table 2

Geographical Distribution of Stigmatics and Saintly Corpses Found Incorrupt

Location:	Stigmatics, 1274–1890	Saintly Corpses Found Incorrupt, 1100–1933
Italy	40%	57%
France	22%	17%
Germany/Austria	10%	1%
Spain	15%	12%
British Isles	–	3%
Poland	–	3%
All other European locations	12%	1%
All non-European locations	1%	5%
	100%	100%
	(N = 321)	(N =94)

decomposition. Usually, incorrupt corpses are made the object of special veneration at some particular church. Even now, there are dozens of Catholic churches which claim to possess the incorrupt body of some saint. Thus the incorrupt body of St. Rita (d. 1457) rests in the Basilica at Cascia, Italy; the incorrupt body of St. Catherine of Bologna (1463) rests in a Bologna chapel; the incorrupt body of St. Mary Magdalene de'Pazzi (d. 1607) can be found in a Florentine convent; and so on. More recent cases of incorruption would include St. Jean Vianney (d. 1859), whose incorrupt body rests in the Basilica at Ars, France; St. Catherine Labouré (d. 1876), whose incorrupt body rests in a convent in the Rue du Bac in Paris; and St. Bernadette Soubirous, the visionary of Lourdes, whose incorrupt body rests in a convent at Nevers, France. I have elsewhere speculated on just what "incorruption" means in the Catholic tradition, and upon the likely psychological appeal of this belief to Catholics.[32] My only concern here, however, is with the geographical distribution of these incorrupt corpses.

Cruz tracked down every reference that she could locate in the Catholic devotional literature to incorruptibility, and ended up with 102 cases.[33] If we limit ourselves to corpses declared incorrupt sometime after 1100, we are left with 94 cases, the

---

32 Michael P. Carroll, "The Catholic Belief in the Incorruption of Saints," unpublished.

33 Joan Carroll Cruz, The Incorruptibles, Rockford, Illinois, Tan Books and Publishers, 1977.

last of which is St. Catherine Labouré (who died in 1876 and who was "found incorrupt" in 1933). If we accept the reports surrounding these 94 cases at face value, then in virtually all these cases the attribution of incorruption appears to have been endorsed, either explicitly or implicitly, by Church authorities. By this I mean that Church authorities are reported as having presided over the exhumation during which the corpse was discovered incorrupt, or at the very least, installed the incorrupt corpse on church property and allowed it to become the object of veneration.

The geographical location at which each of these 94 corpses were first declared incorrupt (based upon the information provided in Cruz) is given in the second half of Table 2. Here again Italy predominates, accounting for 57% of all cases. Although "incorruptibility" is obviously different from "apparitions" and "stigmatization" in some obvious ways (not the least of which being that incorruption involves a corpse, not a living person), all three phenomena are similar in that a belief in each reinforces the notion that individuals can in some clear and unambiguous way experience direct contact with the sacred.

* * * * *

What the data in Tables 1 and 2 indicate, then, is that regardless of whether we assess "direct experience with the sacred" by looking at (1) apparitions of the Virgin Mary, (2) stigmatics or (3) instances of alleged incorruptibility, we find that *an emphasis upon such "direct experience with the sacred" has long been far more a feature of Italian Catholicism than any other variant of Catholicism.* In particular, it seems worth emphasizing that on these measures Italian Catholicism scores significantly higher than, say, Spanish Catholicism, with which it certainly shares certain features[34] and to which it is often compared.

Conclusion

In summary, it seems that Italian Catholicism is characterized by many layers, some of which bear little organic relationship to those which lie below. In the top layer, the one that seems most obvious, we find those occult beliefs and practices that have so fascinated journalists and a great many scholars. Digging a bit deeper

---

34 Local religion in Spain, for instance, is also characterized by strong devotion to Mary and by a tendency to splinter that devotion into a range of separate devotions. My sense is that this splintering of Marian devotion is not quite as extensive as it is in Italy, but I would have a hard time proving that in some systematic way. See William A. Christian, *Person and God in A Spanish Valley*, New York, Seminar Press, 1972; and by the same author, *Local Religion in Sixteenth-Century Spain*, Princeton, Princeton University Press, 1981.

we come upon those beliefs and practices which to some degree involve the official participation of the local Catholic church and whose most obvious manifestations are the festas in honour of the Madonna and the saints and the specialization associated with the cult of the saints. As far as the U.S. hierarchy was concerned, it was this layer, more than the one on top, that most gave rise to the "Italian problem."

But I have suggested that there is a layer deeper still, one that has been the least studied. The outward manifestations of this last layer are (1) the Italian tendency to splinter religious devotions to a single supernatural being, notably Mary, into a range of devotions each separate and complete in itself, and (2) the tendency for Italian Catholics to bypass the institutional church in favor of direct contact with the sacred, as evident in the experience of apparitions and stigmatization, and a belief in the incorruption of corpses. It is here, I think, at this third and final layer that we come upon another important source of the "Italian problem."

Both the tendency to splinter Marian devotion and the predilection for bypassing the institutional church when establishing contact with the sacred suggest that Italian Catholicism possesses a *creative* impulse, that is, a potential for creating new forms of religious devotion, that is missing in other Catholic traditions. I want to argue that it is this creative impulse, or more precisely, the "creative instability" that results from it, that most undermines the spirit of doctrinal and devotional orthodoxy that is part and parcel of romanized Catholicism. In other words, because Italian Catholicism possesses the potential for constantly creating new forms of Catholic devotion that arise outside the institutional Church, it would inevitably present a problem to those romanizers who wanted to standardize Catholicism by promulgating a uniform set of Catholic devotions.

These creative tendencies, to splinter religious devotion and to directly experience the sacred, must of course themselves be explained. Such an explanation would undoubtedly lead us to consider those social and psychological conditions which have historically prevailed in Italy and which have given rise to other features of Italian culture, such as for instance its characteristic political fragmentation.

But just as importantly, a recognition of the creative instability which underlies Italian Catholicism forces us to take a fresh look at the history of this particular variant of Catholicism. For instance, instead of seeing Italian Catholicism as the product of a social order that was stable, traditional and pre-modern, we must consider the possibility that Italian Catholicism has *always* been in a state of flux, and that, as a result, some of the "traditional" practices of Italian Catholics are of relatively recent origin. For example, in Montecastello, Silverman discovered that the single most important festa, in honor of the Madonna dei Portenti, arose only in the 18th century, while a second important festa, involving groups from several different neighborhoods, each honoring the particular Madonna or saint most important to them, was established only in the 1930s.[35] This is only one example,

---

35 Silverman, op. cit., pp. 152–154.

but I suspect that sustained investigation into the history of particular Italian Catholic devotions will demonstrate that a great many of them are far more recent in origin than is generally believed.[36]

36 I would like to thank both Roger O'Toole and Rudolph Vecoli for their constructive comments on an earlier draft of this article. This of course does not mean that they would agree with all the views expressed.

3.

Nineteenth-Century Irish Catholicism, Farmers' Ideology, and National Religion: Explorations in Cultural Explanation

Eugene Hynes

INTRODUCTION

The sociologist interested in understanding Catholicism in nineteenth-century Ireland is faced, on the one hand, with an enormous amount of evidence and, on the other, with the lack of an adequately elaborated framework to explain it.[1] Everybody agrees that it was of crucial importance but the many attempts made to illuminate its many facets have not been notably successful. In this chapter I attempt to provide a better understanding. In doing so, I show why a simple "folk versus canonical"

---

1 Recent years have seen the publication of a spate of important studies of various aspects of Irish Catholic life. Sean Connolly's *Priest and People in Pre-Famine Ireland, 1780–1845* (1982) and James O'Shea's *Priests, Politics and Society in Post-Famine Ireland: A Study of Tipperary, 1850–1891* (1983) are most concerned with the relationship between priests and people. Books by Desmond Keenan (1983) and Tom Inglis (1987: Part 2) attempt sociological explanations of changes in Catholicism, while Desmond Bowen's (1983) biography of Paul Cardinal Cullen focuses upon, by most accounts, the most important bishop of the century. Coldrey (1988) examines the contribution of the Irish Christian Brothers, through their schools and teaching, to the development of Irish nationalism. In addition to these, important evidence and insightful analyses are scattered throughout studies of such topics as emigration (K. Miller 1985), temperance movements (Malcolm 1986), nationalist ideology (Goldring 1982), the Whiteboy movements among the pre-famine rural lower orders (Beames 1983), and others. Not all of these are of equal value. The books by Connolly and O'Shea are rich in evidence but weak in interpretation while those by Keenan and Inglis, by contrast, tend to force the evidence to fit the Procrustean beds of their theories. Bowen and Beames, too, have their own axes to grind.

Catholicism dichotomy is misleading and why changes in nineteenth-century Irish Catholicism cannot be adequately explained by an "ultramontane ecclesiastical campaign" by which orthodoxy was imposed from the top at Rome to the bottom of Irish society. To understand the degree and nature of the success of preaching from the top, we have to understand the audience at the bottom. In nineteenth-century Ireland, this requires an understanding of the ways in which the Catholic clergy and the important tenant farmer class found their interests and aspirations mutually compatible. A similar compatibility of interests and outlooks among aspiring Catholics in the colonial context helps explain how Catholicism and Irish national identity became more closely linked as the century progressed.

SOME CURRENT INTERPRETATIONS
OF NINETEENTH-CENTURY IRISH CATHOLICISM

Structural Differentiation

One way to describe what occurred in nineteenth-century Irish Catholicism is to stress the "differentiation" of society by which "religion" became ever more distinct from the rest of social life and organization and religious functions were taken from the laity and concentrated in the hands of the priests and hierarchy. The roles and statuses of the clergy and laity were differentiated by priests being set apart by clerical garb, by rising living standards, by separate houses, by restriction from common pastimes such as horse-racing, by being forbidden to drink in public houses, by increasingly becoming specialists rather than part-time farmers or cattle-jobbers as many had been. Rites of passage, especially baptisms, marriages, and funerals were increasingly celebrated in church. Church buildings grew larger and more imposing and came to be ever more set apart from the mundane concerns of everyday life. They emerged as centers of religious practices where mass and other religious devotions were more and more accompanied by music, incense, and impressive ceremonial. Finally, Catholicism itself came to be increasingly delineated in ways that stressed its differences from other denominations. (These various observations are made repeatedly by many writers; perhaps the best short guide to the issues and relevant literature is Hoppen 1984:Chapter 3).

As a listing of some changes that need to be explained this is a useful starting point for sociological analysis. As an explanation of change, however, it begs the crucial questions. Based as it is on functionalist claims about internal differentiation of social systems, it never identifies the prime movers, never recognizes conflict, and never concerns itself with the activities of specific people or groups. This analysis simply assumes that change is immanent and to be explained by reference to the needs of the reified "system."

From Folk to Canonical Religion

Change in Catholicism in nineteenth-century Ireland has often been fairly simple-mindedly interpreted as a movement from a "folk" to a "canonical" Catholicism. According to this version of religious history, the Catholicism of the mass of the people was unorthodox in belief and practice at the beginning of the century, but eventually the church succeeded in extending official Roman belief and practices throughout the society. That some such change occurred is undeniable, but its nature and parameters, the process by which it occurred, its cause and results, and its significance are far from clear. The unorthodox took many forms. "Unofficial" Catholicism, for example, included beliefs in a non-Christian supernatural realm and its denizens, such as fairies, who could and often did intervene directly in human affairs and whose power could be used for good or ill by humans who carried out appropriate magical rituals (Jenkins 1977). Additional unorthodox beliefs and practices centered on festivals at turning points in the cycle of the agricultural season or on individuals' rites of passage, especially wakes. These festivities were communal celebrations that included many "pagan" themes and purely secular amusements. Moreover, unofficial religious practices also included pilgrimages to local holy wells or other sacred sites in the local landscape (Johnson 1983).

Undoubtedly, official Catholicism grew in power and influence in nineteenth-century Ireland. Emmet Larkin in 1972 coined the term "Devotional Revolution" to refer to a complex of changes in the people's relationship to the church: regular mass attendance increased from perhaps 40% to over 95% from the 1830s to the 1870s; a plethora of sodalities, confraternities, and other religious groups and observances spread under the auspices of the clergy; the ratio of clergy to laity increased dramatically, clerical discipline and morals improved, and the bishops became more unified and more successful in controlling their flocks and priests.[2] Yet, these changes need to be *explained* as well as described. Moreover, Larkin's

---

2 In his seminal article, Emmet Larkin (1972) argued that in the third quarter of the century the Catholic church, led by Archbishop (later Cardinal) Cullen of Dublin, unified the Irish bishops, improved the numbers and discipline of its own clergy, and turned the laity into devout practicing Catholics. The "devotional revolution" has been the focus for much recent writing in the field. Where Larkin tended to rely on episcopal correspondence and official decrees of bishops' synods, Connolly and O'Shea sought, by contrast, to examine the church from a vantage point outside ecclesiastical circles. By combing sources such as local newspapers, folklore, and travelers' accounts, as well as local archives they amassed huge amounts of evidence on the position of the priest and church in the community before the famine (Connolly 1982) and afterwards (O'Shea 1983). Among many interesting issues, these two books raise questions about the timing of the devotional revolution and its causes, nature, and consequences.

Keenan's (1983) work can be read as a direct response to Larkin's claimed "revolution." Very much a product of "religious sociology," the book is so centrally concerned with the organization of the church that its structure is reminiscent of an organizational

pinpointing of the change, to the third quarter of the century, must be viewed with some scepticism. We need to know *which* people in the society started to "practice" their Catholicism and why and *what* it meant to them. Elsewhere, I have argued that the stratum which became "Catholic" in official practice was primarily the rural farmer class which responded to the commercialization of agriculture that made control of family farms increasingly important (see O'Neill 1984) and that this class became the numerically dominant and socially most powerful stratum in the society when the Great Famine of 1845–49 decimated the other classes in rural Ireland. These farmers needed to control enough land to maintain their living standards and "respectability" in a world of widening horizons and thus selectively accepted Catholic teachings that corroborated their own felt need for family unity, discipline, and order (Hynes 1978, 1988).

Alliance with the Modernizing State

Rather than debate details of when and where (or even whether) reform occurred, Inglis (1987) argues that in the nineteenth century the Catholic Church achieved a "moral monopoly" in Irish society and sets out to explain how and why this was attained. Recognizing that the devotional revolution was not as easily demarcated in time as Larkin maintained, Inglis sees the growth of Catholic discipline as the Irish expression of a general European expansion of "civilization." He attributes the success of the church to the fact that it was entrusted by the British state with the

---

chart. After an early section describing the formal relationship of the Irish church to the "Latin Patriarchiate," i.e., The Papacy, the book devotes subsequent chapters to ecclesiastical structures, diocesan government, the clergy, changes involving the hierarchy, and finances. The laity are considered in chapters on "Parish Life" and "Changes in Parish Life." Throughout, an orthodox organizational perspective influences the selection and interpretation of evidence. In the eyes of another sociologist, the same evidence can be interpreted quite differently. Keenan's stress on formal organizational features leads him to stress continuity in the Catholic Church: "The first and most overwhelming conclusion is that there was no 'reform' of the Irish church in the nineteenth century . . . It was orthodox in doctrine . . . Its organization was complete and uniform" at the beginning as at the end of the century (Keenan 1983:240). To buttress this claim to continuity, Keenan takes an "establishment" view of evidence. For example, he characterizes non-Christian beliefs among the peasantry as "harmless" and concludes that "popular beliefs of any kind did not contradict official beliefs at any point, except perhaps on Purgatory" before noting that a "similar mixture of beliefs persisted in Ireland until our own time" (Keenan 1983:23–24). Keenan's argument for continuity is not, however, the only one in his book. A more interesting but distinctly secondary theme emerges from his examination of the social location and self-image of the church and how these changed. Though not a "reform," Keenan writes that "enormous changes came over the Irish church in the course of the century . . . most characterized by a tendency to emphasize 'Catholicism'" (1983:241–242). This growing exclusiveness is an important part of the story to which we will return below.

task of "civilizing the wild Irish" who were uncouth, superstitious, and rebellious. The church was progressively enabled to extend its influence through ever more institutional areas of life, especially education and family life. Inglis does not neglect the questions of the people's receptivity to the teachings and practices their church was presenting to them but his emphasis is on the way that the church, by disciplining the minds and bodies of Irish lay people, produced and reproduced conservative practicing Catholics.

Another historian argues that a "mutually beneficial" relationship between the British State and the Catholic Church developed as threats to England's security come more and more from social revolution from within rather than invasion by Catholic European states. "The Catholic Church as a centralized national body in a country with diffuse political tradition had a great deal to gain from working within the colonial system; the state, on the other hand, enjoyed the weight of its influence in controlling the violent and subversive elements within the society" (Beames 1983:187). It would be wrong, however, to see the church as just an ideological appendage of the British state. True, the clergy did actively oppose the frequently violent "Whiteboy" agitation throughout the pre-famine decades. Such agitation was used by those peasants whose access to land was curtailed, whose communal identification was undermined, and whose lives were reduced to misery when land, increasingly treated as a commodity, had its price raised by the profitability of raising food for export rather than local consumption (Beames 1983: 186–197). However, the crucial base for the growing power of the church was its alliance, not with the state, but with those peasants who did have and wanted to keep control of farms and who accordingly were among the targets of the Whiteboys. As we will see, it was this stratum of rural society that provided the church with most of its clergy, its staunchest followers and most committed believers, and its financial support.

Bishops' Unity and Cardinal Power

Other writers have looked elsewhere for their explanations of the growing power of the church. Emmet Larkin has continued his projected fifteen-volume history of the Irish Catholic church in the nineteenth century. His main source of evidence for this massive work is the correspondence of Irish ecclesiastics, especially bishops, often with each other and with various Vatican departments. In his latest volume (1987) he argues that the Catholic church was able to consolidate its power in the 1860s largely because the bishops were first able to act as a corporate body with individual bishops refraining from public disagreement with positions the majority supported.

Bowen (1983) emphasizes the impact of Paul Cardinal Cullen in shaping the church into Roman ultramontane ways stressing Catholic separateness and triumphal-ism. After three decades in Rome, Cullen returned to Ireland as Archbishop of Ar-magh (1850–52) and later of Dublin (1852–1878), the most important and populous diocese. Through his Vatican contacts, he was able to engineer the promotion to episcopal rank of men who shared his vision to various dioceses as they fell vacant. Known and trusted by the Pope as a loyal ultramontane and armed as he was with the power of a papal legate he was, according to Bowen, able, through the hierarchy, to extend Roman discipline, devotions, and practice throughout the church.

It would be mistaken, however, to assume that the extension of "orthodox" belief and practices was a simple "top-down" imposition of official doctrine and that the gradual elimination of "folk" elements in the people's Catholicism is to be fully explained either in terms of ecclesiastical alliance with the state or in terms of the power of particular churchmen. In response to Bowen's view of the personal importance of Cardinal Cullen we should note that many of the Roman ways and devotions that Bowen attributes to Cullen's initiatives were widespread long before his arrival, so much so, in fact, that Keenan (1983:243) thinks the credit belongs to Cullen's predecessor as archbishop of Dublin (see also Hoppen 1984:197–208; Kerr 1982: Chapter 1). So great indeed is Keenan's admiration for Archbishop Murray that his book is dedicated to his memory.

THEORETICAL CONSIDERATIONS

Sociologists of Catholicism need to cast their nets widely. As Roger O'Toole has argued in the introduction to this volume, they need to move beyond "religious sociology"—to transcend traditional concerns with ecclesiastical policy and with the development and working of institutions, usually at the local level. The challenge is not to ignore such topics but to link them to the activities of ordinary believers in their various local contexts and to show how the various levels of experience from the people to the papacy are linked. We need to examine the actual religious experience of those who built and sometimes filled the churches, who contributed to the support of the clergy and hierarchy by their donations, and who selectively followed church teachings.

Like sociologists of religion generally, those interested in Catholicism have much to learn from debates and advances in many diverse areas of sociology. By recognizing the complexities in different research traditions, by paying attention to their points of contact and overlap, and by being alert to how their strengths and weaknesses complement each other, we can elaborate a sociology of religious belief and practice that benefits from the insights of many traditions. Thus, for example, by pointing out the similarities between Durkheim's sociology of religion and the theory of ideology developed by Althusser, a recognized neo-Marxist, Susan Strawbridge (1982) has shown that the two traditions are not as separate and different as often presented and understood. Both Durkheim and Althusser, for example, stress religion's role in maintaining and reproducing the *status quo*. It is possible to evaluate the contributions of neo-Durkheimians and select those modifications or elaborations of Durkheim's thought that seem justified by logic and evidence.

Similarly, we can appraise the large body of research on "ideology" carried out by neo-Marxists, critical theorists, post-structuralists, and others such as Foucault. Because much writing in the sociology of religion has neglected post-structuralist and neo-Marxist debates about ideology, subjectivity, power, knowledge, and legitimacy, the field has lost the central importance it had among classic writers and has according to one critic been reduced to a "theoretical side-show" (Turner 1983:4–5). Because of the way it can connect all these issues and topics, a sociology of Catholicism can contribute to resolving sociology's most central questions.

The various perspectives current in sociology, and particularly recent debates in certain subfields of research, have much to teach us about how to explain or understand any Catholic belief or behavior. From the Marxist tradition we learn, first, to locate systems of beliefs within specific social contexts, articulated with the economy, the state, and class struggles (Thompson 1986:14; see also Boswell, Kiser, and Baker 1986). Second, we recognize that the apparent cultural unity of any collectivity hides the reality of past and ongoing class conflict and contradictory values and beliefs (Thompson 1986: Chapter 2; Lears 1985). "Shared" beliefs are always in process, always in flux, subject to contested interpretations and selective acceptance, a point perhaps made most forcibly by Gramsci (1971).[3]

If there is a single overwhelming lesson to be learned from the many works of Michel Foucault it is that power is inextricably bound up with the social construction of meaning. What we take to be rational, true, and good is rooted in relations of power, domination, and subjugation (see e.g. Foucault 1981). Though infrequently interpreted in this way, Durkheim's views are not at all incompatible with such a stress on power (Lacroix 1979). Usually, however, functionalist analysts have not stressed conflict and thus have avoided discussing how beliefs (religions, ideologies, worldviews, or whatever we label them) play a role in legitimating relations of domination (Thompson 1986:44–45). Many neo-Marxist writers, on the other hand, tend to err by simply reducing beliefs to class interests (Boswell, Kiser, and Baker 1986). We cannot assume that there is an automatic and mechanistic relationship between class interests and beliefs such that there is always a dominant ideology (Abercrombie, et al 1980). This is a recent version of a more venerable and widespread tendency in sociology to reduce individuals' interests, identities, and ideas to their social or economic positions. We need to see humans as socially constituted and thus appreciate their beliefs and orientations as the result of an his-

---

3 Durkheim's original paradigm, however, is flexible enough to incorporate these insights. It needs modification by reconceptualizing the social context of belief as including patterns of economic relationships rather than just demographic factors (Hynes 1975:45) and by balancing Durkheim's stress on values (what ought to be) with greater attention to shared views of what exists and what ought to be, i.e., cognition and imagination (Thompson 1986:14). In part these changes result from adapting Durkheim's account of religion in general to account for religion in specific socio-historical contexts.

torical development in particular contexts. That individuals are socially constituted is, of course, a very Durkheimian idea, but this view is also supported by writers in other traditions and in many disciplines, Therborn (1980) in Marxism, for example, Sewell (1980) in history, and MacLeod (1987) in sociology (see Sewell 1987:168).

Durkheim's analysis of religion is often criticized, quite fairly, for its teleological arguments and for its functionalist orientations. There is, however, another strand in his thought that has been fruitfully elaborated by others. This is his emphasis on the symbolic nature of religious understandings and his sketches of the ways in which symbols are linked together into systems of meaning. We can use Durkheim's structuralism rather than his functionalism to understand how collective representations transcend individual and sectional interests by creating a "community" of individual members united under authority figures. Furthermore, Durkheim's recognition of "boundary-mechanisms" can fruitfully be utilized for its contribution to understanding how religious (and other cultural) beliefs can articulate differences and oppositions as well as unity (see Thompson 1986:45, Douglas 1966; 1972). We need, however, to recognize that, contrary to the view of some structuralists, the component symbols in a worldview are not necessarily coherently integrated or internally consistent (see Moore 1975). Rather, elements in belief systems are open to a variety of interpretations and their meanings are ever in flux (Thompson 1986: Chapter 2). The cultural field is contested terrain (see Gottdiener 1985).

Besides those who approach culture with either an explicit neo-Marxist or neo-Durkheimian perspective there are others who have sought to transcend both and to examine the development of cultural items in particular contexts. Many of these writers, themselves influenced by a variety of sociological and anthropological traditions, see culture not as a unified entity but as a "tool-kit of symbols, stories, rituals, and worldviews, which people may use in varying configurations to solve different kinds of problems" (Swidler 1986:273). Not only is there a "repertoire of cultural options" available (Fine 1979) but these options will be "culturally felicitous to different degrees for different groups insofar as they engage some of each group's presuppositions and thus allow meanings to be constructed from what is known and what is new" (Griswold 1986: 1111). These approaches, first, direct attention to the audience of potential followers for new beliefs, religious or otherwise, and, secondly, require us to recognize the active ways in which people together weave their religious worldview out of their old and newly acquired understandings.

From diverse starting positions, therefore, students of religious ideologies, worldviews, or culture have arrived not at unanimity but at basic agreement on some points. They recognize that culture is not a transcendent seamless web but something woven out of diverse elements that are more or less integrated. The weaving is done by people together over time but the weavers do not all have equal power and they disagree about what they "see" in their product. Seams and tears may be hidden, but they indicate past disagreements and may be highlighted by others at any time.

ORTHODOXY FROM TOP TO BOTTOM?

Studies of Catholicism elsewhere, as well as the social scientific theories of culture and ideology discussed above, provide us with overwhelming evidence of the complex interaction of the local and the orthodox, of interpenetration of the little traditions and the great, of culture-continuity in the face of seemingly overwhelming change, and of the active rather than passive stance of ordinary people in creating their own cultural and religious understandings. To understand how these interactions and complexities worked themselves out in the context of nineteenth-century Ireland we will examine some areas of Catholic life and practice.

Mass attendance rose dramatically from the early decades of the century to over 95% by the 1870s. Much has been made of the devotional revolution lying behind these statistics (D. Miller 1975, Larkin 1972, and Hynes 1978; characteristically Keenan 1983:97–99 minimizes the change). Despite the fact of significant devotional changes, we must realize that there were strong elements of continuity at many levels. In terms of involvement, the tenant-farmer class had long been the practicing heart of the church and merely continued its churchgoing ways after the Famine. A considerable part of the increase in churchgoing is due simply to the pattern of mortality during the Great Hunger of the 1840s—deaths being concentrated in the lower classes who were least likely to be regular churchgoers. Survivors did not, in fact, dramatically change their behavior (O'Shea 1983:33). Much of the basic infrastructure of church buildings was in place before the famine (Keenan 1983) and the new Roman devotions were already widely practiced (Kerr 1982:Chapter 1). Even in terms of worldview there was continuity between old and new. The new devout churchgoing orthodox Catholic was already familiar with a supernatural world whose members could be asked for help and protection and whose intervention in the form of miracles or graces granted was expected and common. The "new devotions" such as the Rosary, or Praying for the Souls in Purgatory, or adoring the Blessed Sacrament, were in important ways very like the "old devotions," beliefs in fairies, local saints' cults, and pilgrimages to holy wells. Both presupposed a belief in "the nearness of the other world" and provided for a close relationship with supernatural beings and a means for interacting with them (Taves 1986:62, 47). There is little reason to believe that ordinary people found the different orders of belief irreconcilable or even particularly discordant. For example, at a holy well in Donegal, a traveler in 1837 noted that the sick left crutches and rags both "to the saint and to the nearby fairy whose assistance also demanded formal acknowledgment" (Hoppen 1984:216). Perhaps the most important change was less a matter of changed content of beliefs and practices than the fact that the new devotions were controlled or at least promoted by the clergy. Religious practices moved slowly and fitfully from the outdoors, associated with specific features of the local landscape or with agricultural processes, to church buildings and individual homes. By granting apostolic indulgences for specific devotions, the official church tended to centralize and standardize practices. Why should believers go only to the holy well—different in each locality and on different calendars—when they could gain indulgences for some "new" devotional practice? (Taves 1986:96, 102 and passim). "Under the old system, the individual had direct access to graces and favor through divine interme- diaries while under the new system all graces and favors were mediated through the clergy" (Taves 1986:102, paraphrasing Christian, 1972, and others on 16th to 19th century Europe. See also Michael Carroll's chapter on Italian Catholicism in this volume.) This new monopoly in the dispensation of the means of salvation was an important source of the increased power of the clergy in the purely spiritual realm.

As the church and its priests increasingly gained power as mediators between the people and the supernatural it became ever more important for both clergy and laity to stress the importance of attending mass. This insight suggests a resolution to an apparent paradox in the evidence: Miller (1975) shows that church attendance was low, perhaps 40% in pre-Famine days, yet Keenan (1983:97–99) suggests that, because the clergy and hierarchy did not seem particularly upset about the state of religious practice, mass attendance might have been higher than Miller's data show. The paradox can be explained, however, if we assume that in the early nineteenth century mass attendance was of less importance, even in the eyes of the clergy, than it was later to become. Relevant evidence is difficult to come by, but what we have is supportive. Hoppen (1984:217) notes that in pre-Famine days "priests, indeed, often adopted a comparatively relaxed approach in front of their congregations" as opposed to the solemn atmosphere in churches in later decades. Not just the people but even the clergy at times treated the mass as optional or at least not of overwhelming importance. "Abuses" in the pre-Famine period included widespread failures of priests to say mass at all (Connolly 1982:63–65 and passim; Bowen 1983; O'Shea 1983:33).

Because the mass was the centerpiece of the priests' mediation between God and people, as this mediation increased so did the importance of the mass. The mass itself served to link heavenly and earthly hierarchies in a way that increased the centrality of the church as an institution in the worldview of the believer. "The Catholic understanding of the mass as the unbloody repetition of Jesus' sacrificial death on Calvary and hence of Jesus' real presence in the wafer was the linchpin connecting the supernatural hierarchy (of Jesus, Mary, the Saints, and the faithful) to the earthly hierarchy (of pope, bishop, priest, and laity)" (Taves 1986:103). Sig- nificantly, among the new devotions promoted by the clergy were Veneration of the Blessed Sacrament and meditation on the Sacred Heart of Jesus. Permanently displaying the consecrated host in churches, rare before the famine, became the norm in later decades (Connolly 1982:97). The increasing size and architectural impressiveness of church buildings as the century progressed attest not only to the improving economic circumstances of those who built and supported them but also to the increasing acknowledgment by the laity of the claim that the church building was uniquely "God's House" to which they should go for communion with their God. As God was no longer immediately available but required priestly mediation, so simultaneously churches came to be set apart more and more from mundane affairs, their architecture reflecting the architecture of the people's minds. Pre-Famine churches, poor, unadorned buildings, were often used for secular purposes such as political meetings, or even farm work (Connolly 1982; Hoppen 1984:216) but this would change in later decades (even though electioneering continued just outside the church gates—as it does to the present day).

For theorists who stress the simple suppression of folk Catholicism by orthodox practices a significant problem is the origins and development of specific orthodox beliefs and devotions. All orthodox "universal" features of Catholicism must, originally, somewhere, have been local. The relation between local and universal features is not simply unidirectional. There has been a two-way relation between local and universal religion throughout the history of Catholicism (see Christian 1972; Froeschle-Chopard 1982; Taves 1986). Some local rituals or devotional practices are appropriated by the church hierarchy and ultimately sanctioned for "universal" use throughout the church, while others are suppressed, co-opted, redefined, ignored, or dealt with in other ways. Which particular holy places, shrines, apparitions, practices, or devotions are blessed by the church and ultimately accepted, tolerated, or promoted for wider or even universal use is the outcome of a complex interaction between local and church-wide politics and felt needs. Much probably depends on the strength, within the church organization and hierarchy, of those individuals, religious orders, or others, who promote a given devotion or belief. (For a case study of one local priest's unsuccessful attempt to get the Brazilian Catholic hierarchy to recognize a claimed miracle, see Della Cava 1970.) Of course, the strength of any particular interest group and its chances of success are influenced by what authorities in Rome perceive to be the needs and interests of the universal church and by Roman judgment of how receptive its various flocks might be to a suggested innovation. We need to explain how particular "local" practices increase the repertoire of cultural options (Fine 1979) and how new options are more or less congenial to different groups depending not only on their existing cultural "tool-kit" (Swidler 1986; Griswold 1986) but on their location within society and, in the case of the Catholic church, their position in its organizational structure. For example, in the nineteenth century the Catholic Church, especially during the long papacy of Pius IX, found itself on the defensive, under attack in a world that was growing more liberal and democratic, more urban and industrial, and more secular and scientific. Among the beliefs and practices that found acceptance by the papacy are several that can be understood in the context of the church's position in the world of that time. The Doctrine of the Immaculate Conception, defined in 1854, is a good example. It said that the Virgin Mary was herself born without original sin. Building on Mary Douglas's (1966) insight that concern with bodily purity reflects the importance of social boundaries, Taves argues that "The concern with Mary's inviolability and purity reflected, most specifically, the papacy's concern with the political inviolability of the church in the Italian context. In broader terms, however, it expressed the papacy's need to defend its authority to define truth in the modern world" (Taves 1986:109). A similar analysis explains the formal adoption of the claim to papal infallibility during the First Vatican Council in 1870. This claimed a unique access to fundamental truth on the part of the Pope, and thus by the Roman Catholic Church, a claim made understandable by the various ways in which the claimed authority of the Pope and church to teach "truth" was being threatened—by biblical literalists among Protestants, by scientists, by advocates of democracy and popular rule, and generally by the various heirs of the Renaissance, the Reformation, the Enlightenment, and the revolutions in science and in society. Just as priests increasingly controlled access to divine grace and intercession so the church hierarchy increasingly claimed a monopoly on access to truth.

THE CLERGY-FARMER ALLIANCE

In rural nineteenth-century Ireland, the tenant farmer class provided the primary social foundation for Catholicism. For reasons that are complex and which I have described elsewhere (Hynes 1978, 1988) this farmer class developed a family system in which the father was the authoritarian head, the mother's role was separate but subordinate, sexuality was rigidly controlled, and family unity was important but problematic. I have argued that such a family constellation made people receptive to those elements in Catholicism that stressed obedience to authority, family unity and loyalty, and the evils of sex. Looking at the wider picture here we can understand why Rome was successfully formulating and promulgating such congenial doctrines. For their own respective reasons, Irish farmers and the papal bureaucracy in Rome each had a vested interest, because of their positions and experiences in the world, in emphasizing the authority of the head, the necessity of obedience, and the special asexual nature of the ideal woman. It was the coincidence of the felt needs of the Roman Catholic hierarchy and its most committed Irish members that made the audience especially receptive to official teachings that stressed obedience, familism, and the subordinate but special moral role of mothers as teachers.

These teachings were authoritative not only because of their contents but also because of the very way in which they resonated with the people's everyday situations and experiences. For example, the Virgin Mary was presented as a personification of the church. Loyalty to the Pope was, by some at least, conflated with the new devotion to the Sacred Heart. Moreover, the two, Blessed Mother and Holy Father, served to facilitate the generalizing of emotions that individuals experienced in their own relationships with parents. Such emotions were now directed toward the Church and the Pope, seen as inseparable. "This conflation of Mary and the Church, like the conflation of the Sacred Heart and the Pope, allowed the emotions aroused by devotion to Mary, 'Mother of the Faithful,' to attach themselves to the institutional, or 'mother' church" (Taves 1986:109–110).

Such an analysis as this suggests the complexity of interaction between beliefs and practices at many levels: local and universal; emotional, cognitive, and behavioral; organizational and theological. But such an analysis still leaves unexamined several other areas in which a simple "top-down" imposition of orthodoxy does violence to the evidence we have. The laity did not just passively accept church teachings. They could, and did, adopt and adapt the new teachings and practices to their own religious worldview. "New" devotions could be used to achieve purely instrumental ends. What went on in individuals' minds and hearts at mass we will probably never be able to grasp but we know that the laity could and often, perhaps usually, did engage in "private devotions," perhaps saying the rosary, while "hearing" the Latin mass. There was a perhaps inevitable discontinuity between the worship of the clergy and the laity at mass (see Taves 1986:44–45). Taylor shows that in rural Ireland even today, individuals attending mass do so with diverse understandings (Taylor, Forthcoming a). Other "orthodox" beliefs could be reinterpreted: particular priests, for example, were identified as possessing special magical powers. Priests themselves often did little to squelch popular beliefs in their magical power (see Hoppen 1984:220, 247 for priests' curses during election campaigns) but even orthodox priests, such as the Temperance leader, Father Matthew, had magical power widely ascribed to them. Drunken priests seem to have been seen as particularly potent magicians especially if they were "silenced" by their bishop, an action that, according to one folk interpretation, released the priest's magic from the bishop's control (Taylor, forthcoming b). The result of this reinterpretation was that such priests often gained popular followings precisely to the degree that they did not follow official orthodox expectations.

The clergy was relatively successful in getting the laity to "practise" their Catholicism if by "practice" we mean the people attended mass on Sundays and observed other canonical requirements for membership. But this in no way implied that the people had their ethical consciousness raised. A good illustration of this is the exploitation of farm laborers by the farmer class that was the backbone of the church's support. Schemes to provide cottages for these laborers were vehemently opposed by farmers, but only a minority of priests spoke out against the farmers (O'Shea 1983:Chapter 5; also Hoppen 1984:179–180). In many areas of life, indeed, church teaching, as interpreted by priests, was little more than a justification for the behavior that the farmer class in rural Ireland found to be in their own interests.

Priests were increasingly influential in nineteenth-century Ireland primarily because they articulated and supported the aspirations and interests of a specific social class, the tenant farmers, that increasingly became dominant. These farmers, caught between their landlords above and the landless masses below, endeavored to gain and keep control of enough land to support those dependent on it in a "respectable" manner. These farmers knew that landlessness led, increasingly and inexorably, to nothing but misery, a lesson powerfully taught by the sporadic food shortages from the 1820s that culminated in the massive starvation of the late 1840s. A farm had to generate enough cash to pay the rent to the landlord. Thus, understandably, land, to such people, was life, to be striven for and clung to like life itself. In each generation the family farm was passed undivided to only one heir who was typically a son and who married a daughter of a similar family. In the usual case one son and one daughter would marry; other children either remained life-long celibates or emigrated. This stem family system, far from being "traditional," was itself a response to the commercialization of agriculture (O'Neill 1984) and the consequent destruction of older more communal patterns of residence and land-use (Taylor 1980, McCourt 1971). Because the Famine of 1845–48 devastated the landless stratum, the farmers became the most numerous class in the post-Famine era—and increased in size relative to the population as artisans and agricultural laborers declined in numbers. As this farmer class grew and prospered in the post-Famine decades so it increasingly came to undermine landlord control of local government (Feingold 1984) and eventually challenged the landlords for control over the land it farmed.

The emergence of the Land League, founded in 1879, led to a situation where the doctrines of both church and state conflicted with the interests of the farmers. Legally, the land was owned by the landlords who were free to charge rents as determined in a free market. To question this was to question the very basis of law, "the rights of property" and the operation of the market—central ideas in official state ideology of the time. The Papacy too taught the rights of property and the duty to obey legitimately constituted authority. Yet Irish farmers, in a sustained effort to control their farms, increasingly challenged landlords' rights to fix rents, evict tenants for nonpayment of rent, and exercise other "rights of property." These farmers were heir to another tradition that saw land not just as a commodity to be bought and sold on the open market but as a resource to be used by each generation, held in trust, and passed along to future generations (see Knott 1984; MacDonagh 1983: Chapter 3). Where the earlier tradition saw land as a community-wide resource, the farmers now reinterpreted it not as community-wide but as a *family* resource—and the family was perceived as persisting through generations into the future. As was the case with "religious" ideas and understandings, "traditional" folk views of property were thus modified and transformed. In the case of views about property-rights in land we can even trace how these "neo-traditional" farmer views ultimately prevailed over official views of property. Irish farmers' views impressed the Irish economist Cairns who in turn influenced John Stuart Mill to change his orthodox views (see MacDonagh 1983:34–51). The farmers ultimately prevailed, however, not because they had mightier pens but because of violence or, more often, the threat of violence.

The Land League used many tactics during the "Land War." A common practice was for members of the League in a given locality to meet and unilaterally decide what constituted a "fair rent" and then to offer this invariably low amount to the landlord with the warning that if he refused it he would receive no rent at all. These threats were backed up by "boycotts"—the ostracizing of anybody who paid the rent the landlord asked, who rented farms from which others had been evicted for nonpayment, or who cooperated in any way with landlords or their agents. When the Pope himself condemned such tactics he was not heeded.[4] Bishops found theological arguments to show why the condemnation did not really mean what it said or why it could be ignored. Thus, for example, it was suggested that the Pope was ill-informed, or that what he condemned was not in fact practiced (MacDonagh 1983). Meanwhile, "public opinion, that is, tenant-farmer opinion" was decisive in evoking clerical support for the farmers' attempts during the 1880's to gain control of their farms, and "the priests in succumbing to popular pressure were at pains to propose a general moral justification for the use of boycotting" (O'Shea 1983:94, 108). The contrast with the behavior of priests in opposing Whiteboy movements in the pre-Famine years is glaring. "Whiteboys were clearly powerful local purveyors of an independent and antagonistic view of the world who had to be eliminated," a recent historian has written, adding, "there is clear evidence of priests pursuing the

---

4 If the Pope could be ignored or misrepresented, so also could individual bishops deviate from the decisions of the hierarchy as a body. As already noted, some writers have stressed the growing ability of the bishops to act together and have pointed to the work of Paul Cardinal Cullen, Archbisop of Armagh and later of Dublin from 1850 to 1878. Yet the "cohesion" Cullen brought to the hierarchy was only a surface one and he was outlived by another archbishop, John MacHale, who had doggedly resisted much of what Cullen sought. At times, for example, MacHale simply refused to attend episcopal meetings or agree to "joint" episcopal letters (see Hoppen 1984:188–195; Bowen 1983:232,296).

If the hierarchy was often split in dogmatic and political opinion, bishops seem to have had increasing influence on their priests. Though numerous anomalies can be pointed out, it seems that priests generally were likely to listen to, or at least to avoid public disagreement with, their bishops. Of course this is understandable: priests and bishops were both blown by the same winds of public opinion and so were likely to have similar sympathies. Moreover, "since bishops held the power of promotion, transfer, and suspension, the clergy were naturally sensitive to their views" (O'Shea, 1983:240) but, once this power was lessened, there was little that bishops could do to keep priests in line that would not create more problems than it would solve. An astute observer noted, "The fact is, his bishop can do very little with a treasonable man when once he has been inducted a parish priest" (quoted in Hoppen 1984:192). Generally, however, priests would cooperate, perhaps unenthusiastically, with their bishop's initiatives and relapse to their old ways after the bishop died. Other bishops, anticipating at best lukewarm reception by their priests and people, stayed silent on potentially embarrassing issues. (In the area of anti-drink movements, see Malcolm 1986.)

logic of this position quite consciously and ruthlessly" (Beames 1983:190). Priests and bishops were notably subject to the influence of farmer public opinion. "The priests initiated no policies: they *followed* lay trends" (Keenan 1983:194, original emphasis). If they were led by their training or calling to question farmer behavior the clergy rarely voiced their reservations. However, their training was hardly designed to raise such doubts in their minds (cf. Hoppen 1984:183–185; Connolly 1982:35–45). Significantly, we find that those very few priests who worked for farm laborers' rights or the urban poor had atypical backgrounds, with either nonfarmer or urban origins or seminary training in Europe (McMahon 1981:282; O'Shea 1983).

As Oliver MacDonagh put it, "A priest deviating in public purpose from his people soon lost all influence in, and even most of his income from, his parish" (1983:93) and the same was true of bishops (Hoppen 1984: 191). However, it was not just because of their economic dependence that priests hewed to the line of their tenant farmer congregations. The vast majority of priests themselves came from tenant farmer backgrounds (O'Shea 1983: Chapter 1; Hoppen 1984:176) and as post-Famine rural Ireland was increasingly dominated by this class the priests found themselves surrounded by "their own kith and kin." "Not only could this clergy identify with this class on a social and spiritual level, but their respective politics were, as might be expected, comfortingly compatible" (O'Shea 1983:232).

The Catholic clergy and church increased its power to the extent that it artic-ulated the needs and aspirations of the farmer class. That its power derived to a considerable degree from this ability is apparent when we consider the situations where other interests and/or other groups competed for public expression and alle-giance. In the early part of the century, priests often had to share influence with poets or hedge schoolmasters who voiced different sentiments (O'Fiach 1975, cited in Hoppen 1984:249; Cullen 1969). O'Connell's political organizations of the 1820s used the priests as a "lever"; the "motor working the lever was the lay leadership of the Catholic Association" (O'Ferrall 1981:317). The priests, far from being the power wielders, were recruited by the lay leadership to provide organizational skills in areas lacking middle-class lay Catholics. With the devastation of the lower or-ders by the Famine the reservoirs for support of alternative visions of society were drained. Teachers in the new state-supported schools were effectively controlled by the clergy, indeed very often they were themselves priests, nuns, or brothers. "Na-tional" education became denominational in practice. In rural Ireland over much of the century there were few others with the education or social standing to chal-lenge the priest, provided the priest voiced the concerns of his flock. In the later decades, a lower-middle class of shopkeepers, publicans, and merchants emerged but rather than competing with priests for influence, these tended to cooperate with them. These new traders typically originated from the same comfortable farmer class from which the priests came and like the priests they still essentially reflected its interests and aspirations. For example, in not a few cases priests opposed anti-alcohol movements because their own relatives were involved in the drink trade. (On this "alliance of whiskey and holy water" see Malcolm 1986:298.) Similarly, attempts to organize a system of cooperatively owned enterprises to sell to farmers and buy, process, and market their produce was vehemently opposed by the clergy in no small part because of the threat such cooperatives posed to the welfare of their trader cousins (Kennedy 1978; Hoppen 1984:181). Where a truly urban catholic professional or merchant class existed the clergy lost or never gained their "moral monopoly" (see e.g. Woods 1980, on the role of the clergy in the movement against Parnell in the 1892 election). But the numerical dominance of the farmer class in society as a whole ensured that the clergy most reflected *their* attitudes and aspirations.

When the needs of church organization coincide with the interests of followers, then we can expect growth in church membership and devotion. An alliance of mutuality develops in which each uses the other for its own ends. In the first half of the nineteenth century the Catholic clergy and bourgeois nationalist Catholics mobilized the peasantry for their own ends. Disillusioned with the 1800 Act of Union which had failed to provide promised Catholic Emancipation in legal and political contexts, they were able to play on traditional peasant hostility to the English as conquering usurpers, alien in language and religion. A vivid oral tradition preserved the memories of a dispossessed people and Catholic ecclesiastics who anathematized Protestantism were not creating sectarian divisions (as Bowen 1983 suggests for Cardinal Cullen) but merely corroborating this folk memory (see K. Miller 1985:Chapter 3). The coincident interests of the Roman Catholic Church and of Irish farmers explains their alliance throughout the century.[5]

CATHOLICISM AND IRISH NATIONAL IDENTITY

Several aspects of Irish Catholicism which I have not yet considered can also be understood by examining the wider political and socioeconomic context. Ireland was a colony with all the ambivalence that colonial status involves. As a dominated but rising class in this colonial situation the political views of the farmers, and thus of the clergy, were shot through with ambivalence. (See Memmi 1965 for a useful introduction to the complexities of colonial relationships and identities.) In their nationalism and abhorrence of revolutionary violence that threatened to undo their stake in the current establishment "the priests were but the populace writ large" (MacDonagh 1983:102). The result was what MacDonagh (1983:97–101), building on O'Shea's work, has described as a "triple ambiguity": a profound ambivalence by the clergy toward "nationalist" movements. While condemning violence by liv-

---

5 One historian suggests that the Church reflected larger farmer views not only because of the background, training, and financial dependence of its clergy but because of the church's political interests in getting along with a class that would hold power in a new state that, from the 1880s on, appeared about to be born (D. Miller 1975:94).

ing nationalists they praised similar violence by dead ones. "The more ancient the patriot—the more hearty the retrospective benediction" (O'Shea, quoted in MacDonagh 1983:98). The church allowed a cemetery monument to Charles Kickham years after denying his body admittance to Thurles Cathedral (O'Shea 1983:236). Second, the clergy could make gestures that were anything but empty, such as boycotting a visit by the Prince of Wales. Thirdly, while condemning violence by nationalists such as Fenians they could simultaneously condemn government treatment of Fenian prisoners and campaign for their release. In addition, as Keogh (1986) observed for a later period, while most clerics opposed violent nationalists a minority was always available to minister to their spiritual needs (see also Newsinger, 1978). As MacDonagh stresses, "In all this the church did not stand apart from the great body of its people. Its dilemmas were their dilemmas . . . Its evasions were their evasions" (1983:101).

Within Ireland the farmers' prosperity depended on selling to the British market, yet they did not identify themselves as "British." Within the United Kingdom of Great Britain and Ireland the whole question of "British" identity came to be intertwined with specific denominational stereotypical identities in the various component "nations"; the Welsh were "Methodist," the Scots "Presbyterian," the Irish "Catholic" and the English "Anglican" (Robbins 1982). Those Irish who were not "Catholic" identified themselves as "Protestant" and stressed their British connection. In Ireland "Protestant" and "Catholic" became, in the language of the majority, a set of terms that also connoted English/Foreign and Irish/Native (O'Farrell 1971). The church and its clergy articulated this growing identity but did not create it. Its roots must be sought in the social worlds of the farmer class and others who became nationalist and in the repertoire of cultural options available to them. As a chain of discourse Catholicism not only created an identity for the individual believer but it provided a language adaptable to the task of drawing boundaries between "us" and "them," thereby creating a "community." As Durkheim, Douglas (1966), and many others have noted, this boundary-making process tends to downplay any conflict within the community and, as writers in the Marxist tradition have argued, enables the class whose beliefs become dominant within a society to present their claims as disinterested and universal in nature. In the way the Irish church came to view itself, it incorporated much of the self-definition of its followers, primarily the farmers but also other smaller groups of "nationalists." In the "invention of tradition" (Hobsbawm and Ranger 1983) "the priests were the main agents in propagating the belief in a poverty-stricken, overworked peasantry, ground down by relentless, tyrannical landlords" (O'Shea 1983:56) although modern economic historians generally agree that rents in the post-Famine era were not exorbitant. The new politico-religious idea presented a picture of a nation with a glorious and holy past that had long suffered persecution for its faith. It stressed Ireland's innocence and purity and the wrongs done to her throughout the centuries (Keenan 1983:24–34). A popular hymn recalled the "Faith of our Fathers, living still in spite of dungeon, fire, and sword" and vowed "we will be true to thee till death." But, as we have seen, clerical support for nationalist or quasi-nationalist movements was at best ambivalent—except in the invented traditions common to both priests and people.[6] The social construction of an ideological community involves not just an invention of tradition but ongoing definition and reconstruction of boundaries. In the Catholic Church generally in the nineteenth century there was increasing emphasis on specifically Catholic doctrines and ritual that served to set it apart from Protestantism (see Taves 1986). The appeal of such boundary generating and sustaining emphasis in Ireland is apparent where the religious divide could be superimposed on the colonized/colonizer self-identification of the people who stressed their Catholicism. Keenan notes that Protestants or, later, "pagan" England "formed the 'black' counterpart to the 'white' concept of a stainless church" (1983:32) and, he could have added, a stainless nation, evidenced as such by faith to the true church. Ireland's self-definition like that of the Roman Catholic church came to stress her special position as a reservoir of and defender of spiritual values in a materialistic world.

Catholicism provided a language useful to the task of creating a "national community." Its clergy were defined by themselves and others as representatives of that nation (see Taylor 1985). However, this very idiom could be used by the clergy itself for goals that had little to do with nationalism. A recurrent theme in clerical hostility to temperance movements was that they were Protestant inspired and a priest such as Father Matthew who cooperated with Protestants in opposing drink was progressively isolated within the ranks of the clergy (Malcolm 1986). Similarly, priests' arguments against farmer cooperatives linked them to the Protestant landlord, Horace Plunkett, who pushed for their development.

The reciprocal definitions of good Ireland and bad England contributed to, and reflected, the glorification of "rural" values and lifestyle (i.e., the farmer family system) and the concomitant equation of "urban" with evil. Through the logic of binary opposition England was defined as urban, Protestant, evil, and materialistic; Ireland as rural, Catholic, holy, and spiritual (see Hoppen 1984:182). This romantic,

---

6 According to the testimony of Quaker neighbors, the father of Cardinal Cullen, a prosperous farmer, remained "loyal" during the bloody rising of 1798 in the southeast part of the country where the Cullens lived. Yet "oral tradition in the family ensured that he was pictured as both a deserter from the yeomanry and a leader of the '98 rising" (Bowen 1983:3). As a child in rural Ireland, the present writer attended the 1961 unveiling of a monument to a local man hanged in 1820 for Whiteboy-type agrarian agitation. The monument was blessed by a priest who also addressed the large gathering. Both the priest and the people who heard him would likely be shocked to learn that priests in the 1820s were active in opposing the Whiteboys, even to the point of turning them in to the "English" authorities (see Beames 1983:192 for an instance of a priest in Oranmore in County Galway doing this; Oranmore is about 15 miles from Seefin Hill where the 1961 monument to Anthony Daly was erected).

anti-modern ideology was not unique to Ireland, of course, but in Ireland, because of its colonial heritage and subordinate position in the current sociopolitical and economic establishment, it was particularly appealing to many (see Garvin 1986). One group particularly sensitive to their standing in the colonial context was the small Catholic middle class of the cities. It was from this background that the early members of the Irish Christian Brothers were drawn. This organization of Brothers developed a network of schools which were among the most important institutions through which the view of Ireland as a holy nation wronged by evil England was articulated and propagated. It was not a large step to the reasoning that, because both had survived centuries of persecution and had been sanctified by the blood of martyrs, Irish nationalism and Catholicism were equally legitimate and compelling. This intermingling and conflation of the two was to lead, of course, to the conception by Patrick Pearse and others of insurrection as a sacrifice by a few to redeem the nation (O'Neil 1987; Newsinger 1978). When such a rising was indeed carried out, at Easter 1916, and was followed by the execution of its leaders, the general population rallied to the cause of the "martyred patriots." "Pearse's conception of revolution had triumphed, and the Irish people, in his terms, had indeed been redeemed." And, as Newsinger adds, "The clergy were by no means immune to the great conversion that took place" (1978:618).

THE EXPLANATION OF EMIGRATION

Catholicism, like any cultural system, could be used in different ways, for different reasons, by different groups. As we have seen, it could articulate a national identity while diverting attention from internal conflict and division. It could be selectively adopted and adapted by farmers in light of their needs to maintain their family farms. It could be used by the clergy in ways that promoted their specific interests. Many writers have pointed out one or another of these "utilizations" of Catholicism in the Irish context. A very important point, however, is that Catholicism could do *all* these simultaneously. We need to recognize what Thompson (1986:77) has called the "multi-accentuality of the ideological sign." How the "nation-building" and "family-sustaining" uses of Catholicism were interlinked can be seen most clearly in the church's response to emigration. The farmer class who provided the church with most of its money, personnel, and followers also practiced impartible inheritance which condemned most children to either lifelong celibacy or emigration. Because emigration implied going to live abroad in evil cities, perhaps in pagan England itself, we might expect the Church to have vehemently opposed it. Yet to have done so would have raised other troublesome questions. If emigration ceased, how would the people live? Landlords were an easy target in clerical support of farmers' attempts to own their land but attacks on landlords did nothing to reduce emigration. Periodic movements by smaller farmers or of the landless demanding that large farms be subdivided were invariably co-opted by movements promoting the interests of tenant farmers vis-à-vis landlords. The clergy often spoke against the "graziers," those large farmers whose land supported few people but in practice the church supported the interests of the tenant farmers, including most graziers (see D. Miller 1973:17, 45, 70–75; Hoppen 1984:182).

The consolidation of power by the farmer class inevitably implied a parallel growth in the emigration of its noninheriting children. Yet the willing departure of so many potentially undermined faith in the goodness of rural Catholic Ireland. Thus, the "hegemonic necessities of family, church, and middle-class nationalism" (K. Miller 1985:129) combined to produce and sustain an explanation of emigration which was congenial to the various parties involved. This explanation blamed the exodus on inexcusable fate or, more commonly, English malevolence, rather than Catholic parents and rural bourgeois or the individual emigrants themselves. "Thus emigration, albeit lamented, could continue without challenging . . . the hegemony of the very forces which helped impel departures; indeed, the continued conceptualization of emigration as exile served to buttress that hegemony by heightening popular loyalty to Catholic Ireland's clerical and political defenders against the 'alien' elements deemed culpable for emigration as well as for all the other ills afflicting the island since Norman times" (K. Miller 1985:129; see also Bowen 1983:297ff, for Cardinal Cullen's views along these lines).

CONCLUSION

By examining the social positions and experiences of diverse groups of Catholics and the cultural options available to them, we can explain why they behaved and believed as they did. We have seen how threats to Catholicism generally in the nineteenth century led Rome to stress its authority and distinctiveness. Irish farmers, also because of their life situations, found convincing such teachings on authority and the need for unity. A rising middle class, of farmers and others, in the Irish colonial context also found convincing the church's stress on its distinctive and superior nature. These conjunctures of experiences, felt needs and convincing available teachings explain why the vast majority of Irish Catholics became "practicing" in the nineteenth century and why so many of their children willingly became priests, nuns, and brothers to devote their lives to the work of the church as they saw it. Similar in background to their congregations and economically dependent on them, the clergy helped articulate their interests. But neither the people nor the clergy were passive reflectors of the attitudes and beliefs of the other. Where teaching from the top was uncorroborated by the experiences of everyday life, it was ignored or evaded as in the Papal condemnation of boycotting. Where the people's experiences gave rise to ambivalence, as in middle-class attitudes toward violent nationalism, the clergy faithfully reflected this ambivalence. But the church, nevertheless, consistently condemned secret societies, many of which were nationalist. We sociologists need to recognize such active selection and recombination of beliefs that people make, whether they be lay or clerical. It is unacceptable either to reduce the people to mere objects of an ecclesiastical campaign to romanize them or to dismiss church teaching and practice as simply an ideological cover over something more basic, be it class, nation or state interests and power.

REFERENCES

Abercrombie, Nicholas, Stuart Hall and Bryan S. Turner. 1980. *The Dominant Ideology Thesis*. London: Allen and Unwin.

Beames, Michael. 1987. *Peasants and Power: The Whiteboy Movements and Their Control in Pre-Famine Ireland*. New York: St. Martin's Press.

Boswell, Terry E., Edgar V. Kiser and Kathryn A. Baker. 1986. "Recent Developments in Marxist Theories of Ideology." *The Insurgent Sociologist*, 13:5–22.

Bowen, Desmond. 1983. *Paul Cardinal Cullen and The Shaping of Modern Irish Catholicism*. Dublin: Gill and Macmillan.

Christian, William. 1972. *Person and God in a Spanish Valley*. New York: Seminar Press.

Connolly, Sean J. 1982. *Priests and People in Pre-Famine Ireland, 1880–1845*. Dublin: Gill and Macmillan.

Coldrey, Barry. 1988. *Faith and Fatherland: The Christian Brothers and the Development of Irish Nationalism*. Dublin: Gill and Macmillan.

Cullen, Louis. 1969. "The Hidden Ireland: Reassessment of a Concept." *Studia Hibernica*, 9:7–47.

Della Cava, Ralph. 1970. *Miracle at Joseiro*. New York: Columbia University Press.

Douglas, Mary. 1966. *Purity and Danger. An Analysis of the Concepts of Pollution and Taboo*. London: Routledge and Kegan Paul.

——————— . 1972. *Natural Symbols: Explorations in Cosmology*. New York: Random House.

Feingold, William L. 1984. *The Revolt of the Tenantry: The Transformation of Local Government in Ireland, 1872–1886*. Boston: Northeastern University Press.

Fine, Gary Alan. 1979. "Small Groups and Culture-Creation: The Ideoculture of Little-League Baseball Teams." *American Sociological Review*, 44:733–745.

Foucault, Michel. 1981. *Power-Knowledge: Selected Interviews and Other Writings 1972–1977*. New York: Pantheon.

Froeschle-Chopard, Marie-Hélène. 1982. "The Iconography of the Sacred Universe in the Eighteenth-Century Chapels and Churches in the Diocese of Venice and Gasse" in Robert Forster and Orest Ranum (eds.), *Ritual, Religion, and the Sacred: Selections from the Annales*. Baltimore: Johns Hopkins University Press.

Garvin, Tom. 1986. "Priests and Patriots: Irish Separatism and Fear of the Modern 1890–1914." *Irish Historical Studies*, 25:67–81.

Goldring, Maurice. 1982. *Faith of our Fathers: The Formation of Irish Nationalist Ideology 1890–1920*. Dublin: REPSOL.

Gottdiener, Mark. 1985. "Hegemony and Mass Culture: A Semiotic Approach." *American Journal of Sociology*, 90:979–1001.

Gramsci, Antonio. 1971. *Selections from the Prison Notebooks*. New York: International Publishers.

Griswold, Wendy. 1987. "The Fabrication of Meaning: Literary Interpretation in the United States, Great Britain and the West Indies." *American Journal of Sociology*, 92:1077–1117.

Hobsbawm, Eric and Terrence Ranger (eds.). 1983. *The Invention of Tradition*. New York: Cambridge University Press.

Hoppen, K. Theodore. 1984. *Elections, Politics, and Society in Ireland 1832–1885*. Oxford: Clarendon Press.

Hynes, Eugene. 1975. "The Sociology of Knowledge: The Views of Emile Durkheim." *Understanding* 4:33–58.

—————. 1978. "The Great Hunger and Irish Catholicism." *Societas*, 8:137–156.

—————. 1988. "Family and Religious Change in a Peripheral Capitalist Society: Mid-Nineteenth-Century Ireland." Chapter 9 in Darwin Thomas (ed.), *The Religion and Family Connection*. Salt Lake City: Bookmark for Brigham Young University Religious Studies Center.

Inglis, Tom. 1987. *Moral Monopoly: The Catholic Church in Modern Irish Society*. New York: St. Martin's Press.

Jenkins, Richard. 1977. "Witches and Fairies: Supernatural Agression and Deviance Among the Irish Peasantry." *Ulster Folklife*, 23:33–56.

Johnson, E. M. 1983. "Problems Common to Both Protestant and Catholic Churches in Eighteenth-Century Ireland," pp. 14–39 in Oliver MacDonagh, W. F. Mandle, and Pauric Travers (eds.), *Irish Culture and Nationalism, 1750–1950*. London: Macmillan.

Keenan, Desmond J. 1983. *The Catholic Church in Nineteenth-Century Ireland: A Sociological Study*. Dublin: Gill and Macmillan.

Kennedy, Liam. 1978. "The Early References of the Irish Catholic Clergy to the Co-operative Movement." *Irish Historical Studies*, 21:55–74.

Keogh, Dermot. 1986. *The Vatican, The Bishops and Irish Politics, 1919–1939*. New York: Cambridge University Press.

Kerr, Donal A. 1982. *Peel, Priests, and Politics: Sir Robert Peel's Administration and the Roman Catholic Church in Ireland, 1841–1846*. Oxford: Clarendon Press.

Knott, J. W. 1984. "Land, Kinship and Identity: The Cultural Roots of Agrarian Agitation in Eighteenth-and-Nineteenth Century Ireland." *Journal of Peasant Studies*, 12:95–108.

Lacroix, B. 1979. "The Elementary Forms of the Religious Life as a Reflection on Power (*Objet Pouvoir*)." *Critique of Anthropology*, 4:87–103.

Larkin, Emmet. 1987. *The Consolidation of the Roman Catholic Church in Ireland 1860–1870*. Chapel Hill: University of North Carolina Press.

—————. 1972. "The Devotional Revolution in Ireland, 1850–75." *American Historical Review*, 77:625–652.

Lears, T. J. Jackson. 1985. "The Concept of Cultural Hegemony: Problems and Possibilities." *American Historical Review*, 90:567–593.

MacDonagh, Oliver. 1983. *States of Mind: A Study of Anglo-Irish Conflict 1780–1980*. London: Allen and Unwin.

MacLeod, Jay. 1987. *"Ain't No Makin' It": Leveled Aspirations in a Low-Income Neighborhood*. Boulder, Colorado: Westview.

MacMahon, Joseph N. 1981. "The Catholic Clergy and The Social Question in Ireland 1891–1916." *Studies* LXX:263–288.

Malcolm, Elizabeth. 1986. *"Ireland Sober, Ireland Free": Drink and Temperance in Nine-*

teenth-Century Ireland. Dublin: Gill and Macmillan.

_____ . 1982. "The Catholic Church and the Irish Temperance Movement, 1838–1901." *Irish Historical Studies*, 23:1–16.

McCourt, Desmond. 1971. "The Dynamic Quality of Irish Rural Settlement" in R. H. Buchanan, Emrys Jones and Desmond McCourt (eds.), *Man and his Habitat: Essays Presented to Emrys Estyn Evans*. London: Routledge & Kegan Paul.

Memmi, Albert. 1965. *The Colonizer and the Colonized*. Boston: Beacon Press.

Miller, David W. 1973. *Church, State, and Nation in Ireland, 1898–1921*. Pittsburgh: University of Pittsburgh Press.

_____ . 1975. "Irish Catholicism and the Great Famine." *Journal of Social History* 9:81–98.

Miller, Kerby A. 1985. *Emigrants and Exiles: Ireland and the Irish Exodus to North America*. New York: Oxford University Press.

Moore, Sally Falk. 1975. "Epilogue: Uncertainties in Situations, Indeterminacies in Culture." pp. 210–239 in Sally Falk Moore and Barbara Myerhoff (eds.), *Symbol and Politics in Communal Ideology: Cases and Questions*. Ithaca: Cornell University Press.

Newsinger, John. 1978. " 'I Bring Not Peace But A Sword': The Religious Motif in the Irish War Of Independence." *Journal of Contemporary History*, 13:609–628.

O'Farrell, Patrick. 1971. *Ireland's English Question: Anglo-Irish Relations 1534–1970*. London: Batsford.

O'Ferrall, Fergus. 1981. "The Only Lever. . . ? The Catholic Priests in Irish Politics 1823–29." *Studies* LXX (Winter):309–324.

O'Fiach, Tomas. 1975. "Irish Poetry and the Clergy." *Léachtai Cholm Coille* (Maynooth, Ireland) 4:30–56.

O'Neil, Daniel J. 1987. "The Secularization of Religious Symbolism: The Irish Case." *International Journal of Social Economics*, 14:3–24.

O'Neill, Kevin. 1984. *Family and Farm in Pre-Famine Ireland: The Parish of Killeshandra*. Madison: The University of Wisconsin Press.

O'Shea, James. 1983. *Priests, Politics, and Society in Post-Famine Ireland: A Study of Co. Tipperary, 1850–90*. Dublin: Gill and Macmillan.

Robbins, Keith. 1982. "Religion and Identity in Modern British History," pp. 465–487 in S. Mews (ed.), *Religion and National Identity*. Oxford: Blackwell.

Sewell, William H. Jr. 1980. *Work and Revolution in France*. New York: Cambridge University Press.

_____ . 1987. "Theory of Action, Dialectic, and History: Comment on Coleman." *American Journal of Sociology* 93:166–172.

Strawbridge, Susan. 1982. "Althusser's Theory of Ideology and Durkheim's Account of Religion: An Examination of Some Striking Parallels." *Sociological Review*, 30:125–140.

Swidler, Ann. 1986. "Culture in Action: Symbols and Strategies." *American Sociological Review*, 51:273–286.

Taves, Ann. 1981. *The Household of Faith: Roman Catholic Devotions in Mid-Nineteenth-Century America*. South Bend, IN: University of Notre Dame Press.

Taylor, Lawrence. 1985. "The Priest and the Agent: Social Drama and Class Consciousness in the West of Ireland." *Comparative Studies in Society and History*, 27:696–712.

_____ . 1980. "Colonialism and Community Structure in Western Ireland." *Ethno-*

history 27:169–181.

_____ . forthcoming a. "The Mission: An Anthropological View of an Irish Religious Occasion" in Chris Curtin and Thomas Wilson (eds.), *Ireland From Below*. Galway: University of Galway Press.

_____ . forthcoming b. "Stories of Power, Powerful Stories: The Drunken Priest in Donegal." In Ellen Badone (ed.), *Folk Religion and Orthodoxy in Europe*. Princeton: Princeton University Press.

Therborn, Goran. 1980. *The Ideology of Power and the Power of Ideology*. London: New Left Books.

Thompson, Kenneth. 1986. *Beliefs and Ideology*. New York: Tavistock.

Turner, Bryan. 1983. *Religion and Social Theory*. London: Heinemann.

Woods, C. J. 1980. "The General Election of 1892: The Catholic Clergy and the Defeat of the Parnellites," pp. 289–319 in F. S. L. Lyons and R. A. J. Hawkins (eds.), *Ireland Under the Union: Varieties of Tension. Essays in Honor of T. W. Moody*. Oxford: Clarendon Press.

4.

Containing the Luciferine Spark:
The Catholic Church and Recent Movements for
Social Change in the Republic of Ireland

John A. Hannigan

While the secularization of modern society has been a ubiquitous theme in the sociology of religion, the specific influence, both positive and negative, of the established churches in this transformative process has been inadequately analyzed. In particular, scant attention has been paid to the actions of lay elements in promoting or retarding the social forces which fan the sparks of secularism and modernity.

In this chapter, I examine how the Catholic Church in contemporary Ireland has confronted increasing demands for change in matters of morality and family life and assess its continued ability to impose its doctrine and ideology in a society which is undergoing a period of social, economic, and demographic transition. Empirically, the paper will focus on the "moral politics" surrounding two recent national referenda in the Irish Republic—the 1983 constitutional referendum on abortion and the 1986 referendum on divorce.

1. Theoretical Approaches

For heuristic purposes, two main types of theoretical approaches can be identified in the scholarly literature on the adaptation of the Catholic Church to secularization and social change—the evolutionary/typological model and the dialectical model.

In the evolutionary/typological approach, the Catholic Church at first seeks to deny the development of a civil society or to neutralize it by taking an absolutist, aggressively defensive posture. When this fails, then the Church attempts to come to terms with the secular-pluralist society by penetrating the new order and establishing a distinctive "Catholic ethos" organized around a form of "social Catholicism" or "religious socialism."

Donald Smith (1970), for example, in his book, *Religion and Political Development*, proposes a three-stage developmental model. In the first stage, the Church, confronted by the modern world, responds by aggressively affirming its role as the "divine authority in the midst of human sociey with power to direct, guide, and judge all temporal institutions." In the second stage, the Church retreats from this absolutist position and takes a more "humanist" approach. Smith calls this stage a "religious socialist society," although Sanders (1974:284) points out that, in practice, this is more properly a form of reformist society based on religious inspiration. In the third stage, the Church becomes part of a "secular pluralist" society.

Vallier's (1970) five stage "typology" of Catholicism is somewhat similar. In the second half of the nineteenth century, the Catholic Church lost its position as the "monopoly" church, and, in the face of a "liberal" threat, formed a series of short-run coalitions with conservative forces (the era of the "political church"). As the Church moved into the present century, its leaders increasingly recognized that these conservative coalitions alienated many of the laity, and, as a result, began to look inward. In this third "ghetto church" stage, specialized structures (trade unions, youth groups) were established to insulate Catholics from the outside world. In the fourth stage ("the servant church"), the Church moves back into the external world in the role of "social worker," mounting social and economic programmes for the betterment of society-at-large. In the fifth and final stage, the "pastoral church" becomes a source of community leadership and the emphasis is placed on "teaching" the faithful their social responsibilities.

In a chapter in the present volume, assuming a perspective derived from the work of the German neo-functionalist, Luhmann, Peter Beyer has presented an account of the role of Catholicism in the modernization of Quebec society which constitutes another version of this evolutionary model. He suggests that, for a century, the Catholic Church in Quebec successfully enforced a kind of "communicative isolation" wherein French Canadians were excluded from industrial pursuits and culture and incorporated into a distinctive religio-familial-cultural system which neutralized the most typical manifestations of the developing modern structures. As in Latin America, the Church erected and maintained its own institutions, notably the Catholic trade unions, schools and universities, and various social action groups which reflected a sort of social Catholicism. When this strategy of "neutralization" lost its effectiveness during the Quiet Revolution of the nineteen-sixties, the Church withdrew for the most part from direct management and guidance of educational, health, and cultural institutions. However, Beyer argues that withdrawal did not spell irrelevance and that "Ultramontane Catholicism" left a legacy—a distinctive, French-Canadian, cultural identity which continues to interpenetrate the economic and cultural spheres.

The dialectical model is based on the application of the ideas of the Italian Marxist theorist, Antonio Gramsci. Gramsci's review of the role of the Church in social developments occurring in Catholic Europe in the nineteenth and early twentieth centuries (see Fulton, 1987) is on one level similar to the evolutionary perspectives discussed above. However, his focus on the relationship between religion and power in society suggests an approach which is less unidirectional, less historically idiosyncratic, and more open to a cross-cultural application.

Gramsci's comments on religion and the State have been most fully developed by the Brazilian scholar Paulo Krischke (1985) who builds on the work of Portelli (1977). In the Krischke model, the Catholic "ideological *bloc*" in contemporary societies is made up of three elements—the ecclesiastical apparatus (hierarchy), lay militant movements, and Catholic institutions (unions, political parties). The Church's relationship with the polity takes the form of a centripetal-centrifugal dialectic. Catholic political and union leaders disseminate the Church's influence externally while lay movements and the hierarchy "receive and organize the ideological external influences within the Church's own priorities" (Krischke, 1985:410). Under normal circumstances, the Church is not a major political player in a secular society. However, in times of social and political "crisis," for example, Brazil in 1964, the Church's actions may either reinforce or weaken the trends of the classes in opposition and ultimately "weigh heavily on the final results of the crisis" (Krischke, 1985:411). In such a crisis, the Church is said to be acting within an occasional or "conjunctural" context rather than an "organic" one where the "stakes" involve a fundamental transformation of the main contending classes in their dispute for "hegemony" (the cultural power for social control). Nevertheless, in such a crisis, the church can contribute decisively to the process of the rise and fall of the main contending social classes.

The Irish case provides an interesting context for the application of this dialectical model. For historical reasons to be discussed below, Ireland has not secularized as rapidly as most of the rest of the Western world and contains a majority Roman Catholic population which appears "to still be dominated by a church embracing a hegemonic view of its role in the cultural values of the state" (Fulton, 1987:214). Yet, on closer consideration, this cultural control is intermittently under siege. Increasingly, hegemony must be negotiated rather than assumed. In particular, the coalitions and conflicts within and beyond the Catholic ideological bloc determine how successfully religion can continue to operate as a hegemonic force within Irish society. In order fully to assess this present situation, it is first necessary to understand why the Church became the primary ideological agent in the south of Ireland and how closely Church and State have been linked in the historical past.

2. Historical Background: Church-State Relations in Ireland

In the past, the privileged position of the Catholic Church in Ireland has often been explained as the product of the confluence of a set of idiosyncratic historical circumstances. Within the borders established in 1922, Protestants represented under

10 per cent of the population of the new Irish Free State. This opened the way to the formation of a more or less homogeneous society whose ethos was overwhelmingly Catholic. Why it remained so can be explained in ideological, political and economic terms. Ideologically, Catholicism

> gave to Ireland a sense of identity which reinforced its separateness from Britain and gave to the Irish a strong sense of self-confidence and mission in a secularizing world. (Girvin, 1986:63)

In political terms, it has been suggested (Keogh, 1985) that during the early years of the fledgling Irish state, politicians from both sides of the Civil War competed for the *imprimatur* of the Church in order to gain legitimacy with a population which was deeply Catholic in belief and obedience. Economically, the Church was one of the few sources of mobility in a society which was characterized by "underemployment and incomplete industrialization" (O'Connell, 1982:197).

Scholarly opinion in recent years has put the influence of the Catholic hierarchy[1] on state policy in Ireland as lying in an intermediate zone conforming neither to the theocratic-state model nor to a simple interest group model. Whyte (1971:370), in his landmark historical study, argues that the difficulty in defining the hierarchy's influence in Irish politics is that "it is not a constant, of equal importance on all subjects and at all periods." He cites three variables which affect the influence of the hierarchy: party traditions, changes in the climate of public opinion, and the nature of the issues on which they are seeking to exert influence. More recently, Girvin (1986:63–64) uses the analogy of the business community in a market economy; the Church's special position makes it more than just another interest group but state autonomy does exist, albeit often weakly.

The intrusion of the Church into affairs of state has often been considered in relation to the "Mother and Child Scheme" of 1950. After sixteen years of rule by the conservative *Fianna Fail* government of Eamon de Valera, an inter-party government briefly came to power in 1948. The coalition's Minister of Health, Dr. Noel Browne, appointed by the leader of the radical reform party, *Clan na Poblachta*, proposed a scheme[2] which would have provided free family practitioner care, free specialist, consultant, and hospital treatment, free visits from midwives and free dental and optical treatment for Irish mothers—before, during and after childbirth. Suspecting that the scheme would open the way to the loss of Church control over moral education, the hierarchy denounced the plan and Dr. Browne

---

1 The term "hierarchy" is frequently used in Ireland to refer to the bishops as a corporate decision-making body. Traditionally, the hierarchy has met at Maynooth College, the national seminary, to work out matters of policy.

2 Dr. Browne's plan, in fact, imitated the new British National Health Scheme approved in 1948 and guided through Parliament by Aneurin Bevan, Minister of Health in the Labour government of Clement Attlee.

was pressured to resign by Sean MacBride, his party leader. Whyte (1971:236–7) produced some limited evidence to indicate that the Mother and Child Scheme was unsuccessful not simply because of Church opposition but because the Church became a useful ally for those of Dr. Browne's cabinet colleagues who opposed universalist welfare schemes on entirely non-religious grounds. Ryan (1985:396) cites this as an example of how the "theocratic" model understates the "influence of natural propertied conservatism in Irish politics"—a conservatism which often has found "a ready ally in the Church or at least a ready justification for their own intransigence."[3]

The complexities of politics and religion have been highlighted once again in the constitutional referenda of 1983 and 1986. Unlike previous episodes, however, these campaigns have been characterized by two new factors: (1) a more visible dichotomy between those advocating social change and those committed to a more traditional social order (2) the emergence of right-wing lay Catholic interest groups whose actions are not always directly in accord with the wishes of the hierarchy.

3. The 1983 Abortion Referendum

By most accounts, the 1983 referendum campaign had its beginnings in the late 1970's in an emerging grassroots movement which was opposed to the increasing secularization of Irish society. Kerrigan (1983:7) identifies three specific organizations as being central to this movement. In the 1977 general election. a small group, the Christian Political Action Movement canvassed against Labour Party politicians including the future Minister of Health, Barry Desmond. The following year, the Council for Social Concern, later to be "one of the prime movers in the Amendment campaign," told the *Catholic Standard* that it was:

> deeply concerned about certain undesirable developments in Ireland in recent years
> . . . . we particularly refer to unsubtle attacks on our religion, morality and culture
> by certain women's organisations and by the lobbies for contraception, divorce and
> secular schools. (Kerrigan, 1983:7)

A third organization, the League of Decency, later a constituent element of the Pro-Life Amendment Campaign, participated in the 1978–9 campaign against a new family planning act by sending parliamentary members (TDs) pictures of foetuses.

In the next two years, the movement was reinforced by the active participation of two established Catholic "exclusive" societies—the Knights of Columbanus and *Opus Dei*. These associations, more popularly constituted than the hierarchy, could put pressure on politicians without directly implicating the Church in the political process (Girvin, 1986:68). Their contacts in the media, the civil service and other

---

3 See Eugene Hynes' chapter in this volume for an account of how the 'moral monopoly' of the Irish Church in the nineteenth century was the product of an alliance between the clergy and the "comfortable farmer class."

influential organizations put them in a position to effectively lobby political decision-makers (Kerrigan, 1983:8).

While the idea of a constitutional amendment to prevent abortions being declared legal by the courts was not new, it was revived in earnest at a 1980 conference on medical ethics organized by an obstetrics professor at Trinity College, Dublin who was a leading member of the natural conception movement. This led in early 1981 to the formation of the Pro-Life Amendment Campaign (PLAC) which "brought together various right-wing Catholic groups eager to press for an amendment to the constitution guaranteeing the right to life of the unborn" (Cooney, 1986a:62). PLAC was initially a coalition of conservative doctors' groups, notably the Catholic Doctors' Guild, and the exclusive societies discussed above. The "structural link" between the doctors and the pressure groups was provided by the Council of Social Concern, an umbrella group which included the League of Decency and the Christian Political Action Movement (Kerrigan, 1983:12). Later, the coalition was expanded to include the Catholic Nurses' Guild, *Muintir na Tire*, a traditional Catholic group, and the Irish wing of SPUC (Society for the Protection of the Unborn Child), a British organization known for its anti-abortion activism. The most prominent member of PLAC was Professor Eamonn de Valera, a leading Irish gynecologist and the son of the revered *Fianna Fail* founder, *Taoiseach* (Prime Minister) and President.

PLAC chose to launch its campaign just prior to the General Election of 1981 and in doing so was able to exploit a political weakness in *Fine Gael*, the more liberal of the two major Irish political parties. *Fine Gael*, once the party of conservative middle-class rural landowners and small town professionals, had split by the 1980's into a moderate "urban" party with a conservative wing, somewhat similar to the Democratic Party in the United States in the sixties. The party leader, Garret Fitzgerald, fearful that his "constitutional campaign" to promote reconciliation between Catholics and Protestants in both the north and south of Ireland would be jeopardized by PLAC charges that he was 'soft' on abortion, agreed to calling a referendum. Fitzgerald and his cabinet colleagues quickly had misgivings about the referendum but were unable to postpone the vote, nor did they succeed in substituting an alternative wording[4] to that originally proposed by the *Fianna Fail* leader, Charles Haughey.

The attitude of the hierarchy to this point was guarded. While none of the bishops could be said to favour abortion in any form, there were divisions over the

---

4 The *Fianna Fail* wording read "This State acknowledges the right to life of the unborn and with due regard to the right to life of the mother guarantees in its laws to respect and as far as practicable by its laws to defend and vindicate that right." By contrast, the defeated *Fine Gael* version read "Nothing in this Constitution shall be invoked to invalidate or deprive of force or effect any provision of a law on the grounds that it prohibits abortion."

advisability of a nationwide referendum on this issue. Some of the more conservative prelates, notably Archbishop Ryan of Dublin and Bishop McNamara of Kerry, vocally supported the pro-amendment campaign, but others, echoing the position of a number of Vatican officials,[5] felt that the risks were not worth the possible benefits (Carroll, 1983:6). In particular, they feared that the referendum campaign would irrevocably open up a national debate on a topic hitherto beyond public discourse. In retrospect, this perception proved to be accurate.

In mid-August, 1983, the three-week constitutional referendum campaign began.

By this time, another grassroots movement had emerged in opposition to the Amendment. The Anti-Amendment Campaign was a coalition of three elements: left wing political organizations (Democratic Socialists, Communist Party of Ireland, Socialist Workers' Party), women's health groups (Irish Family Planning Association, Well Woman Centre), and centrist political groups and representatives (the *Fine Gael* youth group, Labour Party). Local branches of the Anti-Amendment Campaign were set up, largely in Dublin and Cork, and members actively canvassed to defeat the proposed constitutional change. While not actively involved in the campaign, leading *Fine Gael* politicians (Dr. Fitzgerald, the Ministers of Finance and Education), the *Tanaiste* (Deputy Prime Minister), Dick Spring, and Protestant church leaders, notably Dean Victor Griffin of St. Patrick's Cathedral, Dublin (Church of Ireland) all publicly announced their opposition to the Amendment. With support from doctors, lawyers, academics, and journalists, the Anti-Amendment Campaign "presented their case skillfully in the media, particularly on television, and, as the campaign progressed, 'their objections were being taken seriously'" (Girvin, 1986:74).

The developing polarization of opinion was evident in many occupations and organizations. For example, a rift developed in the Irish Farmers' Association when eleven members who spoke out against the Amendment were suspended along with the organization's president, Donal Cashman.

In the face of what was perceived as mounting opposition, the hierarchy began to play a more active role. After a meeting at Maynooth with the Papal Nuncio, Dr. Alibrandi, sitting in to hear the discussions, a statement was published on August 22, 1983 which recognized the right of each person to vote according to conscience but stated that it was the episcopal conference's considered opinion that the Amendment would safeguard the right to life of both the mother and the unborn child. This final wording was, evidently, a compromise between the hard line position of the Ryan-McNamara caucus and the more cautious approach of other colleagues. It was crafted so as not to appear excessively heavy-handed, yet, at the same time, not to give the impression that "it did not matter how you voted" (Carroll, 1983:7).

The response of some individual prelates was less subtle; Cooney satirically

---

5 The Vatican, no doubt, remembered all too well the recent (i.e. 1978) rebuff dealt the Church in the Italian divorce referendum.

(1986a:68) describes it as being "a Carmelite on one hand and a ballot box in the other."[6] Archbishop Ryan and Bishop McNamara took a hard-line stance against the Amendment. The former described the issue in a pastoral letter read at all masses in the Dublin diocese as a matter of "life and death" and the latter, at a special mass in Killarney to mark the conclusion of the Irish Medical Association's annual congress, argued that the Amendment was not sectarian and warned that not to implement it would be the thin edge of the wedge, leaving the door open to selective abortion in the future. The rank and file clergy were equally open in their opposition. A Franciscan in Archbishop Ryan's own parish, for example, implored the congregation to vote "yes" and offered personally to "take the responsibility before God" (Carroll, 1983:7).

On September 7, 1983, referendum day, nearly two thirds of those who went to the polls (66.45%) voted in favour of the Amendment. Voter turnout, however, was quite low (54.6%).[7] Opposition to the initiative was concentrated in Dublin, where five constituencies voted down the Amendment, and in the cities of Cork, Galway and Limerick where sizeable minorities voted against it. By contrast, in rural areas, especially in the West of Ireland and in traditional urban working-class constituencies the "yes" vote was consistently high. These latter constituencies are characterized both by traditional close relationships with the clergy and by a tradition of *Fianna Fail* support (Girvin, 1986:79).

While the Amendment passed into law, it may well have been a pyrrhic victory, for, despite numerous incidents of media censorship, abortion was debated openly for the first time. As Gibbons (1983:28) has noted:

> even to open debate on such a closed topic, to allow people choice on the matter is in fact to break the old mould of unquestioning obedience and silence in the face of authority.

The low turnout, particularly in Dublin, was interpreted by some as a similar indi-

---

6 This is a wordplay on "the armalite and the ballot box," a term used to describe the recent Irish Republican Army strategy wherein military action and political mobilization are jointly pursued without contradiction (see Hannigan, 1985:32).

7 There has been some debate over how best to interpret this high abstention rate. Walsh (1984) presents data which suggest that the low turnout resulted in an understatement of the "true" level of support for the proposed amendment; that is, actual support for the amendment in the population seems to have been higher than that indicated in the Referendum results. Believing the result to be inevitable, such voters did not feel the urgency to cast their ballots. O'Donnell and Brannick (1984), however, dispute the validity of Walsh's methodology, arguing that it is impossible to assign statistically a preference for or against the amendment to those who abstained. Girvin (1986:77) concludes that a more likely explanation than Walsh's is that resistance to holding a referendum is reflected in the abstention rate and that some of the abstainers distinguished between personal opposition to abortion and the necessity of holding a referendum.

cator that "the bishops' influence was on the wane." One bishop observed:

> It was a very sobering kind of result. There were very few unaware of the attitude of their bishops and priests and yet so many voted the other way. The size of the "No" vote was depressing, a sign of the spirit of secularism that we have to work against. (Carroll, 1983:6)

Finally, despite displaying the persisting power of Catholicism in Ireland, the 1983 referendum publicly confirmed what survey data had previously found: that there is a growing liberal constituency in Ireland as well as a smaller, committed anti-clerical movement (Girvin, 1986:81).

4. The Divorce Referendum of 1986

Three years later, the voters went to the polls once again to decide whether to accept or reject the Government's proposal to remove the civil ban on divorce and to permit the *Oireachtas* (Legislature) to introduce a limited form of divorce.

In several ways, the complexion of this vote was at least superficially different from the earlier one. While only a relative few in Irish society were in favour of abortion, support for divorce was considerably more widespread. For example, an *Irish Times*/MRBI opinion poll in May, 1986 showed that 61 per cent favoured the Government's limited divorce proposal (Cooney, 1986b:1). In light of this, the Catholic bishops saw the divorce issue as a crucial rubicon in their fight to preserve a traditional morality. Thus, unlike in the 1983 referendum, the hierarchy did not depend upon lay organizations such as PLAC to assume the front-line position in the battle against social change. Nonetheless, the grassroots activism so evident during the 1983 referendum campaign continued to be of significance, especially in the West of Ireland. Inglis (1987:88) suggests that this anti-divorce Lobby "helped transform the central issue from minority 'civil' rights for non-Catholics to an issue about the common good of Irish society." Finally, the political context of this referendum was somewhat different. This time *Fine Gael* was directly sponsoring a measure which was opposed by the Church, although there were splits both within the cabinet and the party. While a majority of *Fianna Fail* members opposed the divorce amendment, the leader, Mr. Haughey, freed TDs to make up their own minds and to participate personally in whatever way they wished in their individual capacities. Informally, however, *Fianna Fail* members were allegedly urged to "embarrass" the Government by ensuring the defeat of the Amendment (Walsh, 1986:6).

The hierarchy's campaign against divorce actually began in 1982 prior to the abortion referendum. In June of that year, the Irish Theological Commission, a body consisting of the top echelon of Irish Catholic theologians including six bishops, published a twenty-five page document entitled *What God Has Joined* in which the threat of divorce was said to "leave no room for complacency" and a new family court system was proposed as a practical alternative. Nearly three years later, in anticipation of an all-party committee report on marriage breakdown,[8] the Catholic bishops ordered a pastoral letter entitled *Love is for Life* read in all the parish churches on three successive Sundays. The message was similar. In May, 1986 the bishops published and distributed over a million copies of a new fifteen page pastoral letter, *Marriage, the Family and Divorce*, which likewise argued that a marriage in the sight of God could not be undone by the State. Dr. McNamara, now promoted to Archbishop of Dublin, warned Catholic politicians on September 29, 1985 not to dismiss the guidance offered by the bishops on moral issues and announced his total opposition to the introduction of civil divorce in the Republic (Cooney, 1986a:107).

During the referendum campaign, the direct involvement of the hierarchy in the anti-divorce campaign was evident. During a pastoral visit to Ballyfermot, Dublin, Archbishop McNamara urged that "people should pray to God to save marriage and the family in Ireland from the great evil of divorce." Opening a school in County Limerick, Dr. Dermot Clifford, the Archbishop of Cashel and Emly, told an audience that "while children dream day and night of reuniting their parents, divorce destroys these hopes completely" (*Irish Times*, June 14, 1986:8). The hierarchy statement, issued two weeks before the vote, was, as in the 1983 referendum, more cautious. While rejecting the divorce option, it nevertheless recognized the extent of marital breakdown in the Republic and made it clear that, if their conscience so dictated, Catholics could vote "Yes."[9]

On referendum day, nearly two out of three voters (63.1 percent) rejected the government's proposal to lift the ban on divorce. This time 63 percent of the electorate turned out to vote as compared to only just under 55 percent in the abortion referendum. Despite the early polls showing a majority in favour of the amendment, the "Yes" vote turned out to be only slightly higher than the "No" vote in the 1983 referendum, although the reverse was true in several areas of Cork, Ireland's second largest city (*Irish Times*, June 28, 1986:9). Analyses of why support for the amendment reversed so dramatically concentrated on four main factors: the influence of the Catholic hierarchy, its clergy and lay pressure groups, the social fears that once divorce was allowed it would open the door to a more permissive divorce law in the future, the fears of women about their property rights, and the

---

8 The Committee's report appeared on April 2, 1985. While it recommended a referendum to remove the constitutional ban, it made no proposal about the kind of divorce law which would be appropriate, instead, opting for recommendations concerning education, counselling services and legal remedies open to those whose marriages had broken down (see Cooney, 1986a:104).

9 The new article in the Constitution would allow a court of law to grant a dissolution in certain circumstances, i.e. where the marriage had failed for a period of at least five years, where there was no possibility of reconciliation, and where adequate provision was made for any dependent spouse or child (see Inglis, 987:86).

failure of proponents to campaign aggressively coupled with the *de facto* opposition of *Fianna Fail* politicians (Cooney, 1986b:8).

In the aftermath, many of those on the "Yes" side addressed their comments to the first of these factors (*Irish Times*, June 28, 1986), referring to the triumph of the "confessional state" (a spokesman for the SDLP, the "moderate" Catholic party in Northern Ireland), to the "enforcement" of a Catholic "ethos" (a Presbyterian Church statement) and to the decision to keep the Republic "a Catholic state for a Catholic people"[10] (a Divorce Action Group representative).

5. Discussion

Rather than a straightforward progression from one stage to another, the Church's relationship with state and society in Ireland is better described in Krischke's terms as a "centripetal/centrifugal dialectic." In this depiction, the Church is increasingly dualistic—conservative in matters of morality and family life (abortion, divorce, contraception, illegitimacy) and liberal in matters of economic and social justice (unemployment, social welfare, nuclear weapons, foreign policy). Dissent within the Church is more likely to be tolerated on issues pertaining to the latter than those connected to the former. In part, this reflects the historical position of the Catholic Church in Ireland as a "popular" church (Girvin, 1986:62) in the political sense but a privileged body in terms of its ability to impose its doctrine and morality.

This duality is reflected within the Catholic "ideological *bloc*." For example, the second element of this *bloc*, the lay Catholic movement branches in two directions. On the right, there are the grassroots groups centrally involved in the 1983 constitutional referendum: *Opus Dei*, Knights of Columbanus, Christian Political Action Movement, League of Decency. On the left are those Catholic organizations which focus on social justice issues, especially those related to the Third World. The latter movement arose largely as a response to the human rights violations and abuses witnessed by Irish missionaries in Central America and the Phillippines. The ideological currents generated by these lay movements spin out in a centrifugal fashion into the wider Irish society. During the two referendum campaigns, the right-wing movements successfully articulated the defense of a traditional morality regarding contraception and marriage. Yet, on other occasions, the more left-wing ideology has triumphed. For example, during U.S. President Ronald Reagan's 1984 tour of Ireland, a popular protest campaign against American policy on nuclear arms and Central America was legitimized by the refusal of the Irish Catholic bishops to attend all official ceremonies involving Reagan.

In such matters, the interests and policies of the Church have by no means always been coterminous with those of the State. With the exception of several

---

10 The irony here is unlikely to be accidental; this is a paraphrase of the famous statement made by Lord Carson at the founding of "Stormont," the now suspended legislature of Northern Ireland: "a Protestant parliament for a Protestant people."

well-known parliamentarians on its conservative wing, most of the ruling *Fine Gael* party in varying degrees opposed the 1983 abortion referendum as did most in their coalition partner, the Labour Party. Similarly, as Ryan (1985:397) has observed, lay Catholic movements whose goal it is to promote justice and peace in the Third World (the best known of these groups is called *Trocaire*) represent a view which is "totally at variance with the thinking of the two largest Irish political parties."

What would happen, then, if what the Krischke-Portelli model terms a social or political "crisis" should occur? Such a crisis will most certainly arise within the economic rather than the moral sector. Ireland faces a battery of serious economic problems: high youth unemployment, escalating de-industrialization, a *per capita* debt which is the highest in Europe and higher than many Third World nations. Indeed, the Association of Irish Priests has identified unemployment as the "main challenge to Christians" (Cooney, 1986a:82). If elements from within the Catholic ideological *bloc* (liberal prelates, a "social justice"-oriented lay movement which has applied the lessons of the Third World to the internal political situation) were to ally with reformist political elements this could significantly affect, and perhaps realign, the power relations between the main contending social classes in their dispute for hegemony in Ireland.

6. Conclusion

In this chapter, I have noted the roots of the Catholic Church's hegemonic position in Irish society and shown how this position has recently been challenged by secular forces seeking to initiate changes relating to morality and family life. While the hierarchy has been in the forefront of those seeking to snuff out the spark of this change, it has been aided by the initiative and support of a number of grassroots lay movements wishing to defend traditional ideologies of family life and sexual relations. Using concepts drawn from the Krischke-Portelli model of church-polity relations, I have suggested that Irish life today is best described by a dialectical model wherein various official and lay groups within the Catholic ideological *bloc* compete for cultural primacy.

The picture of contemporary Irish Catholicism which emerges, then, is an increasingly complex one. As Inglis (1987:224–25) has observed, the monolithic Church which brought a holistic view to Irish social, economic and political life is beginning to fragment. While it is still the major moral force in Irish society, the Church can no longer take for granted that its teachings on moral matters will be uniformly accepted.

With the pane cracked, one finds many different breezes blowing in the window. Some are the currents of secular change but others come from very different directions. As the 1983 and 1986 referenda indicated, lay religious organizations and movements are increasingly taking the initiative in setting the political agenda in Ireland. At present, these efforts are generally congruent with the wishes of the hierarchy, but, as Michael Cuneo's chapter in this volume illustrates, conflict can easily develop between the bishops and lay elements in the Church. Furthermore, as Cuneo found for the "pro-lifers" in Canadian Catholicism, these lay groups do not find it inconsistent to be intensely conservative on matters of family life and morality (private life) but to be quite the opposite in matters of economic and political policy (public life).

Secularization, then, has not proceeded in Ireland in an evolutionary, linear fashion. While it is possible to interpret this in a Luhmannian fashion (i.e. the cultural and religious subsystems have not yet caught up with the economic and political spheres), it appears more useful to conceptualize secularization in Gramscian terms as a process of ideological contestation in each of the main societal sectors. In the moral politics of the nineteen-eighties, as has been shown, this contest pitted all three elements within the Catholic ideological *bloc* against the forces of secularization. However, potentially, this configuration may look quite different in the next decade with alliances and conflicts developing both within and across the boundaries of the Church. The end-product may well be a variety of secularization somewhat different from any so far observed in Western Europe and North America.

REFERENCES

Carroll, Joe. 1983. "Wrong Battle, Wrong Time." *The Sunday Tribune* (Dublin), October 16:6–7.

Cooney, John. 1986a. *The Crozier & The Dail: Church & State 1922–1986*. Cork and Dublin: The Mercier Press Ltd.

————— . 1986b. "Voters Reject Divorce by Massive Majority." *Irish Times*, June 28:1,8.

Fulton, John. 1987. "Religion and Politics in Gramsci: An Introduction." *Sociological Analysis* 48(3):197–216.

Gibbins, Luke. 1983. "Man Bites Dogma: The Press and the Amendment Campaign." *Magill*, April: 28–30.

Girvin, Brian. 1986. "Social Change and Moral Politics: The Irish Constitutional Referendum 1983." *Political Studies* XXXIV:61–81.

Hannigan, John A. 1985. "The Armalite and the Ballot Box: Dilemmas of Strategy and Ideology in the Provisional IRA." *Social Problems* 33(1):31–40.

Inglis, Tom. 1987. *Moral Monopoly: The Catholic Church in Modern Irish Society*. Dublin: Gill and Macmillan.

Keogh, Dermot. 1985. *The Vatican, the Bishops and Irish Politics: 1919–1939*. London: Oxford University Press.

Kerrigan, Gene. 1983. "The Moral Civil War." *Magill*, September:6–16.

Krischke, Paulo J. 1985. "The Role of the Church in a Political Crisis: Brazil, 1964." *Journal of Church & State* 27(3):403–427.

O'Connell, Declan. 1982. "Sociological Theory and Irish Political Research," pp. 186–198 in Mary Kelly, Liam O'Dowd and James Wickham (eds.), *Power, Conflict & Inequality*. Dublin: Turoe Press.

O'Donnell, Rory and Teresa Brannick. 1984. "The Influence of Turnout on the Results of the Referendum to Amend the Constitution to Include a Clause on the "Rights of the Unborn": a Review of Walsh's Findings." *The Economic and Social Review* 16(1):59–69.

Portelli, Hughes. 1977. *Gramsci: y la Cuestion Religiosa: Una Sociologica Marxista de la Religion*. Barcelona. Ed. Laia.

Ryan, Brendan. 1985. "The Church and Justice." *Studies: An Irish Quarterly Journal* 74 (296):393–401.

Sanders, Thomas G. 1974. "The New Latin American Catholicism," pp. 282–302 in Donald E. Smith (ed.), *Religion and Political Modernization*. New Haven & London: Yale University Press.

Smith, Donald E. 1970. *Religion and Political Development*. Boston: Little Brown.

Vallier, Ivan. 1970. "Extraction, Insulation and Re-entry: Toward a Theory of Religious Change." In Henry A. Landsberger (ed.), *The Church and Social Change in Latin America*. Notre Dame, Indiana: University of Notre Dame Press.

Walsh, Brendan M. 1984. "The Influence of Turnout on the Results of the Referendum to Amend the Constitution to Include a Change on the 'Rights of the Unborn.'" *The Economic and Social Review* 15(3): 227–234.

Walsh, Dick. 1986. "The Enemies of the Republic May Now Gloat." *Irish Times*, June 28:6.

Whyte, J. H. 1971. *Church and State in Modern Ireland: 1923–1970*. Dublin: Gill and Macmillan.

5.

Refugees from the National Myth:
The English Catholic Odyssey

Roger O'Toole

Introduction

Two unrelated events recently placed English Roman Catholics in an unaccustomed limelight. The unprecedented visit of a pope to Great Britain and the television serialization of Evelyn Waugh's novel *Brideshead Revisited* generated, at least fleetingly, a widespread public interest in the phenomenon of English Catholicism, even on the American continent. These events offer a useful means of introducing a discussion of the evolution of English Catholicism and the formation of its distinctive character.

The Papal Visit

Ironically, while the visit of Pope John Paul II to Britain in the Spring of 1982 was an undoubted personal triumph for the Polish pontiff, it could also be interpreted as the culmination of a process of profound *secularization* in which "religious thinking, practice and institutions (have lost) social significance."[1]

The explicit awareness that such a visit would have been unthinkable only a few short years previously was a theme continuously reiterated through the national media in the days preceding, during and following the momentous event. The sense of near disbelief which permeated reports of the meeting with Queen Elizabeth II and the visit to Canterbury Cathedral suggested as much about changes in British public opinion as it did about the Pope's personal credibility as an advocate of peace and goodwill. Clearly, the factor of public opinion was strategically crucial in the tense days immediately preceding the long-planned visit when the war in the

---

1 Bryan R. Wilson, *Religion in a Secular Society*, Harmondsworth: Penguin Books, 1969, p. 14.

South Atlantic cast its shadow over British national life and threatened eleventh-hour cancellation. For, while a trip to a constitutionally Protestant country engaged in hostilities with a predominantly Catholic nation presented the pontiff with a complex of delicate diplomatic problems, the likely nature of his *public reception* by ordinary British people outside his flock undoubtedly loomed large in his deliberations and in his urgent consultations with the Roman Catholic hierarchy of Great Britain. The decision to proceed with, rather than postpone, the visit appears to have been made in terms of a perceptive and accurate assessment of contemporary public attitudes to the papacy in particular and the Roman Catholic Church in general. The unquestionable triumphal success of this papal pastoral visit, at least from the standpoint of public relations, must, therefore, be at least partly attributed to a *contemporary* British public tolerance for Catholicism which stands in sharp contrast to the *traditional* national perception of its character. The most likely basis of such tolerance would seem to be an indifference bred of an underlying process of secularization which has inexorably banished all formally religious concerns to the margins of everyday life, personal interest and national consciousness.[2]

The discussion of the history of English Catholicism below underlines the novelty and singularity of such a state of affairs by illustrating the centrality of religious controversy in British national life during the past four centuries. More specifically, it indicates that "popery" has played a far from marginal part in the lives of British people for much of this time, and that this fact is crucial to an understanding of the general character of British Roman Catholicism. Marx may have exaggerated when he observed that "the tradition of all the dead generations weighs like a nightmare on the brain of the living."[3] It is indisputable, however, that the relationship of British Catholics to their compatriots has, until very recently, been patterned according to religious and political animosities of greater and lesser degrees of antiquity.

Evelyn Waugh Revisited

Nearly four decades after its original appearance in print, Evelyn Waugh's classic *Brideshead Revisited* recently fascinated and intrigued an audience of millions of television viewers on both sides of the Atlantic by its portrayal of the fortunes of an aristocratic English Catholic family during the inter-war years.[4]

Viewed through the eyes of the narrator, the middle-class and agnostic Charles

---

2 The notion of secularization is not embraced by all sociologists of religion. For a recent overview see Phillip E. Hammond (ed.), *The Sacred in a Secular Age*, Berkeley: University of California Press, 1985.

3 Karl Marx, "The Eighteenth Brumaire of Louis Bonaparte" in Karl Marx and Friedrich Engels, *Selected Works* (Vol. 1), Moscow: Foreign Languages Publishing House, 1958, p. 247.

4 See Evelyn Waugh, *Brideshead Revisited*, Harmondsworth: Penguin Books, (rev. edition), 1962. John Mortimer adapted the novel for television.

Ryder, the family of Lord Marchmain appears mysterious and alien, despite its worldly display of fashionable conspicuous consumption. Intimidated by a suffering and legalistic God of crushing immanence, its members appear simultaneously elevated, isolated and imprisoned in a strange, murky world of absolutes, incense, Latin, private chapels, rosary beads, taboos, dietary restrictions and the writings of G. K. Chesterton.

Recently relived vicariously in humbler settings, the fascination, seduction and repulsion experienced by Ryder are rooted in a specific image of English Catholicism; one which is of central importance in the history and mythology of the Roman Catholic community in Britain. The unique legitimating role played by the country gentry in the ideology of English Catholicism is an indispensable element in any attempt to furnish an account of the character of that minority community which was the main official focus of the Pope's pastoral visit to the United Kingdom.

Stereotypes and Secularization

The concerns expressed regarding the timing of the Pope's visit to Britain reflected an acute consciousness, on the part of some observers, of the historical importance of Catholicism in the *political* life of the nation. They betrayed the anxiety of certain Catholics and non-Catholics that an ill-timed pontifical appearance might undo much recent good work by inflaming old and politically sensitive religious prejudices by conjuring up largely forgotten or repressed sentiments regarding "popery" and its perfidious and even diabolic foreign character.

Whether such sentiments were, in fact, provoked among non-Catholic British viewers of a dramatized *Brideshead Revisited* is a matter of conjecture. It is not inconceivable that the serialized depiction of country-house Catholicism may have rekindled long suppressed fears, suspicions and animosities within at least some of those schooled broadly in the British Protestant tradition and versed in the rudiments of the national mythology. The world depicted by Waugh is one of eccentric privilege permeated by an atmosphere of uncompromising and inescapable religiosity. To Charles Ryder, the outsider afforded an intimate, prolonged glimpse into this world, its religious life seems shrouded in secrecy and superstition. Splendidly isolated and smugly exclusive, it is a strange, unknown territory of absurd dogma, doubtful certainty, clerical casuistry, confessors, crucifixes and candles. To the modern British viewer, a secular stranger seeing this alien land darkly through a television screen, the religious life of Brideshead and Marchmain House may well have been as repugnant and infuriating as it was to Waugh's fictional central character.

It may be suggested, however, that a public prepared to welcome a pope into its midst might well have been prepared to extend its tolerance to the doings of the Flyte family. If this was indeed the case, and if the hitherto historically predictable responses were not evoked by the revival of Waugh's narrative, this may well be interpreted as a measure of the high degree of secularization of British public opinion.

A Historical Sketch of English Catholicism

It is impossible in this short chapter to attempt to provide even an outline history of English Catholicism. Instead, taking its cue from the themes raised above, subsequent discussion will focus upon two main topics and will endeavour to indicate their significance for a general appreciation of the character of English Roman Catholicism until recent times.[5] These topics are inextricably intertwined with each other, and with others which cannot be treated here.

The first topic which merits exploration is that of "popery," broadly conceived as a religious and political epithet calculated to incite suspicion, indignation and hostility. As a derogatory depiction of a specific religious tradition, this term has a virtually unparalleled recurrent and tenacious importance in British history. Indeed, it may be regarded without question as denoting a vital ingredient in the British national myth.[6]

The second worthy subject for investigation concerns the part played by the landed gentry and nobility in the history and a fortiori the mythology of English Catholicism. Clarification of its role within the Catholic community and vis-à-vis the wider society is a prerequisite of an adequate understanding of the peculiar evolution of Catholicism in England.

The British National Myth

To those sceptical of consensualist and functionalist views of society the rather Durkheimian notion of a "national myth" may appear inappropriate or unhelpful in sociological analysis.[7] On the other hand, it may be suggested that, in defining and understanding the nature of English Catholicism, this concept has a utility which may be perceived far beyond the ranks of structural-functionalism. The term

---

5 The most recent general historical treatments of English Catholicism are Edward Norman, *Roman Catholicism in England*, Oxford: Oxford University Press, 1986; John Bossy, *The English Catholic Community, 1570–1850*, London: Darton, Longman and Todd, 1975 and E. E. Reynolds, *The Roman Catholic Church in England and Wales: A Short History*, Wheathampstead: Anthony Clarke Books, 1973. Other useful sources are David Mathew, *Catholicism in England*, London: Eyre and Spottiswoode, 1948 (Second edition, first published 1936); E. I. Watkin, *Roman Catholicism in England*, London: Hutchinsons, 1957 and George A. Beck (ed.), *The English Catholics, 1850–1950*, London: Burns Oates, 1950.

6 See for example E. R. Norman, *Anti-Catholicism in Victorian England*, London: George Allen & Unwin, 1968 and John Miller, *Popery and Politics in England, 1660–1688*, Cambridge: Cambridge University Press, 1973.

7 See Emile Durkheim, *The Elementary Forms of the Religious Life* (trans. J. W. Swain), New York: Collier Books, 1961 (first published 1912).

has recently been employed most usefully by the distinguished British sociologist David Martin who notes that, while Christianity condemns the worship of Caesar or the exaltation of the ethnic group, in order to retain "even the possibility of suggesting more worthy objects of praise" it is necessary that it be "positively related to the national consciousness, particularly as this is highlighted in a myth of national origins."[8] According to Martin, a lively and widespread attachment to religion requires "positive overlap" with this myth because "the majority of people cannot bear too sharp a contradiction between their universalistic faith and their group identity." Where religious faith stands in contradiction to national myth, the faith which survives the contest seems "likely to be composed of refugees from the national myth working for a sectarian haven capable of creating an alternative society."[9]

In most European countries, notes Martin, it is "of enormous importance that the existence of the nation and its heroic folk memory is either rooted directly in religion or positively related to it." This is true of all northern Protestant nations, although in some cases the link between Protestantism and "national self-consciousness" was less marked in the sixteenth and seventeenth centuries than in the nineteenth-century period of "liberal nation-building." In England the national myth was forged early. There, as in the Netherlands, "the events of the Reformation itself and the wars which succeeded it indelibly welded together a land and a people."[10] Thus, although a profound Protestantism was a vital aspect of the *Pax Brittanica* of the nineteenth century, the founding myth of the English nation is of sixteenth-century origin and concerns the defeat of the Spanish Armada by Sir Francis Drake in 1588.

The defeat of the great Armada sent by Philip II is a heroic tale of national glory as familiar to every English school child as the story of the "Gunpowder Plot" of 1605 which, itself a key element in the national myth, is still celebrated with appropriate incendiary activity each November the Fifth. Like the lifting of the siege of Leyden for the Dutch, the defeat of the Spanish Armada concisely symbolizes what is being asserted and defended as the national "way of life." Thus, victory over the Spaniards represents proof that God is on England's side and guides her destiny; it indicates that He is a *Protestant* God opposed to the Pope and Catholic princes; and it confirms a divine commitment to defence of the island race against external religious or political interference. In identifying loyalty to the nation state with allegiance to the legally established national religion, the memory of Drake's victory over Catholic sea power underlines the role of Protestantism as the *sine qua non* of the national myth.

Moreover, it may plausibly be argued that a national myth which, from its incep-

---

8 David Martin, *A General Theory of Secularization*, New York: Harper & Row, 1978, p. 101.

9 *Ibid.*, p. 101.

10 *Ibid.*, p. 101.

tion, incorporated a notion of the English as an "elect nation" inhabiting God's island fortress, can only be interpreted through the language of Protestant apocalypticism. Paul Christianson has observed that even those seventeenth-century English reformers who rejected the notion of a national church nevertheless "found it difficult to escape from the fixed belief that the Almighty would reveal His reformation first to His Englishmen, then to the rest of the world."[11] But such a revelation would be part of a more fundamental apocalyptic vision. Apocalyptic thought, therefore, contributed one of the "most mighty thrusts in nascent English nationalism" charging with eternal significance "such important symbols of national pride" as the victory over the Armada. Apocalyptic logic "created a means of categorizing all foreign powers into either the camp of good or that of evil" reinforcing an existing tendency to perceive moral causes for domestic problems. In terms of the conspiratorial logic of apocalypticism such troubles "resulted from the machinations of evil people, of the agents of Antichrist."[12] Hence, as Christianson comments:

> In an age of religious and political dispute, the ideological component of foreign and domestic policy gained a strongly polarized momentum from the apocalyptic tradition.[13]

Popery

If Protestantism and apocalypticism are essential ingredients of the British national myth, "popery" is of crucial importance in both these systems of ideas. Indeed, the intensity of the English hatred of "popery" in the century following the Reformation, and in three centuries beyond, may only be fully grasped "by placing it firmly within the context of that standard justification of a break with Rome, the apocalyptic interpretation of the Reformation."[14] As proponents of "popery," English Roman Catholics have, since the Reformation, languished for the most part as "refugees from the national myth."[15] They have, however, been outcasts in a very special sense, for they have not merely been rejected on the basis of the national myth; more fundamentally, their exclusion from the national life has been an *integral part of the myth itself.* To the extent that they have, in David Martin's terms, inhabited a sectarian haven and embarked upon at least some attempts to create an alternative society, their plight has been a direct consequence of the logical foundations of the national myth.

Throughout the last four centuries, almost up to the present day, the term "pop-

---

11 Paul Christianson, *Reformers and Babylon: English Apocalyptic Visions from the Reformation to the Eve of the Civil War*, Toronto: University of Toronto Press, 1978, pp. 246–247.

12 *Ibid.*, p. 247.

13 *Ibid.*, p. 247.

14 *Ibid.*, p. 5.

15 Martin, *op. cit.*, p. 101.

ery" has remained a pivotal term of political and religious abuse in England. In its matchless sustained ability to provoke an immediate emotional response combining suspicion, fear, indignation and hostility, "popery" has been one of the most powerful epithets in English history. Accordingly, over time, its condemnation has been justified on grounds, not only of "pure" religion, but of patriotism, scientific rationalism and political liberalism. In the minds of ordinary Englishmen, for several generations "popery" has represented a vague though profound threat to the core values of the "English way of life." Imbued, in a mythical manner, with diabolical malevolence, subversive sublety and insidious intent, "popery" has been the stuff of nightmare, evocative of the sinister world of the dungeon, judicial torture and the *auto-da-fé*.[16] Failure to appreciate this makes it impossible to understand the marginal position of Roman Catholics in English society and the peculiarly sensitive nature of this marginality.

To the contemporary secular sociologist or historian, a stark contrast is apparent between "popery" as a mythical entity and the actual nature of English Catholicism. If it is true that few Bishops of Rome have measured up to the demanding description of the Antichrist, it is even more evident that the English "papists" have made a pitiful showing in the role of those "brats of Babylon" with which they have been identified by apocalyptic Protestantism. The scattered flock of English Catholics barely surviving under conditions of semi-feudal domesticity, secrecy, illegality and social stigma from the sixteenth to the nineteenth centuries hardly seem to have presented a threat sufficient to justify the attention, let alone the fears of their compatriots.[17] Yet, alone among English religious dissenters, over three centuries Roman Catholics were unable to shake off their reputation as alien, subversive, perfidious, disloyal, treacherous enemies of the *political* as well as the religious life of the nation. Try as they might to couple their desire for religious dissent with an enthusiasm for political conformity, their quest for legal emancipation and full citizenship proved fruitless time and time again. Despite their willingness at times to interpret their allegiance to the papacy in the most minimal terms, English Catholics were unable, for over two hundred years, to convince their fellow countrymen that they deserved even second-class citizenship in the land of their birth. Popularly perceived as jesuitical political schemers practising bizarre, idolatrous rituals in secrecy, they were despised as willing tools of papal power politics and condemned

---

16 These images were continually re-conjured, for example, by successive re-printings of John Foxe's *Book of Martyrs* (1563). See the depiction in John Henry Newman's famous (1852) sermon "The Second Spring," in *Sermons Preached on Various Occasions*, London: Longmans, Green, 1913, pp. 163–182, and reprinted in many collections of his writings. See also his *Lectures on the Present Condition of Catholics in England*, London: Longmans, Green, 1896. Consult also Denis Gwynn, *The Second Spring, 1818–1852: A Study of the Catholic Revival in England*, London: Burns Oates, 1942, pp. 10–13.

17 See Bossy, *op. cit.* and the discussion below.

as insidious sympathizers of a Catholic foreign diplomacy inherently hostile to the
English nation and the Protestant religion. Thus, their desperate pleas for tolerance
and their fervent declarations of political loyalty were deprecated as the hollow
rhetoric of rascals, liars and potential traitors. Such scoundrels, it was inferred,
were undoubtedly ready, at the strategic moment, to cast off their cloak of duplicity
and reveal the real nature of their allegiance by rekindling the fires of Smithfield.[18]

The hoary sociological aphorism that things defined as real are real in their consequences has a peculiar poignancy when applied to the fortunes of English Catholics.
For most of their history they have been the victims of a myth which has been, in
part at least, of their own making. Their treatment as a religious minority and their
reception as a community have been determined less by genuine knowledge, understanding or appreciation of the nature of their dissent than by a predetermined,
stereotyped perception of their role in a highly formalized cosmic drama. Within the
British national myth, the scriptural apocalyptic element has receded in importance
over time but its basic outline has never been entirely eradicated. In the English
version of the perennial battle between Good and Evil, therefore, it was impossible,
until fairly recently, for English Catholicism as a whole to attain a place among the
forces of righteousness. An appreciation of why this was so may be gained through
even the briefest sketch of the evolution of "popery" in the context of English religious and political controversy. In this process, myth and reality were fused to
such a degree that it is sometimes difficult to distinguish them.

Popery in the Sixteenth and Seventeenth Centuries

From the beginning, the fate of English Catholicism was entwined with the political
doctrine of *Cuius Regio Eius Religio*. Though claiming apostolic continuity with
the pre-Reformation church of Henry VIII, the Romanism which survived in the
reign of Elizabeth I was in a sorry state. Clinging on to life only as a tiny sect[19]
whose congregations clustered fearfully around upper-class nuclei located mainly
in the more remote regions of the kingdom, its spiritual needs were ministered
secretly by missionaries trained abroad and smuggled into their homeland. This
period of dungeon, fire and sword, beloved of later Catholic martyrologists and
myth-makers[20] saw Roman Catholicism become alien to the English people in a

---

18 The site of Protestant martyrdoms during the reign of "Bloody Mary."

19 Bossy has made a persuasive case for the use of this term in the present context. See
   Bossy, *op. cit.*, pp. 25, 60, 108–148. See also reference to seventeenth-century Catholicism as an upper-class sect in Lawrence Stone, *The Crisis of the Aristocracy*, Oxford:
   Oxford University Press, 1965, p. 731. Another sociological use of 'sect' in a Catholic
   context is Thomas F. O'Dea, "Catholic Sectarianism: A Sociological Analysis of the
   so-called Boston Heresy Case," *Review of Religious Research*, Vol. 3, No. 2, Fall 1961,
   pp. 49–63.

20 The cult of "the English martyrs" culminated in the canonization of forty individuals by

number of senses. Those Roman Catholic "recusants" who refused to acknowledge their Queen as "Supreme Governor of the Church in England" were, judging by the laxity with which the penal laws were often applied, frequently viewed as harmless enough eccentrics by their nearest neighbours. In a national context, however, they came increasingly, and not without some justification, to be perceived as part of a dangerous political "fifth column" threatening the peace and security of the realm. Frequently regarded by the Crown as wedded in unholy alliance to the Puritans, Elizabethan papists appeared as potential or actual agents of the papacy and other Catholic foreign powers.[21] Almost subterranean in their seclusion, they were nonetheless seen as internal enemies seeking to undermine the beneficent rule of the Virgin Queen by ceaseless criminal conspiracy. To the understandable dismay of many Catholics this perception was rashly and disastrously reinforced in 1570 with the publication of Pius V's inflammatory Bull *Regnans in Excelsis*. Apart from excommunicating Elizabeth and releasing her Roman Catholic subjects from their allegiance to her, this decree also imposed upon English Catholics, in principle at least, the duty of deposing their heretical monarch. Coming on the heels of the ill-fated Northern rebellion, accompanying the intrigues of Mary, Queen of Scots, and immediately preceding the infamous St. Bartholomew's Day massacre of French Protestants, the Pope's pronouncement was a devastating blow to those Catholics who sought the acceptance and esteem of their compatriots and who insisted that their religious dissent did not compromise their political loyalty.[22] As David Mathew, one of the most eminent historians of English Catholicism remarked, the "change of feeling consequent upon the Pope's action" was clearly a factor in "the progressive alienation of the English people from the Catholic Church."[23] In these circumstances, the fervent loyal protestations of a Campion facing a gruesome death as the penalty for his priestly activities were made to sound hollow by the papal-inspired subversive rhetoric of those who hatched plots and uttered threats from the safety of the English seminary in France.[24]

Thus, in Elizabethan England, papists were identified, for the most part unjusti-

Pope Paul VI in 1970 while "recusant history" has long held a paramount place in English Catholic scholarship. In the area of popular fiction, the "penal times" are most notably evoked in Robert Hugh Benson's novel *Come Rack! Come Rope!* New York: All Saints Press, 1962 (first published 1912).

21 See Patrick McGrath, *Papists and Puritans under Elizabeth I*, London: Blandford Press, 1967; and Elliot Rose, *Cases of Conscience: Alternatives Open to Recusants and Puritans under Elizabeth I and James I*, Cambridge: Cambridge University Press, 1975. See also Bossy, *op. cit.*, p. 393.

22 On the extent of Catholic loyalty to the Crown see Arnold Pritchard, *Catholic Loyalism in Elizabethan England*, London: Scholar Press, 1979; and Adrian Morey, *The Catholic Subjects of Elizabeth I*, London: George Allen & Unwin, 1978.

23 Mathew, *op. cit.*, p. 41.

24 See Evelyn Waugh, *Edmund Campion*, Harmondsworth: Penguin Books, 1956, (first

fiably, with the forces of the Counter-Reformation and especially with the military designs of the King of Spain. In fact, subjected to constant political, economic and legal pressure, English Catholics were a numerically insignificant, geographically dispersed, beleaguered and retreatist group of religious refugees harbouring very few seditious intentions. Despite this, however, it is understandable that they should have remained suspect in the eyes of the Crown, and that removal of the immediate threat of a Spanish invasion should have done nothing to remedy this perception. A view of popery as the most likely instrument of a national "stab in the back" persisted and was to persist over the succeeding centuries. It is in the Elizabethan period that a popular English image of Catholicism as epitomized by the crafty, scheming Jesuit originates. The vitality of this image in popular culture three centuries later may be discerned by examination of Victorian mass fiction.[25] By contrast, English Catholic history and mythology depicts the Elizabethan Age as a heroic period of recusants, rack, rope, dungeon, fire and sword in which the ancient Faith of the Fathers was preserved against overpowering odds. It is here that the cult of martyrdom, so central to the ideology of this minority, has its origins.[26]

Although Catholics had anticipated some improvement in their condition under a Stuart dynasty, their hopes were disappointed. No redress from the Penal Laws was obtained during the reigns of James I and Charles I, and the more favourable personal dispositions of Charles II and James II tended, ironically, to work largely to their detriment. In addition, periodic revelation of the existence of scattered small groups of popish conspirators committed to religious counter-revolution by political means made it virtually impossible for the vast majority of law-abiding Catholics to convince their fellow-countrymen of their political loyalty. Thus, the infamous "Gunpowder Plot" of 1605, in which popery was implicated, generated even more severe measures against Catholics as potential regicides; measures with which the average Englishman, with his limited or non-existent contact with Catholics, was unlikely to quarrel. In Stuart times, "gunpowder, treason and plot" became so associated with Catholicism that, for generations to come, English schoolchildren would reaffirm this connection in the annual autumnal ritual of "Bonfire Night."[27]

---

published 1935).

25 See Margaret Mary Maison, *Search Your Soul, Eustace: A Study of the Religious Novel in the Victorian Age*, London: Sheed and Ward, 1961, especially Chapter 8, "The Wicked Jesuit and Company," pp. 169–182. The (literally) incendiary power of this image is also evident in the effects of the British "No Popery" crusades of such renowned Victorian agitators as the Italian Alessandro Gavazzi and the Irishman William Murphy.

26 See, for example, Lady Catherine Ashburnham, *The Witness of the Martyrs*, London: Sheed and Ward, 1929. For a different view consult H. R. Trevor-Roper, "Twice Martyred: the English Jesuits and their Historians" in his *Historical Essays*, London: Macmillan & Co., 1957, pp. 113–116.

27 The ritual of burning an effigy of Guy Fawkes persists though its anti-Catholic symbolism

In the reigns of Charles II and James II, following the Cromwellian Protectorate, English national enmity shifted from Catholic Spain to Catholic France and it was thus as a fifth column for Louis XIV that popery, as perceived by the popular mind, continued to perform its evil work of subversion. The threat of a self-confessed papist ascending the English throne had the effect of generating a great fear among the English populace, the result of which was a naive public receptivity to stories of plots, conspiracies and political sabotage. In this climate of anxiety, the Great Fire of London of 1666 was officially blamed upon popish arsonists while the transparently malicious and fabricated discovery of a dreadful "Popish Plot" by Titus Oates in 1678 resulted in a national hysteria which those who recognized Oates' account as perjury were unable to control. The trials, executions, witch-hunts, panic and paranoia set in motion by Oates' accusations shook the kingdom, leaving even the monarch, the supposed target of this treason, incapable of quelling the public outcry.[28]

The "Glorious Revolution" of 1688 which removed the Catholic James II from the English throne entailed a political settlement which carefully circumscribed the rights and activities of members of the tiny Roman Catholic sect, ensuring that papists would exist outside the political, professional and religious life of the nation for another century and a half. Thus, under William of Orange, Queen Mary, and Queen Anne a general public perception of popery as alien and seditious was given specific constitutional confirmation. Not for nearly a century was there any softening of this official attitude.[29]

Popery in the Eighteenth and Nineteenth Centuries

Though, under the Hanoverian dynasty, Catholics were naturally under suspicion as Jacobites, sympathizers of the exiled Stuart pretenders who had staged rebellions in 1715 and 1745, their presumed preference for these popish princes "over the water" was, in official eyes, little more than an irrelevant anachronism by the last quarter of the eighteenth century. An informed appraisal of the political impotence of English papists combined with an equally accurate assessment of the serious-ness of the American revolutionary threat to promote the English government to contemplate and negotiate a parliamentary Act for the Relief of His Majesty's Ro-man Catholic Subjects. Inspired specifically by a desire to recruit Catholic Scottish Highlanders for service in the war against the Americans, the Act was designed to allow Roman Catholics to demonstrate their loyalty to King and Country by service in the armed forces. At the price of a loyalty oath it also offered them a small measure of legal relief. Yet, the proponents of the Catholic Relief Act of 1778

has evaporated.

28 See J. P. Kenyon, *The Popish Plot*, London: William Heinemann Ltd., 1972.

29 Norman observes that William III's Disabling Act of 1695 "more or less completed the removal of Catholics from Public Life." *Roman Catholicism in England*, p. 40.

had seriously underestimated the persisting vigour of popular hostility to popery as an affront to Englishmen and an abomination in the eyes of God. In the midst of rumours of jesuitical malice and popish pyromania reminiscent of the hysteria of a century earlier, the public outcry led by Lord George Gordon's "Protestant Association" culminated in the "Gordon Riots" directed against Catholics and their property.[30] Once again, the members of this marginal, minuscule sect found themselves identified with "popery," that monstrous entity which played a devilish role in the national myth. Such was the power of this myth that any real knowledge of the actual social and political conditions of English Catholics was utterly irrelevant to the patriots who feared them so greatly. After delicate and indeed humiliating negotiations aimed at finding a formula by which they could assert their genuine loyalty to the Crown while retaining their spiritual allegiance to the Holy See, English Catholics suffered vilification and physical attack as the most dangerous threat to the peace and security of the realm. Not surprisingly, the retreatist inclination within the Catholic community was somewhat reinforced by this experience; discretion continued to be regarded as the better part of valour in its relations with the wider society. Sensitive negotiations aimed at distinguishing loyal "Protesting Catholic Dissenters" from "Papists" still subject to the full force of the Penal Laws culminated in the Catholic Relief Act of 1791.[31] Within a very few years of its passage, however, complete political emancipation was to become a possibility for all "His Majesty's Roman Catholic Subjects."

The battle over "Catholic Emancipation" was waged against the backdrop of the Napoleonic Wars, but it was won only in 1829, and then only as a result of a Catholic victory on Irish soil. A consequence of Pitt's Act of Union which, in 1800, legally united England and Ireland under one parliament, was the inextricable linkage of the destinies of English and Irish Catholics. Following Pitt's inability to persuade George III to approve Catholic Emancipation in his now United Kingdom of Great Britain and Ireland, English Catholics remained second-class citizens in the land of their birth. To their dismay, however, their quest for emancipation was now legally contaminated in the bottomless bog of Irish politics. With characteristic English distaste for things Irish, therefore, they were at pains to distance themselves from what they perceived as the genuinely alien and disloyal sentiments of their Irish coreligionists. For generations English Catholics had struggled to be accepted as full, loyal members of their own society; incapable of threats or blackmail, they had sought this as humble petitioners, confident that justice would ultimately be their lot. Now, just as it seemed that such an acceptance was almost within their reach, the

---

30 Various riots occurred in Scotland and England in 1779 and 1780. In fiction they provide the background to Charles Dickens' *Barnaby Rudge*.

31 The act allowed the practice of Roman Catholic ritual in legally registered chapels by clergy willing to take a loyalty oath. It removed certain restrictions on Catholic participation in public life but other restrictions, notably on Crown office-holding, remained.

old accusations of perfidy and disloyalty appeared doomed to resound again with a vengeance. For English "papists" would unfortunately be judged by public opinion, not on their own merits, but as spiritual brethren of an unspeakable Irish peasantry whose Catholicism combined ignorance, superstition, and even rebellion. In such circumstances, "popery" was likely to prove as unpalatable as ever to English taste. When, therefore, legal emancipation came to English Catholics, it did so as a by-product of Irish unrest. The Emancipation Act of 1829 resulted not from *trust* in papists but from *fear* of them, in Ireland at least. The election of the leader of the Irish Emanicipation movement, Daniel O'Connell, to a parliamentary seat which, as a Catholic, he was not legally entitled to hold, created a constitutional crisis which threatened to deteriorate into open rebellion. Judging that only an Emancipation Act (which would allow O'Connell to take his seat) could prevent an Irish revolution, the Duke of Wellington and Sir Robert Peel fought the necessary political battle to ensure its passage into law. Opposition to the Emancipation Bill was heated and virulent so that by the time George IV was persuaded to ensure the security of his Kingdom by giving it the necessary Royal Assent, English public life had been polarized over the ancient issue of popery.[32]

For English Catholics, these were the very worst circumstances in which to receive their long-sought political and legal rights. An image of popery as alien, seditious and threatening had been vigorously revived in English popular culture and English Catholics had received the rights of citizenry not because of their loyalty but because of Irish disloyalty. Delivered by the hand of a self-styled Irish "liberator" with whose cause they had little sympathy, emancipation had a bitter taste for the Catholic community in England.[33] The circumstances surrounding the Emancipation Act provided something of an omen, however, by underlining the existence of an unwanted but unavoidable link between English Catholics and their Irish brethren. This connection was to prove even more significant in the decades to follow as famine and poverty drove wave upon wave of Irish Catholics onto English shores.

Due in part to its expanding numbers, and changing social and ethnic composition, discussed in more detail below, Catholicism in England in the decades following emancipation began to shed much of its retreatist character in a manner which did

---

32 See G. I. T. Machin, *The Catholic Question in English Politics, 1820 to 1830*, Oxford: Clarendon Press, 1964; Fergus O'Ferrall, *Catholic Emancipation: Daniel O'Connell and the Birth of Irish Democracy*, Dublin: Gill & Macmillan, 1985; Denis Gwynn, *The Struggle for Catholic Emancipation*, London: Longmans, Green, 1928; and Bernard Ward, *The Eve of Catholic Emancipation* (3 vols.), London: Longmans, Green, 1911–1912. See also Ursula Henriques, *Religious Toleration in England, 1787–1833*, Toronto: University of Toronto Press, 1961, pp. 136–174.

33 This was true especially of O'Connell's wealthier and more socially elevated English coreligionists. A proposal to elect him to membership of the prestigious Catholic "Cisalpine Club" was blocked in the weeks following the granting of royal assent to the Act.

little to endear it to an evangelically-minded Victorian public. From this point of view, the low point in its public popularity was undoubtedly the "Papal Aggression" crisis of 1850 when the newly-styled Archbishop of Westminster, Nicholas Wiseman, issued his insensitive and provocative pastoral letter from Rome immediately prior to the "restoration" of the English Roman Catholic hierarchy. For many English Catholics, the establishment of a formal hierarchy of bishops became, as a result of Wiseman's triumphalist rhetoric, less a cause for celebration than an occasion of embarassment and even fear. Eliciting stern rebuttal from no less a person than the prime minister himself, Wiseman's intemperate pronouncement succeeded in reviving all the old nightmares about popery in the popular press and the public mind. English popery once again attained mythical dimensions as it was revealed, apparently by its own admission, as an alien force bent upon turning back the religious clock three centuries. At countless, outraged public meetings, many expressed the view that Catholic Emancipation had been a grave error. In popular culture, all the stock popish stereotyped characters reappeared, nowhere more effectively than in the pages of *Punch* where such cartoons as "The Thin Edge of the Wedge" and "Guy Fawkes 1850" induced an immediate and predictable anti-Catholic response. Wiseman thus succeeded in rallying the English to their national myth by arousing religious prejudices which had lain dormant for two decades. He revived a grotesque image of popery which was to persist in the English mind well into the next century to the distress of the Catholic community in England. It is undoubtedly true that the public image of English Catholicism as alien, insidious and seditious was not enhanced, during the latter half of the nineteenth century and the first half of the twentieth century, by an Ultramontane clergy and hierarchy, an increasingly Irish composition, and a typical public attitude of intolerant exclusivism. Yet it is true, nonetheless, that Wiseman ensured the persisting marginality of Catholics in English society by seeming to confirm their role as servile but arrogant vassals of an alien Pope.[34]

So central has been the role of a stereotypical popery in the English national myth, and so out of proportion to the numerical, social, political or economic significance of English Catholics that it is by no means surprising that, more than a century-and-a-half after Catholic Emancipation, a proposed visit to England by a Pope should have been a matter of the greatest anxiety on the part of its organizers.

The Catholic Gentry

The role of the country gentry is a crucial element in any adequate analysis of English Catholicism for two reasons: the first historical, the second mythical. It is undeniable that the tiny sect of "papists" which emerged in Elizabethan times owed its existence primarily to the unwillingness of a number of wealthy landed families

---

34 See the account in Norman, *Anti-Catholicism in Victorian England*, pp. 52–79.

to tailor their religious beliefs and practices to suit the temper of the times.[35] Stubborn in their resistance to religious reforms, these families, some of them of noble pedigree, were the nuclei around which all Catholic activity revolved during the periods of enforcement of penal laws against popery. In "penal" times, their country estates were the cells of an underground religious resistance movement while their retainers comprised its rank-and-file membership. It was in their great houses that missionary priests were hidden and masses celebrated in secret. Here too, government informers and *agents provocateurs* were planted and, on occasion, dramatic arrests were made. By their willingness, not only to pay the hefty economic penalty of religious nonconformity, but to risk their lives and property on behalf of hunted priests ministering to a scattered flock of religious dissidents huddled in the more remote regions of the country, these "recusant" families earned a preeminent place in English Catholic history and mythology.[36] Leadership evolved naturally and early upon the recusant landed gentry so that it is only a slight exaggeration to perceive English Catholicism, for much of its history, as a geographically isolated upper-class sect whose numbers were supplemented almost feudally by a loyal rural tenantry. Thus, while recent research reveals that English Catholicism, at least by the eighteenth century, was more socially heterogeneous than hitherto believed, the role of the gentry as leaders of, and spokesmen for, the English Catholic community was unchallenged, even by the clergy, for at least three centuries.[37] Characteristically conservative, doggedly patriotic and loyal to the Crown despite all their difficulties, the Catholic gentry were nonetheless intensely proud of their family traditions of religious deviance and defiance. Though they numbered heroes and even martyrs among their ancestors, their characteristic posture toward the wider society was a considered, strategic retreatism. Eschewing provocation and ostentation in their public lives as much as in their private devotions, they exercised a style of leadership which relied on subtle persuasion grounded in a gentlemanly code of honour. Prepared to risk humiliation in negotiation rather than to lose ground by provocation or threats, the Catholic gentry and their aides from the small papist semi-professional class perceived the quest for emancipation essentially as an educational enterprise. Content to improve the status of their community by one small favour at a time, they sought primarily to convince the English public, initially through its legal, political and religious representatives, of their unquestionable and unswerving political reliability. In their view, political credibility constituted a necessary though by no means sufficient condition for the legal emancipation of English Catholics. Complete freedom to practise their religion publicly without penalty or stigma thus

---

35 Consult Bossy, *op. cit.*, pp. 77–107.

36 See W. B. Patterson, "The Recusant View of the English Past" in Derek Baker (ed.), *The Materials, Sources and Methods of Ecclesiastical History*, Oxford: Basil Blackwell, 1975, pp. 249–262 and consult the scholarly journal *Recusant History*.

37 See Bossy, *op. cit.*, pp. 60 and 74.

seemed dependent upon official acceptance of Catholics as loyal and trustworthy subjects of the Crown, unencumbered by any taint of dual political allegiance.

The degree to which upper-class laymen serving on the "Catholic Committees," engaged in negotiating terms of relief or emancipation with the government, were prepared to retreat in minimizing or circumscribing the nature of their allegiance to the papacy occasionally offended or alienated certain members of the clergy.[38] It is significant, however, that in all the internal diplomacy of the late eighteenth and early nineteenth centuries, it was deemed entirely proper that eminent laymen from the Catholic gentry and nobility should be entrusted with the fate of the Catholic community while the clergy played a merely supportive role.

The above exposition of the diplomatic strategy of those gentlemen of the Cisalpine Club[39] who represented the English Catholic community should make clear the reluctance of English Catholics to receive emancipation at the hands of O'Connell. Many must have felt with repugnance that their goal had been reached at the sacrifice of that credibility and respectability which had been within their grasp, and which they had striven for generations to attain.

The manner in which emancipation was achieved independently of their efforts might have served as an omen for the English Catholic gentry in more than one sense. For not only did it forewarn them that the Irish factor would soon be paramount in English Catholicism, it also hinted more subtly that their preeminence as the effective leaders of the Catholic community might soon be eroded. The event which symbolically tolled the death knell of the unbridled rule of the gentry within the English Catholic community was Wiseman's provocation of the "Papal Aggression" crisis. For while he succeeded in outraging and alienating the old Catholic lay elite by the intemperate, insensitive and triumphalist tone of his incendiary episcopal missive, he also did much more. He implicitly stated the claim of the clergy, and specifically the new hierarchy appointed by Pope Pius IX, to be the sole spokesmen and leaders of English Catholicism. The second half of the nineteenth century was, indeed, to witness the waning of the effective power of the gentry, whilst a

---

38 Notably John Milner. See Norman, *Roman Catholicism in England*, pp. 58–59; Bossy, *op. cit.*, pp. 334–337; and Mathew, pp. 153–156.

39 Literally denoting its genesis in lands North of the Alps, the Cisalpine outlook was akin to Gallicanism in church-state matters. Mathew observes that "Cisalpines were accustomed to concentrate attention on their moral obligations towards the State. In theory they accepted the dogmatic teaching of the Holy See; but they regarded all other forms of papal action with chill reserve" (p. 150). The Club was formed in 1792 by leading members of the "Catholic Committee" which had negotiated the Catholic Relief Act and Norman observes that it "stressed the benefits of the British Constitution and loyalty to the Crown. It was anti-papal in the sense that its members articulately eschewed 'foreign' interference both in English Catholicism and in the life of the nation generally" (*Roman Catholicism in England*, p. 60). "Cisalpinism" is generally considered the antithesis of "Ultramontanism" (see below).

self-confident hierarchy and a clergy no longer willing to be kept "in its place" by well-born laymen expanded their prerogatives and tightened their grip on the Catholic community in England.[40]

Coinciding with the rise and triumph of Ultramontanism on an international scale within the Catholic Church, the establishment of an English episcopacy could not have been more badly timed from the point of view of the Catholic gentry. The two decades between the "Papal Aggression" crisis and the promulgation of the doctrine of Papal Infallibility saw the gentry outmanoeuvred and alienated by clerical forces dedicated to an ostentatious brand of militant papalism.[41] In the church of *Pio Nono*, the role of caution, discretion, circumspection and retreatism, qualities which had characterized the policies of the Catholic gentry, was restricted at best. Yet this clerical defeat of the gentry would have been less easy had not the Catholic community in England been itself changing so rapidly and profoundly. It is difficult, if not impossible, to cite a case of sect development which comes close to comparing, in either depth or scope, with the transformation undergone by English Catholicism during the nineteenth century. At this time, what had been a tiny, withdrawn, largely rural indigenous community led by landed gentry and composed of a mixture of agricultural workers, artisans, merchants and minor professionals, expanded and metamorphosed into a predominantly ethnic, urban, proletarian and boisterous body dominated and led by a clerical elite. In a few short years the church of the rural estate became that of the Irish ghetto.[42]

This transformation did not mean, however, that the Catholic gentry were merely consigned to the rubbish heap of history as antiquarian relics. On the contrary, though their political demotion was virtually complete, they nonetheless retained a crucial importance in the English Catholic community. This importance, however,

---

40 Norman describes the Cisalpine Club as "in reality the last expression of gentry management of the Church" (*Roman Catholicism in England*), p. 60; while Trevor-Roper describes the lay recusant gentry as having been "finally crushed" in the last century by a "new Irish and Italianate clergy." See H. R. Trevor-Roper, "Sir Thomas More and the English Lay Recusants" in *op. cit.*, p. 92.

41 Ultramontanism, literally implying an orientation towards Rome beyond the mountains, contrasts with the Cisalpine and "liberal" perspectives. It stresses the independence of the Church from all civil authorities and the absolute supremacy of the papacy in all matters of church doctrine and ecclesiastical organization. The Ultramontane movement succeeded almost completely in imposing its vision on the Roman Catholic Church in the century between the elections of Pius IX and John XXIII. At its extreme, Ultramontanism became essentially papolatry. See August Bernhard Hasler, *How the Pope Became Infallible*, (trans. P. Heinegg), Garden City, N. Y.: Doubleday & Co., 1981.

42 1850 may be conveniently regarded as the watershed in this respect. Beyond this point, argues Bossy, "the old English Catholic community . . . may be said, if not to have ceased to exist, at least to have been transformed beyond recognition" (*op. cit.*, p. 296). See John Hickey, *Urban Catholics*, London: Geoffrey Chapman, 1967.

was now of a symbolic rather than a practical nature, a fact well appreciated by the
new masters of English Catholicism. Though to colder clerical eyes the Catholic
gentry must surely have seemed mere Cisalpine curios, their visible presence was
nonetheless a priceless asset to what was now, in effect, a new immigrant church of
the urban slums. As a living link with the glorious era of the Elizabethan mission,
and indeed with pre-Reformation times, the gentry provided this religious community with a clearly visible symbol of continuity and legitimacy. In a communal
context now more Irish than English, their presence offered reassurance that, far
from being merely a recent alien import, English Catholicism was *authentically*
English, as well as of distinguished pedigree.[43]

English Catholicism of the late nineteenth and early twentieth centuries was decidedly ambivalent in character. On the one hand it aspired to be "more Roman than
Rome" in its clerically-inspired Ultramontanism,[44] while on the other, it seemed to
claim to be more English than the Anglicans. It may be suggested that in asserting
the prerogatives of the papacy and in espousing the new flamboyant Italianate Latin
ceremonies and devotions, a lower-class Irish immigrant population was able to pro-
claim symbolically its *non-English* character. The subcultural or even contracultural
spirit of exlusivist triumphal intolerance generated within English Catholicism at this
period was thus heavily embedded in ethnicity. Politically as well as religiously
provocative, it hinted strongly at that very disloyalty from which earlier generations
of English Catholics had been at pains to dissociate themselves. Thus, the new,
proletarian English Catholic community appeared to revel in alien ritual, to rejoice
in a divided loyalty and to emphasize rather than minimize its challenge to the
national myth. In such a context, the periodic revival of popular anti-Catholicism
with all its gory folklore may be at least partly understood.

At the same time, however, this community was also intensely preoccupied with
establishing an unassailably English character by tracing its ancestry and selectively
exploring its history. In this enterprise, relatively recent Cisalpine labours doggedly
aimed at winning the trust of the wider society were ignored while the events of Elizabethan times were obsessively reexamined. In a version of history which inverted
the national myth, the contemporary English Catholic community was depicted as
the lineal descendant, not merely of the heroic recusants and martyrs who struggled
to preserve the "old faith" against the innovations of the Reformation, but as the
legitimate heir of the pre-Reformation English church with which continuity had
never been broken. Portraying English ecclesiastical history as a story of persecution, seizure, confiscation and plunder, this reading of history seemed implicitly
to question the right of the Protestant established Church of England to its ancient

---

43 See Trevor-Roper, *op. cit.*, pp. 92 and 97.

44 See Derek Holmes, *More Roman than Rome: English Catholics in the Nineteenth Century*,
London: Burns & Oates, 1978; and Edward Norman, *The English Catholic Church in the
Nineteenth Century*, Oxford: Clarendon Press, 1984.

churches, cathedrals and foundations. A largely Irish congregation naturally espoused this simplified, ideological, and indeed mythological account of Protestant usurpation and Catholic suffering with an empathic enthusiasm. From its point of view, an image of Elizabethan martyrs as resistance fighters braving rack and rope to thwart a ruthless, superior Protestant usurping force had an immediate, intutitive and timely appeal.[45]

Thus, while neither the new clerical elite nor the rank-and-file membership among the English Catholics had great sympathetic interest in the long, quiet struggle for Catholic civil rights waged by the gentry over three centuries, they nonetheless accorded "old Catholics" of the landed class a unique esteem. For whatever assessment was made of its political strategy over the generations, the gentry's very existence within the Catholic fold was a boon of inestimable value to a church now avowedly bent on nothing less than the "Conversion of England." Not only did the gentry provide elements of prestige, dignity and even nobility to a community sadly lacking in them, it provided (in the most prestigious social form) living examples of the indigenous papist tradition which had survived, though sometimes barely, since the Reformation of the sixteenth century.

As shadowy figures on the margin of society, the Catholic country gentry had long held a certain repellant mystique for members of the wider society. Their mystique was fostered by the new clerical leaders of the Catholic community, eager to derive legitimacy from their involvement, however minimal or token, in church affairs. Thus, before the end of the nineteenth century, they began to exert a peculiar fascination for literary aesthetes and romantic Catholic converts, a pattern which persisted well into the present century. None of this should be allowed to obscure one crucial fact, however: in the second half of the nineteenth century the old English Catholic lay elite were reduced to the status of "decoy-ducks,"[46] camouflaging under a cloak of ancient pedigreed respectability the true nature of contemporary English Catholicism as a clerically-dominated urban sect of lower-class Irish immigrants. Their position was not to improve in the century which followed.

Popery, Gentry and the Character of English Catholicism

Beginning with a consideration of the reception accorded both Pope John Paul II and the television serialization of *Brideshead Revisited*, this essay has traced the career of "popery" in English life while exploring the special mystique exerted by the Catholic landed gentry. It is hoped that this has facilitated greater appreciation of the character of English Catholicism in the century following the "restoration" of its hierarchy. In this period, the Catholic community in England grew through Irish influx rather

---

45 Throughout the nineteenth century "the Irish Question" dominated British politics. See Alan O'Day, *The English Face of Irish Nationalism*, Dublin: Gill & Macmillan, 1977.

46 In Trevor-Roper's apt phrase, *op. cit.*, p. 92.

than through anything remotely resembling the "Conversion of England." Newman's hopes of a Catholic "Second Spring" were proven intellectually and culturally over-optimistic as an Ultramontane and increasingly Irish clericalism consolidated its control over its flock. Led by a hierarchy unschooled in English institutions, English Catholicism evidenced a preoccupation with its special educational needs which, combined with its essential endogamy, gave it the character of a distinct subculture. Prone to a provocatively inappropriate religious rhetoric and a posture of exclusive intolerance, it presented an image to the wider society which was in no way improved by a smug, patronizing attitude towards its "separated brethren" within the Protestant fold. During this time, therefore, the Catholic community did little to dispel the prevalent outsiders' view that it was somehow still marginal or alien to English society. Rooted in a base of antagonistic ethnic difference which continued to constitute a refuge from the national myth, English Catholicism on the eve of the Second Vatican Council still exhibited essentially those same characteristics of a minority sect which it had evolved during the third quarter of the previous century.[47]

The social as well as spiritual forces which would soon converge in the process of *aggiornamento* were, of course, already quietly at work at this time. The waves of immigration having subsided, English Catholics in the mid-twentieth century were more geographically and socially mobile, more educated and articulate, more involved in the wider society, and in some cases more resentful of being clerically patronized as the "Simple Faithful."[48] Dramatic and profound though the transformation or denominalization of English Catholicism has been in the last two decades, it is nonetheless unclear whether Catholics have yet fully succeeded in establishing themselves as entirely trustworthy participants in the national life. Though difficult and painful, the work of theological renewal may have been easier to accomplish than the task of political reinstatement. To the extent that it has been successful, it may be suggested that removal of the stigma deriving from the national myth probably owes less to the generously motivated dialogue of ecumenism than to a more general process of secularization in English society.

Conclusion

It is worth considering whether the visit of a real Pope has finally broken the spell of "popery," and whether prime-time television exposure has at last divested the Flytes of their esoteric mystery. Recent sociological research paints a rather more

---

47 Note the rather complacent tone of the concluding section in Mathew, *op. cit.* and the rather bewildered epilogue to Reynolds, *op. cit.* See also Holmes, *op. cit.*, pp. 249–257 and Antony Archer, *The Two Catholic Churches: A Study in Oppression*, London: SCM Press, 1986. Note also the general tone of Beck, *op. cit.*, published at mid-century.

48 Antony Archer has astutely focussed on this term, entitling a chapter "Vatican II and the Passing of the Simple Faithful," *op. cit.*, pp. 126–146. See also his article "The Passing of the 'Simple Faithful'," *New Blackfriars*, Vol. 56, No. 660, May 1975, pp. 196–204.

prosaic portrait of contemporary English Catholicism,[49] but it would be interesting to discover to what extent awareness of this sheer ordinariness has penetrated popular culture and neutralized stereotypical prejudice. If, in a profoundly secular society, English Catholics have indeed completed the metamorphosis from mythical creatures into ordinary men and women, such a demystification represents the ultimate stage in the long journey of Catholic emancipation.

49 See, for example, Michael P. Hornsby-Smith and Raymond M. Lee, *Roman Catholic Opinion: A Study of Roman Catholics in England and Wales in the 1970s*, Guildford: University of Surrey, 1979; and Michael P. Hornsby-Smith, "A Typology of English Catholics," *Sociological Review*, Vol. 30, No. 3, 1982, pp. 433–459; and Michael P. Hornsby-Smith, *Roman Catholics in England: Studies in Social Structure Since the Second World War*, Cambridge: Cambridge University Press, 1987.

6.

The Quandary of Dissent
on the Catholic Right

William D. Dinges

The Second Vatican Council signaled a historic shift in the Roman Catholic Church away from a position of long-standing opposition to many cultural and intellectual dynamics of modernity. Although the nature and scope of this accommodation remains contested (Seidler, 1986), the transition has been marked by considerable organizational dysfunction and conflict, elements of which are evident in widespread public dissent from Magisterial authority, in the emergence of a highly privatized and selective appropriation of Church doctrine, and in spreading factionalism and polarization among Catholics.

While much of the public and academic attention surrounding change and conflict in the postconciliar Church has focused on aspects of social movement organizations associated with liberal Catholic dissent, feminist and "liberation" theology movements, and Catholic Charismatic Renewal, far less attention has been given to organizational initiatives on the Catholic right. As Cuneo (1987: 4) has noted, in an era of resurgent fundamentalism, movements on the Catholic right have almost entirely escaped the notice of sociologists of religion.

In this paper, I will address several sociological issues relating to dissent on the Catholic right. My analysis will center on Catholic traditionalism, a movement that is international in scope, segmented, and loosely organized. While there are a number of different traditionalist organizations, all share common objectives in seeking to reaffirm and restore ideational, symbolic, ecclesial, and cultic patterns that have been altered, discredited, or abandoned in the wake of the Second Vatican Council. The culture symbol around which traditionalist dissent has galvanized is the Latin Tridentine Mass. Although traditionalism lacks centralized leadership, the movement's most visible symbol of authority is the aging French Archbishop Marcel Lefebvre and his priestly fraternity—the Society of St. Pius X (Dinges,

1983a, 1983b). Archbishop Lefebvre's initiatives will be the primary focus of the discussion of traditionalism in this paper.

The first issue I will address concerns the ideological repertoire with which Archbishop Lefebvre legitimates his dissent from Vatican authority. Legitimation pertains to the problem of "explaining and justifying" (Berger and Luckmann, 1966: 93). Legitimation is important in the life of religious movements, especially where there are conflicting claims with regard to who speaks with the purity of faith and for the "true" Church. At a more pragmatic level, legitimation is also important because it is a type of "moral resource" which, once obtained, facilitates access to other more tangible resources instrumental to the success of a social movement (Harrison and Manika, 1978: 217).

Dissent is problematic within Roman Catholicism when it is marked by an institutional challenge to Magisterial authority—as is clearly the case with regard to Archbishop Lefebvre's traditionalist initiatives. Within the Protestant tradition, dissent is easier to legitimate because it is a classical tradition of the Reformation to appeal over the heads of human authority directly to the scriptures. Access to the Word of God is open to all (Dillenberger and Welch, 1988: 3). Catholics, on the other hand, have long accepted a two-source theory of revelation: scripture and tradition. In practical terms, however, much greater weight has been given to tradition—where the Pope and the bishops of the Church acting collectively are the ones to whom is entrusted the responsibility and the charisma for deciding what is ultimately the "true" faith and what is not.

As a dissenting movement claiming continuity with the One True Church and the authenticity of the faith, Catholic traditionalism challenges the power and legitimacy of those who currently exercise hierarchical authority in the Church. Traditionalist leaders like Archbishop Lefebvre profess the high ground of orthodoxy while simultaneously trying to recruit and hold members to a counter-church movement on the basis of an appeal to "tradition"—but against the statements of the living Magisterium of the Church from which "tradition" cannot, by definition, be separated.

This quandary of dissent on the Catholic right is a classic illustration of cognitive dissonance (Festinger, et al., 1956). Because it is characterized by inconsistencies in belief and action, the traditionalist position presents an opportunity to examine both how unconventional beliefs emerge, and how they persist in the face of their contradictory character. With regard to this latter issue, it is commonly accepted that the maintenance of unconventional beliefs necessitates the resolution of cognitive dissonance and/or the existence of elaborate "plausibility structures" (Berger and Luckmann, 1966: 154–155). Snow and Machalek (1983), drawing on the work of Borhek and Curtis (1975), have challenged these assertions by illustrating how certain belief systems contain self-validating characteristics that provide them with immunity from the pressure of events. This latter perspective is highly relevant to understanding Catholic traditionalist dissent.

The second issue I will examine (not unrelated to the above) concerns the opposition, strategies, and tactics surrounding traditionalist conflict with establishment Church authorities, and the manner in which traditionalist dissent and schism are affected by structural characteristics of the Catholic Church.

All social movements have goals and objectives. To achieve these goals and objectives, movement leaders usually adopt a combination of bargaining, coercive, and persuasive tactics (Turner, 1970). Archbishop Lefebvre is unique among traditionalist leadership elites in that he has had (up until the June 1988 schism) some measure of success in extracting concessions from the Vatican in furtherance of his traditionalist ideals. This situation evolved largely because of Lefebvre's command of an exchange resource—i.e., the power to ordain. On the issue of how structural characteristics affect traditionalist dissent, attention will be brought to the dialectical nature of schism and the manner in which instrumental and expressive concerns are readily transformed into issues of authority in undifferentiated social systems—a situation more likely to precipitate the type of conflict that leads to schism.

Examination of the above issues sheds light on the dynamics of sectarianism, on the sociology of dissent, on issues surrounding the acquisition and maintenance of unconventional belief systems, and on the construction of social movement ideologies.

Archbishop Marcel Lefebvre

Although the "Ecône Affair" cannot be treated in its entirety here, the following points are germane to the focus of this paper.

Archbishop Lefebvre's opposition to certain theological currents animating Vatican II was well-known at the time of the Council. He was a founder of the International Group of Fathers (*Coetus Internationalis Patrum*), an organization of conservative prelates who worked to uphold "tradition" against liberal elements pushing for change at the Council. Lefebvre sided with the conservatives in all of the major debates of the Council and refused to sign the conciliar documents on the Church in the Modern World (*Gaudium et Spes*) and the Declaration on Religious Liberty (*Dignitatis Humanae*).

In 1968, Lefebvre resigned as head of the Holy Ghost Fathers in a dispute with members of the Chapter General over reform of the order in keeping with Vatican II directives. He then moved to Rome to retire but, by his own account, was sought out by a group of young men who desired that he direct them in a "traditional" priestly formation. Lefebvre first guided his seminarians to pursue their studies at the University of Fribourg, but abandoned this course of action when he became convinced that the university was "infected" with modernism. He then acquired permission from Bishop Charrière of Fribourg to establish a house for seminarians in that location in June 1969. With the approval of Msgr. Adam, Bishop of Sion, Lefebvre obtained a large house belonging to the Canons of St. Bernard. This property became the Ecône seminary, opening formally on October 7, 1970. The following month, Bishop Charrière canonically established the *Fraternité Sacerdotale de Saint Pie X* (the Society of St. Pius X).

During the next three years, Ecône's reputation as an "orthodox" seminary spread rapidly among Catholics holding to preconciliar conceptions of the Church in Europe and the United States. In the fall of 1974, in response to the archbishop's escalating critique of Vatican II, his continuing use of the (then prohibited) Tridentine liturgy, and in response to pressures from the French bishops, the Vatican announced an Apostolic Visitation to the Ecône seminary. On November 21, in reaction to the "scandal" occasioned by comments of the two Belgian priests who carried out the visitation, Lefebvre issued an acerbic "Declaration" denouncing Vatican II as a reform initiative that "comes from heresy and is founded in heresy, even if all of its acts are not formally heretical" (Lefebvre, 1985: 35). Tension between Rome and Ecône escalated steadily from that point on, culminating in the Vatican removal of the Society's canonical approval following the condemnation of a Commission of Cardinals in May 1975. In July of the following year, Archbishop Lefebvre was suspended *a divinis* for ordaining priests at Ecône in defiance of an explicit Vatican directive (On Lefebvre see Davies, 1979; 1983; Congar, 1976).

The conflict between Archbishop Lefebvre and the Vatican over his repudiation of the Council, his continuing defiance of the ban on ordinations, and over the canonical status of his priestly fraternity remained unresolved for the next twelve years. Finally, on June 30, 1988, following the breakdown of a series of intense eleventh-hour negotiations, Archbishop Lefebvre consecrated four bishops from the ranks of his priestly fraternity without Vatican approval, thereby incurring automatic excommunication.

The Problem of Legitimation

Ideological formulations (doctrines, beliefs, myths) that give meaning to social action and order are among the most discernible products of social movements. Shared beliefs held by participants: (1) reveal the objectives and goals of the movement and the rationale for action, (2) provide a critique of the existing structure which the movement is attacking and seeking to change, and (3) legitimate a group's claim to authority (McPherson, 1973).

The (1) objectives, goals, and ideological rationale for Archbishop Lefebvre's traditionalist initiatives center around the necessity of saving the "true Church" as manifest in pre-Vatican II ecclesial, disciplinary, and sacramental forms. According to Lefebvre, this "true Church" is exclusively essential to the salvation of souls. The "true Church" must be saved because the post-Vatican II "conciliar Church" has capitulated to "modernism" and is now apostate, heretical, and schismatic (See Lefebvre, 1976, 1986). By establishing an international network of traditionalist chapels and mass centers and by continuing to use preconciliar sacramental forms,

Lefebvre and his priestly fraternity preserve the "true Church" until the current era of apostasy has passed and the "errors" of Vatican II are rectified. These traditionalist ecclesial and messianic ideological orientations give expression to the classic sectarian concern with exclusivism, "correct" doctrine, and maintaining the "pure" and "authentic" version of a faith tradition (Troeltsch, 1931; Stark and Bainbridge: 1985: 24). Furthermore, the archbishop has made it clear that the "true Church" cannot be saved without preserving the "true priesthood," the proper instrumentality of the Church's means of salvation. By linking the "true Church" with the "true priesthood," the archbishop's seminaries, foundations, and other organizational initiatives—which constitute the infrastructure of the traditionalist movement—are made perpetually relevant to the objectives of the traditionalist cause.[1]

Archbishop Lefebvre's (2) critique of current Church leadership and the ecclesiology of the Second Vatican Council, and his (3) legitimation of traditionalist dissent are closely interrelated.

Papal Authority

It is first of all noteworthy that Lefebvre has never challenged or repudiated the *nature* of papal authority or questioned that it exists by divine will. He has previously repudiated the more radical *"sedevacantist"* position that recent popes are deposed, excommunicated, or improperly elected, and that the chair of Peter is, therefore, vacant.[2] It is also ironic—in light of his own challenge to papal authority—that Lefebvre has steadfastly opposed collegiality as a "threat" to papal authority (See Lefebvre, 1976: 43–48). Lefebvre's position on dissent has been that he challenges only *certain* acts and orientations (related to the implementation and content of Vatican II reforms) of *particular* popes (Paul VI, John Paul II) who have failed to defend the faith and "what the Church has taught for two thousand years" (Lefebvre, 1986: 138). Lefebvre argues that such dissent is not, *ipso facto*, wrong. When Church leadership uses the institutions and authority of the Church to "endanger" the faith, it is the proper duty of Catholics "to disobey and keep the Tradition" (Lefebvre, 1986: 136). Only a "false" sense of obedience constrains criticism of Church authority under such circumstances. The authority of the Pope is valid, according to Lefebvre, only "as long as he echoes all apostolic tradition and the teachings of his predecessors" (Lefebvre, 1986: 134).

Although Lefebvre places his traditionalist dissent in the context of a proper understanding of the nature of authority in the Church, his appeal to this authority is

---

1 I have elsewhere examined how Lefebvre's traditionalist initiatives give expression to status politics related to the maintenance of clerical power and authority in the postconciliar Church (See Dinges, 1987).

2 Among this *"sedevacantist"* segment are priests ordained bishops by the former Vietnamese Archbishop Ngo-Dinh-Thuc. These priests derive from Palamar de Troya in Spain, and six bishops Thuc consecrated in 1983.

typically in the abstract (i.e., "eternal Rome," "Tradition"), highly selective (derived primarily from the documents of the Council of Trent and papal anti-modernist pronouncements), and oriented around the past—rather than present—exercise of this authority. This legitimating stratagem of playing a selective appropriation of the past against the living present is also evident in the traditionalist use of historical analogy.

In an address in 1968, Lefebvre intimated that a new St. Athanasius would succeed again in "saving the Church" (Lefebvre, 1976: 48). By evoking the memory of a fourth-century Bishop of Alexandria who was wrongfully excommunicated for his stand during the Arian heresy, but who was later vindicated and canonized by the Church, the archbishop prefigured subsequent association of his own "defense of the faith" with that of St. Athanasius. The Athanasius analogy draws the inference that the saint's persecution and exoneration "proves" that during times of general apostasy, Christians who remain faithful to their traditional faith have to function outside established ecclesial channels where they may have to look for "truly Catholic teaching, leadership, and inspiration," not to official channels of authority, "but to one heroic confessor whom the other bishops and Roman Pontiff might have repudiated or even excommunicated" (Davies, 1987: 12).[3]

Vatican II

Archbishop Lefebvre's challenge to Magisterial authority derives first and foremost from his repudiation of the Second Vatican Council as a reform initiative that "begins in heresy and ends in heresy" (Lefebvre, 1976: 190). This repudiation of the Council is more problematic than Lefebvre's challenge to the disciplinary actions taken against him by the Vatican because of the theological consensus regarding the infallible authority of ecumenical councils (See Dulles, 1987: 235–242).[4] It is hardly surprising, therefore, that most of the archbishop's writings and public pronouncements over the past two decades focus on disavowing the Council and the implementation of its reforms. This de-legitimation of Vatican II is accomplished in ways that give distinctive character to the traditionalist movement and that differentiate traditionalist dissent from other critiques of the Council prevalent on the Catholic right.

First, unlike conservative Catholics who have interpreted the Church's post-

---

3 Other historical analogies drawn by traditionalists to illustrate that popes have "erred" in the past and, therefore, can be lawfully disobeyed include the condemnation of Pope Honorius (625–628) for his role in promoting the Monotheletism heresy (See Davies, 1978a: 14–15; 1978b).

4 According to the 1917 Code of Canon Law, an ecumenical council has supreme power in the Church, and thus there is no appeal from its decrees (Canon 228). Dulles (1987: 239) asserts that the teachings of Vatican II are irreformable only where the council repeats what had already been infallibly taught.

conciliar crisis as a consequence of "excesses" and "improper implementations" of Vatican II (See Likoudis and Whitehead, 1981), and who have called for a normative "strict-constructionist" approach to the Council documents,[5] Lefebvre lays blame squarely and uneqivocally on the Council itself. The archbishop has consistently asserted in his writing and public pronouncements that the "destruction of the Church," the "ruin of the priesthood," and the "abolition of the Sacrifice of the Mass and the Sacraments" is a direct result of the Council's embrace of the "false principles" of Protestantism, humanism, liberalism, and modernism (Lefebvre, 1976, 1982, 1986). At the Council, these "false principles" unleashed by the Enlightenment, the Reformation, and the French Revolution were assimilated into the Church. Catholicism's postconciliar "self-destruction" is the fruit of this capitulation to the "poison of heresy" (Davies, 1979: 51). Lefebvre has consistently sought to convince Catholics that the proximate cause of the postconciliar crisis in the Church is not merely a wrong interpretation of the Council, but a direct result of the "heresy" of the Council itself.

It is noteworthy that Lefebvre's repudiation of Vatican II stems from the perception that *aggiornamento* has raised the spectre of "intrinsic contradictions." According to Lefebvre, what was once "unequivocally" held as error and heresy (especially relating to ecumenism, religious liberty, and liturgical reform) is promoted and embraced in the postconciliar Church as truth and correct doctrine. This "contradiction" *leitmotif* animates all of Lefebvre's attacks on the theology of Vatican II and is also present in the archbishop's repudiation of liturgical reform, the symbolic issue around which much traditionalist dissent has galvanized. As is the case with other traditionalist apologists, Archbishop Lefebvre denigrates the *Novus Ordo* Mass by drawing "grim parallels" between the once condemned liturgical changes accomplished by Luther, Calvin, Cranmer and other Protestant reformers in the sixteenth century, and those stemming from the Second Vatican Council (See Davies, 1976). This "contradiction" theme regarding the Council and its liturgical reforms gives clearest expression to the fundamentalist-like doctrinal positivism in traditionalist ideology; a position that presupposes that change or development of doctrine *ipso facto* calls into question the Church's supernatural authenticity (Lefebvre, 1976: 70).

A second ideological stratagem for repudiating Vatican II revolves around the exploitation of the ideal/real gap. It is widely recognized that disjunction between the ideal and the real is an almost universal source of strain in institutions. Religious institutions are particularly vulnerable to such disjunction because they are preeminently symbolic and idealistic in their core structures (O'Dea, 1961). Archbishop Lefebvre has sought to descredit Vatican II by exploiting the ideal-real gap between the positive expectations associated with the Council and the negative institutional

---

5 Cardinal Ratzinger, for instance, has explained traditionalism as a response to the "arbitrariness" and "thoughtlessness" of post-conciliar interpretations of the Council (1985: 31–33).

declension that has followed in some areas of Church life. Thus, the decline in mass attendance and clerical vocations, the exodus of priests and nuns, and other forms of institutional dysfunction are taken to demonstrate (*post hoc, ergo propter hoc*) that the Second Vatican Council has had a "catastrophic effect" on the Church. The Council cannot, therefore, be authentically Catholic because its fruits have been entirely negative (See Lefebvre, 1979; 1982; Lefebvre and Castro Mayer, 1987). Any positive developments that might be attributed to *aggiornamento* are simply ignored.

Lefebvre has also sought to diminish the authority of Vatican II by arguing that the Council was "pastoral" and not "dogmatic" as had been the case with Trent and Vatican I. Because Vatican II did not "present itself as did other Councils," it is only a teaching of the Ordinary Magisterium and, therefore, "not fallible" (Lefebvre, 1979: 15). By inference, neither is it binding (Lefebvre, 1986: 112–113). Where Lefebvre has made a concession to the authority of the Council—primarily in the latter stages of his negotiations with the Vatican—it has been to agree to accept Vatican II, but only as the Council is interpreted in accordance with "tradition"—which Lefebvre clearly relegates to himself the right to define.

Conspiracy

Conspiracy theories and themes of eschatological urgency are a third ideological genre with which traditionalist Catholics legitimate their dissent. Traditionalist leadership elites have a strong predilection for explaining Catholicism's postconciliar malaise in terms of a "plot" or "conspiracy" against the Church. These conspiracy motifs range from explicating the machinations of "liberal" and "modernist" theologians at the Council (Davies, 1977) to full-blown conspiracy theories purporting to show the influence of Masons, communists, and other "sinister" forces on Vatican decision-making (See Kelly, 1976; McKenna, 1977). Within this conspiracy orientation, conflict among Catholics is not interpreted as status or interest group issues, as a product of ideological differences, or as social tension that naturally accompanies initiatives to change ossified institutions. Explanations of this nature are derided as "secular" and lacking insight into the truly eschatological struggle between good and evil currently taking place in the Church. Instead, the turmoil over *aggiornamento* is taken as *prima facie* evidence of the workings of conspiracy and subversion. Conspiracy theories that became more prominent in traditionalist circles in the early 1970's were also accompanied by eschatological themes combining motifs of cosmic conflict and purgation with the sense of election. In the context of dysfunction in the Church and opposition from Vatican authorities, the "remnant faithful" were being called to "hold fast" against the work of Satan and the Great Apostasy (2 Thess. 2:3) (Lefebvre, 1975; 1986: 138).

As is the case with other Christian sectarian movements, traditionalist Catholic conspiracy motifs are partially derived from scriptural passages warning against the dangers of deceivers and "false prophets" within the fold (See Acts 20:29–31; Matthew 7:15). However, as both explanations of institutional dysfunction and as a means of legitimating traditionalist dissent, conspiracy theories on the extreme Catholic right are drawn more directly from, and are reinforced by, constituent features of Catholic religious self-understanding, including Magisterial pronouncements and, at the level of Catholic folk piety, revelations and messages associated with Marian apparitions. As stratagems for legitimating dissent, traditionalist conspiracy theories are also partially a function of the conferring of deviant status on the movement and its subsequent isolation within the postconciliar Church. The case of Archbishop Lefebvre is particularly instructive in this regard.

Lefebvre's stand during and immediately following the Council generally followed "conservative" themes denouncing the manner in which "modernist"-inspired bishops (especially the French and German episcopates) and their theological *periti* maneuvered the Council to adopt a liberal/neo-modernist agenda (See Wiltgen, 1967), primarily by placing ambiguities and equivocations in the texts (See Lefebvre, 1976; esp., 1–73). After 1970, Lefebvre's attack on the Council became more open and direct, culminating in the assertion that Vatican II was entirely responsible for the Church's malaise (Menozzi, 1987: 36). However, it was not until the suppression of the Society in 1975 and the subsequent disciplinary actions against him the following year that Lefebvre's view of the situation in the Church and of the "persecution" of Ecône took its most radical conspiratorial turn. References to "Communist" and "Satanic" influence in the Church now began to appear more frequently in many of the archbishop's public pronouncements (See Lefebvre, 1976). In the midst of his suspension in July 1976, Lefebvre began explicitly denouncing "Masonic" influences that were, by implication, responsible for the suppression of his seminary at Ecône. With regard to the Council, Lefebvre declared that Vatican II's "ill-omened" compromise with modernity had been "an undertaking which originates in a secret understanding between high dignitaries in the Church and those of Masonic lodges . . ." (Davies, 1979: 234). Lefebvre also joined other traditionalists in charging that Archbishop Annibale Bugnini, the head of the Vatican Commission for carrying out liturgical reform, was a Freemason—concluding that "he is not the only one" (In Davies, 1979: 168; see also Lefebvre, 1986: 95–96). Lefebvre's conspiracy theory of social causation finally reached its fullest proportions in the context of the controversy over his consecration of episcopal successors; an act justified by Lefebvre on the grounds that the See of Peter and the posts of authority in Rome were now "occupied by anti-Christs" (Lefebvre, 1988: 38).

While psychological theories of conspiracy orientations (e.g., Toch, 1965) have some utility in explaining their pervasiveness and credibility, such orientations among traditionalist Catholics cannot be solely attributed to "paranoid" personalities within the movement. Nor do such convictions necessitate widespread plausibility structures associated with maintaining the credibility of belief systems.

The trauma surrounding the scope and speed of *aggiornamento* clearly facilitated the tendency to equate change in the Church with conspiracy and subversion, especially in view of the popular perception that Catholicism had been timeless and unchanging for centuries in its disciplinary, doctrinal, and ritual forms. Conspiracy and apocalyptic themes were also reinforced by the ease with which parallels could be drawn between widespread cultural turmoil in the nineteen-sixties, and the concomitant dysfunction within the Church—the one crisis reinforcing and reflecting the other. Furthermore, theories of conspiracy and subversion also found official endorsement in the form of the Vatican's long-running campaign against the cultural and intellectual inroads of "modernism" in the Church.

For nearly a century and a half, a succession of popes and curial authorities had warned against and repeatedly condemned the hydraheaded monster of "modernism" (See, e.g., *Humanum Genus*, 1884; *Lamentabili sane exitu*, 1907; *Divini Redemptoris*, 1937). The Magisterial campaign against modernism came to focus, especially in the latter part of the nineteenth century, not exclusively on external threats, but on those within the infrastructure of the Church itself. As Kurtz (1986) has shown, a major aspect of the Vatican's strategy against modernism was its characterization of the enemy as a conspiratorial group that was endangering the Church while masquerading as its friend (1986: 33). This thinking was brought to a head in Pius X's anti-modernist broadside, *Pascendi Gregis* (1907), in which Catholics were solemnly warned that the twentieth century was one in which the threat to the faith could be found "in the very bosom and heart" of the Church itself.

This long line of anti-modernist vendettas, combined with the campaign of harassment and the intimidation of Catholic biblical scholars and intellectuals tainted with the "virus" of modernism, fostered a widespread perception that Holy Mother Church was forever threatened from within. In the context of the turmoil surrounding the meaning and implementation of Vatican II, this long-standing fear of subversion and conspiracy provided traditionalist apologists with a ready-made, rational, and authoritatively articulated explanation and critique of what was happening in the Church.[6]

At the level of Catholic folk culture, traditionalist conspiratorial and eschatological themes also derived plausibility and legitimacy from revelations and messages—particularly apparitions of the Virgin Mary—portending widespread apostasy in the Church (See Dupont, 1970). These revelations enabled traditionalist leaders like Archbishop Lefebvre to link the post-Vatican II crisis in the Church to "punishments foretold by Mary [at Fatima]" (Lefebvre, 1987: 10–14), thereby casting the necessity of dissent in a symbolic framework of eschatological urgency and tran-

---

6 Menozzi also points out that Archbishop Lefebvre's themes of "Satanic" subversion were given added weight in the wake of Paul VI's assertion in a June 1972 address that turmoil in the Church indicated that the "fumes of Satan had entered the temple of God" (1987: 339).

scendent prophecy.

The point I wish to make here is that traditionalist ideology contains effective and internally consistent stratagems for legitimating dissent and reducing dissonance. These motifs are logically interrelated and derived from constituent elements of Catholic religious self-understanding. They sensitize traditionalists to certain developments in the postconciliar Church and provide them with an integrated interpretation of these events. What traditionalist ideology generally lacks is a hermeneutical vocabulary that explains Catholicism's postconciliar malaise in terms other than pre-Vatican II theological frames of reference or conspiracy theories. Traditionalist ideology also expresses little tolerance for discrepancies between ideals and norms. And positive revitalizations that could be attributable to the Council are simply ignored (See Lefebvre, 1976; 1986), while "Tradition" is appropriated selectively and in a manner that serves traditionalist organizational goals and objectives exclusively.

Conspiracy theories are the most interesting and functionally significant means by which traditionalists legitimate their dissent. These theories simplify and localize ills, focus resentment, and promote solidarity among participants by generating a sense of joint persecution, urgency, and out-group hostility. They provide a rationalization not only for conflict between traditionalists and establishment Church authorities; they also help explain much of the conflict that is endemic among traditionalists themselves. Furthermore, conspiracy theories focus attention on an occupant of hierarchical office in the Church, rather than the nature of the authority of the office itself. By symbolically degrading an occupant of office, therefore, traditionalists avoid calling into question the nature of ecclesiastical authority. This distinction is critical where the exercise of Church authority is challenged in defense of "orthodoxy." Furthermore, by attributing the destruction of the Church to individuals influenced by "Masonic" or "Satanic" forces, it is less essential to seek challenges to their power by normal institutional means since such initiatives would only meet with repeated resistance. Traditionalists are justified, therefore, in pursuing a course of action outside official Church channels.

In the case of Archbishop Lefebvre, the self-validating character of his ideology of dissent is readily evident. Lefebvre has been able to interpret positive Vatican overtures as tacit endorsement for the positions and actions he has taken and as an exoneration of his dissent. Any opposition or disciplinary action, on the other hand, has simply been interpreted as further proof that the current Church leadership is in error, that "wolves" are within the fold, and that extraordinary times call for extraordinary measures. The point here is that conspiracy and subversion orientations facilitate the self-validating character of traditionalist ideology and resolve dissonance arising from dissent; they constitute an orientation wherein the traditionalist position cannot be disconfirmed. This obviates the need for widespread plausibility structures to enhance what is logically self-evident and self-perpetuating.

Opposition, Tactics and Strategies

For the most part, public opposition to traditionalism in general and to Archbishop Lefebvre in particular has come primarily from the hierarchy, and from individuals and organizations associated with conservative Catholic causes (See Likoudis and Whitehead, 1981). The Vatican attitude has varied somewhat, with John Paul II showing a more solicitous position than Paul VI in seeking to reach accord with Lefebvre and accommodate traditionalist discontent.

While Catholic liberals have tended to dismiss traditionalists as a fringe element of antiquarian malcontents, or to chide them for their "separation anxieties" over the departure from the reference points of Post-Reformation religious ritual, formula, and institution (*America*, March 24, 1973: 262), Catholic conservatives have been more ambivalent. This ambivalence stems from the fact that conservatives share a number of ideological affinities with traditionalist Catholics. Both condemn the resurgence of "neo-modernism" in the Church, the "de-sacralization" of the liturgy, and the weakening of Catholic identity and discipline. Both groups also maintain elements of an ideology of cultural decline, a cognitive defiance of modernity, and tendencies toward ethical rigorism and counter-cultural piety (See, for example, Molnar, 1968; Kelly, 1979; Hitchcock, 1974; 1979). Furthermore, Catholic traditionalism did not begin as a discrete social movement, but grew out of diffuse conservative Catholic discontent with Vatican II *aggiornamento* (Dinges, 1983a; 1983b).

The above affinities notwithstanding, however, conservative and traditionalist leadership elites have been at odds over a number of issues relating to the Second Vatican Council, papal authority, and the reform of the liturgy. Conservatives have generally held that the traditionalist movement is an "understandable" reaction to the "excess" and "distortions" of Vatican II [6], but one that diverts attention from the liberal and "neo-modernist" threat to the Church (Likoudis and Whitehead, 1981; see also Morris, 1978; Whitehead, 1979). Conservatives have also chided traditionalists for exercising the "Protestant principle of private judgement" in dissenting from Magisterial authority, and for undercutting, by their more extremist rhetoric and tactics, the credibility of those Catholics working for the "proper" implementation of *aggiornamento* and for the reinforcement of hierarchical (especially papal) authority (See *Triumph*, June, 1970: 25; *The Wanderer*, December 26, 1967: 9). Tensions between conservative and traditionalist Catholics also stem from conflicts over the mobilization of resources, especially where traditionalist organizations have drawn membership and support from the ranks of conservatives disenchanted with the "compromise" policies and pronouncements of the more moderate Catholic right.[7]

For their part, traditionalists acknowledge the affinity between many of their

---

7 In 1974, the president of *Una Voce*, a conservative Catholic group advocating retention of the Tridentine liturgy, complained that the organization was "losing quite a few members" to the traditionalist cause because of the position it had taken on the new liturgy (*Una*

own views of the postconciliar Church and those of conservative Catholics, while belittling conservatives for their failure to challenge hierarchical authority in defense of "true" doctrine and discipline. Traditionalists also chide conservatives for their unwillingness to acknowledge that the crisis in the postconciliar Church is a direct "fruit" of the Council, not a product of "excesses" surrounding its implementation. For many traditionalists, the conservative position is no more than a misguided form of "papolatry" stemming from a "distorted sense of obedience" (See Kelly, 1976: 1–6). Traditionalists have also denounced conservative organizations (e.g., Catholics United for the Faith) for "neutralizing" right-wing opposition—from which traditionalist organizations have drawn constituents—by channeling this discontent into organizations "controlled and manipulated by the hierarchy" (See *The Voice*, February 3, 1973: 2).

Although Church authorities have opposed aspects of the traditionalist movement with warnings and disciplinary actions, they have not been able to suppress it. This opposition did not become extensive until after the prohibition of the Tridentine rite and mandatory implementation of the *Novus Ordo* liturgy in November 1971, as traditionalism became a more ideologically radicalized and self-conscious movement.[8] With the establishment of Archbishop Lefebvre's seminary at Ecône in 1970, the traditionalist movement acquired a more organizationally coherent character. As the network of Society of St. Pius X traditionalist chapels and Mass centers spread internationally, episcopal authorities began to warn of the "unauthorized" and "irregular" nature of these initiatives, and of the potentially schismatic character of the traditionalist movement. Laity were admonished that in attending traditionalist chapels, they were failing to fulfill their "Sunday obligation," while individual priests who affiliated with traditionalist organizations, or those who continued illicit use of the Tridentine rite contrary to the 1971 Vatican Instruction were disciplined and, in some cases, suspended by their bishops (See Dinges, 1983a).

While Catholic traditionalism is, as I have indicated, organizationally diverse, Vatican concern with traditionalist dissent has focused primarily on the initiatives of Archbishop Lefebvre and his priestly fraternity. This concern with the "Ecône affair" stems from the fact that, unlike traditionalist enclaves organized around individual priests (e.g., Fr. Gommar De Pauw's Catholic Traditionalist Movement, Inc.), Lefebvre's efforts are of a "juridically definable common form" (Ratzinger, 1985: 32). The archbishop can both ordain and consecrate, thereby establishing a line of succession and initiating schism—as he subsequently did on June 30, 1988.

Voce Newsletter 42, 30, 1974).

8 One exception was the controversy in the United States beginning in 1965 between Fr. Gommar de Pauw, a professor of theology and academic dean at St. Mary's Seminary in Emmitsburg, Maryland, and Cardinal Lawrence J. Shehan of the Archdiocese of Baltimore over the former's launching of the "Catholic Traditionalist Movement, Inc." in March of that year (Dinges, 1983a).

The desire to avert schism has been a preeminent concern in all Vatican negotiations with the archbishop. This pressure to accommodate Lefebvre (and traditionalism in general) stems, in part, from Catholicism's "church-like" proclivity to tolerate internal diversity, especially so in an atmosphere of greater tolerance for ecclesiastical pluralism following Vatican II. In addition, in the context of the decline in Catholic institutional vitality and the rise of restorationist initiatives marked by conservative anti-conciliarism (See Johnson, 1981; Menozzi, 1987), Church leaders are hard pressed to deny a place to those who vigorously demonstrate their loyalty to traditional Catholic forms and disciplines. Averting schism is also relevant to the maintenance of hierarchical authority; schism casts aspersions on the legitimacy of that authority both by challenging it directly, and by illustrating its ineffectiveness.

Strategies and Tactics

Turner (1970) has noted that social movement leaders usually adopt a combination of strategies and tactics in conflict situations with target groups. These strategies and tactics include coercion, persuasion, and bargaining. Coercion entails the manipulation of the target group in such a manner that any course of action other than that sought by the movement will be met by considerable cost or punishment. Persuasion involves the use of symbolic manipulation wherein a movement identifies its course of action with values held by the target group. To bargain effectively, a social movement constituency must control some exchangeable value sought by the target group (1970: 145–155).

For the most part, Catholic traditionalists have had little success in using coercive or persuasive strategies in their campaign against establishment Church authorities. Traditionalist groups have been too small and too isolated from the communicative and power structures of the Church to be effective in these ways. Bishops have generally avoided public confrontations with traditionalist representatives and have refused contacts or debates that would provide traditionalists with a forum for propagating anti-Vatican II views. Given the more radicalized and value-oriented nature of traditionalist ideology (with its proclivity for literalism, infallibilism, and wooden defense of pre-conciliar theology), there has been little common ground for persuasive dialogue—although certain traditionalist theses regarding the Council and its aftermath are by no means totally unacceptable to Vatican thinking (Menozzi, 1987).

Archbishop Lefebvre, however, has been in a position to effectuate both coercive and bargaining strategies on behalf of the traditionalist cause: he controls an exchange value in the form of his power to ordain priests who, although illicitly ordained, are, nevertheless, valid priests according to Church law.

It will be recalled that the initial disciplining of Lefebvre stemmed from points raised in his 1974 "Declaration" that were deemed by a Commission of Cardinals "impossible to reconcile" with the Second Vatican Council. Although Lefebvre personally issued the "Declaration," his entire order was suppressed—a point over which the archbishop complained bitterly. Lefebvre's subsequent demands for an audience with the Pope were refused unless he first renounced his "inadmissible position" regarding the Council (See Davies, 1979: esp. 35–75).

Following his suspension in 1976, Lefebvre made it clear that he would use his powers of ordination to extract concessions from the Vatican to further his traditionalist initiatives. In June 1977, and on several occasions thereafter, Lefebvre offered to postpone or suspend ordinations if his Society were granted "legal recognition" and permitted to use the Tridentine rite. Publicly the Vatican reacted negatively to these overtures and continued to demand Lefebvre's "submission." However, the archbishop was eventually granted a papal audience with both Paul VI and John Paul II and a review of this case by the Congregation for the Doctrine of the Faith (1978) without any substantive change in the position he had taken on the Council or the new liturgy. He continued to denounce the new Mass as a "Protestant" and "Bastard Rite," and conceded only to sign an acceptance of Vatican II "as interpreted in accordance with tradition" (Menozzi, 1987: 344).

With the election of John Paul II, new Vatican initiatives for rapprochement with Lefebvre were undertaken. The archbishop's public disavowals of the Council, his allegations of "Masonic" influences in the Church, his previously defined "errors and dangerous opinions," and his rejection of the new liturgy were reduced, in the wake of a November 18, 1978, meeting with the new pope, to an instrumental issue: the "canonical" status of his Society.

Throughout the next ten years, however, the "Ecône affair" remained unresolved. The pattern that emerged was one of escalating demands on Lefebvre's part in response to Vatican overtures toward accommodation. As his priestly fraternity grew steadily, Lefebvre's demands went from mere tolerance of his Society and use of the Tridentine liturgy, to demands for a prelature and independence from local episcopal authority, to demands for the consecration of episcopal successors—including specific numbers and a specific date. Throughout the entire period, Lefebvre remained essentially intransigent regarding the Council and the new liturgy, declaring publicly "null . . . all of the postconciliar reforms, and all of the acts of Rome accomplished in this impiety" (Lefebvre and Castro Mayer, 1987: 2–3). His success in keeping negotiations open with the Vatican had the practical consequence of buttressing his self-confidence and tendency to escalate his demands.

In the fall of 1983, Lefebvre raised the bargaining stakes with the Vatican by intimating that "to safeguard the Catholic priesthood which perpetuates the Catholic Church and not an adulterous Church . . ." he would consecrate bishops (Lefebvre, 1988: 36–37). In October of the following year, the Vatican issued an Indult allowing Catholics to return to the Tridentine liturgy, albeit under "strictly controlled conditions."[9] Lefebvre responded to this "appeasement" by declaring it unaccept-

---

9 These conditions required securing permission of the bishop and public acknowledgment "beyond all ambiguity" that those who desired the old liturgy were in no way connected

able and asserting that there would be "no rallying to the liberals" in the Church (Lefebvre, 1987).

In his ordination sermon at Ecône in June 1987, Lefebvre again threatened publicly to consecrate bishops without papal authorization—this time in response to "signs from Providence."[10] This threat provoked a flurry of Vatican initiatives to reach accommodation. On July 28, 1987, two weeks after a personal meeting, Lefebvre received a letter from Cardinal Ratzinger proposing official recognition of the Society, and promising it permission to run its own seminary and use the Tridentine liturgy. A "Cardinal visitor" would perform ordinations and "guarantee the orthodoxy" of—along with having the final word on—candidates for ordination. Lefebvre was no longer being required to sign a specific document acknowledging his adherence to Vatican II (sensu obvio), or his acceptance of the new liturgy.

Following a visitation by Canadian Cardinal Edouard Gagnon in November 1987, and the signing of a May 5, 1988, protocol granting semi-independence from other bishops, authority to consecrate one episcopal successor, establishment of a commission to examine Vatican II interpretations on ecumenism and freedom of conscience, Lefebvre reneged, continuing to press for at least three bishops, a June 30, 1988, consecration date, and majority representation on the Vatican Commission (Remnant, May 15, 1988: 2). Although Lefebvre's age (83) was a factor in his decision to consecrate, the crucial issue centered around power in the form of Lefebvre's perpetuation of his own institutional initiatives and his refusal to allow Vatican juridical authority over his priestly fraternity: "there can be no question of our relinquishing at any point in time our authority over or responsibility for our own seminarians" (See Superior General Letter 33, October 11, 1987). This position ultimately provoked the June 30, 1988, schism.

On Schism

The Catholic traditionalist movement gives organizational expression to sectarian impulses within the postconciliar Church. Sectarianism, however, does not ipso facto result in schism. Social movement theory can also be a useful perspective for illuminating some of the conditions under which movements split off from a parent body.

Smelser (1962) has observed that norm-oriented and value-oriented movements often arise simultaneously during periods of social strain and conflict. Value-oriented movements—like radicalized sects—tend to be generated in social systems with little structural differentiation, and where normative channels of protest or dissent

---

with groups that impugned the lawfulness and doctrinal integrity of the new mass.

10 In his June 29, 1987, "Ordination Sermon" Lefebvre indicated that the Pope's ecumenical prayer meeting held in Assisi in October, 1986, and the reply from Cardinal Ratzinger to Lefebvre's objections concerning religious liberty were these "signs from Providence" (Angelus 10, 7 July 1987: 10–14).

are blocked or nonexistent (1962: 313–348).

As I indicated earlier, traditionalist dissent is rooted in a value-oriented repudiation of the reforms of the Second Vatican Council, rather than in a concern with their normative violations. Dissent of this nature cannot, therefore, be explained solely as the consequence of blocked channels of communication, nor merely as a matter of a mild reform movement being pushed into a more radicalized position by an intransigent leadership. However, it is also clear that Catholicism's structural characteristics and the actions of leadership elites facilitated the emergence of traditionalism as a counter-Church movement outside the normal institutional framework.

In differentiated social systems, structural possibilities exist for demanding normative change without simultaneously appearing to challenge basic values. However, in systems in which all social or normative rules are thought to be part of a comprehensive order, alterations in or challenges to norms are likely to be interpreted as efforts to subvert fundamental values. Although conflict in less-differentiated systems is less likely to occur than in differentiated ones, the conflict will be more intense and value-oriented once it surfaces; any protest against norms will likely appear as a protest against values (Smelser, 1962: 313–382). A structural condition of this nature readily facilitates schism in religious organizations (See Harrison and Manika, 1978).

The structure of Roman Catholic polity is such that, whatever the theological or sociocultural sources animating *aggiornamento*, the "correct" interpretation and legitimation of the Council was inextricably tied to the issue of Magisterial authority through which the "apostolic heritage" of the faith is preserved and guaranteed. The traditionalist refusal of Vatican II reforms, especially in the area of the liturgy, can be viewed as an act of expressive/symbolic dissent, but one that was rapidly transformed into an issue of authority both by the prohibition of the Tridentine liturgy and, on the part of Archbishop Lefebvre, by his refusal of the canonical suppression of his Society, and by his repeated defiance of the Vatican on the ordination issue.

As long as Church authorities permitted use of the Tridentine Mass, Catholics estranged by *aggiornamento*—and its most concrete effectuation in the area of the liturgy—were symbolically and institutionally linked with the establishment Church. However, once the *Novus Ordo* liturgy became mandatory (1971), Catholics committed to the old Mass accrued a deviant status within the Church. Once this deviant status was conferred and sanctions were imposed for adhering to the old liturgy, traditionalists were further isolated. This development, in turn, intensified the ideological radicalism of the movement, especially in regard to the conspiracy and subversion motifs discussed earlier. The logic of traditionalist religious self-understanding was such that they could not simply "leave the Church," or transfer their loyalties beyond Catholicism's ecclesial boundaries. Traditionalist Catholics had no "exit option" given their conviction of the centrality of the Church's sacramental system in the economy of salvation. Unable or unwilling to accept Vatican II reforms, and excluded from institutional legitimacy by their challenge to hierarchical authority, traditionalists undertook organizational initiatives that, in the case of Archbishop Lefebvre and his supporters, eventually led to schism. There is no small irony here in the fact that the kind of authoritarianism and hierarchical order extolled by traditionalists made their rebellion a "zero-sum" game.

Conclusion

In this paper I have applied a number of conceptual and theoretical orientations derived from the sociology of social movements and collective behavior to the analysis of dissent on the Catholic right. The transformation of Catholicism in the wake of the Second Vatican Council provides a rich milieu for further analysis of this nature. In the case of the traditionalist movement, an opportunity is afforded to reexamine many issues regarding sectarianism, unconventional beliefs, schism, and the dynamics of fundamentalism. Much of the previous sociological research on all of these topics has relied heavily on analysis of Protestantism or, more recently, "new" (non-Christian, non-Western) religious movements. It is time for Catholic sectarians, schismatics, and fundamentalists to be given the sociological attention they deserve.

REFERENCES

America. "Temptations to Idolatry," March 24, 1973.

Berger, Peter and Thomas Luckmann. 1966. *The Social Construction of Reality: A Treatise in the Sociology of Knowledge.* Garden City, New York: Doubleday.

Borhek, James T. and Richard F. Curtis. 1975. *A Sociology of Belief.* New York: John Wiley.

Congar, Yves. 1976. *Challenge to the Church: The Case of Archbishop Lefebvre.* Huntington, Indiana: Our Sunday Visitor.

Cuneo, Michael. 1987. "Conservative Catholicism in North America: Pro-Life Activism and the Pursuit of the Sacred," *Pro Mundi Vita: Dossiers* January: 2–27.

Davies, Michael. 1976. *Liturgical Revolution: Cranmer's Godly Order.* New Rochelle, New York: Arlington House.

——————. 1977. *Liturgical Revolution: Pope John's Council.* New Rochelle, New York: Arlington House.

——————. 1978a. *The True Voice of Tradition.* St. Paul, Minnesota: Remnant Press.

——————. 1978b. "Pope Liberius and the Arian Heresy," *The Remnant* (April 30): 14–15.

——————. 1979. *Apologia Pro Marcel Lefebvre: 1905–1976, I.* Dickinson, Texas: Angelus Press.

——————. 1983. *Apologia Pro Marcel Lefebvre: 1977–1979, II.* Dickinson, Texas: Angelus Press.

——————. 1987. "Arianism," *The Angelus X*: 10–13.

Dillenberger, John and Claude Welch. 1988. *Protestant Christianity: Interpreted Through Its*

Development. New York: Collier Macmillan.

Dinges, William. 1983a. "Catholic Traditionalism in America: A Study of the Remnant Faithful," Unpublished Ph.D. dissertation. University of Kansas.

_____ . 1983b. "Catholic Traditionalism," pp. 137–158 in Joseph Fichter, ed. *Alternatives to American Mainline Churches*. New York: Rose of Sharon.

_____ . 1987. "Ritual Conflict as Social Conflict: Liturgical Reform in the Roman Catholic Church," *Sociological Analysis* 48: 138–159.

Dulles, Avery. 1987. "Councils," pp. 235–242 in Joseph A. Komonchak, Mary Collins, and Dermot A. Lane, eds. *The New Dictionary of Theology*. Wilmington, Delaware: Michael Glazier, Inc.

Dupont, Yves. 1970. *Catholic Prophecy: The Coming Chastisement*. Rockford, Illinois: TAN Books.

Festinger, Leon, H. W. Riechen, and S. Schachter. 1956. *When Prophecy Fails*. New York: Harper Torchbooks.

Harrison, Michael and John Manika. 1978. "Dynamics of Dissenting Movements Within Established Organizations: Two Cases and a Theoretical Interpretation," *Journal For The Scientific Study of Religion* 17: 207–224.

Hitchcock, James. 1974. *The Recovery of the Sacred*. New York: Seabury.

_____ . 1979. *Catholicism and Modernity: Confrontation or Capitulation?* New York: Seabury.

Johnson, Paul. 1981. *Pope John Paul II and the Catholic Restoration*. Ann Arbor, Michigan: Servant.

Kelly, Clarence. 1976. "The Catholic Thing to Do," *For You and for Many* (November-December): 1–6.

Kelly, George. 1979. *The Battle for the American Church*. New York: Doubleday.

Kurtz, Lester R. 1986. *The Politics of Heresy: The Modernist Crisis in Roman Catholicism*. Berkeley: University of California Press.

Lefebvre, Marcel. 1975. "Letter to Friends and Benefactors," #9.

_____ . 1976. *A Bishop Speaks: Writings and Addresses 1963–1975*. Belford Park, Edinburgh: Una Voce.

_____ . 1979. "Understanding the Crisis," *For You and For Many* April-May: 15.

_____ . 1982. *I Accuse the Council!* Dickinson, Texas: The Angelus [1976] Press.

_____ . 1985. *Archbishop Marcel Lefebvre: Collected Works, I*. Dickinson, Texas: Angelus Press.

_____ . 1986. *An Open Letter to Confused Catholics*. Herefordshire, England: Fowler Wright Books Ltd.

_____ . 1987. "Ordination Sermon," *The Angelus X*, 7: 10–14.

_____ . 1987b. "In Conformity to God's Will," *The Angelus X*, 7:2–9, 27.

_____ . 1988. "A Public Statement on the Occasion of the Episcopal [1983] Consecration of Several Priests of the Society of St. Pius X," *The Angelus XI*, 7: 36–37.

Lefebvre, Marcel and Antonio de Castro Mayer. 1987. "Declaration," *The Angelus X*, 1: 2–3.

Likoudis, James and Kenneth Whitehead. 1981. *The Pope, The Council, and The Mass: Answers to The Questions The Traditionalists Are Asking*. West Hanover, Massachusetts: Christopher Publishing.

McKenna, Robert. 1977. *Our Vindication: Masonic Prelates in the Church*. Bridgeport, Connecticut: ORCM Reprint.

McPherson, William. 1973. *Ideology and Change*. Palo Alto, California: National Press.

Mennozi, Daniele. 1987. "Opposition to the Council (1966–1984)," pp. 325–349 in Ciusepe Alberigo, Jean-Pierre Jossua, and Joseph A. Komonchak, eds. *The Reception of Vatican II*. Washington, D.C.: The Catholic University of American Press.

Molnar, Thomas. 1968. *Ecumenism or New Reformation*. New York: Funk and Wagnalls.

Morris, Frank. 1978. "What Do Conservatives Really Want?" *The Critic* 36: 18–26.

O'Dea, Thomas. 1961. "Five Dilemmas in the Institutionalization of Religion," *Journal For The Scientific Study of Religion* 1: 30–39.

Ratzinger, Joseph. 1985. *The Ratzinger Report* (With Vittorio Messori) Trans. by Salvator Attanasio and Graham Harrison. San Francisco: Ignatius Press.

The Remnant. May 15, 1988.

Seidler, John. 1986. "Contested Accommodation: The Catholic Church As a Special Case of Social Change," *Social Forces* June: 847–875.

Smelser, Neil J. 1962. *Theory of Collective Behavior*. New York: Free Press.

Snow, David A. and Richard Machalek. 1983. "Second Thoughts on the presumed Fragility of Unconventional Beliefs," pp. 25–45 in *Of Gods and Men: New Religious Movements in the West*, edited by Eileen Barker. Macon, Georgia: Mercer Press.

Stark, Rodney and William Sims Bainbridge. 1985. *The Future of Religion: Secularization, Revival, and Cult Formation*. Berkeley: University of California Press.

Superior General Letter. October 11, 1987.

Toch, Hans. 1965. *The Social Psychology of Social Movements*. New York: Bobbs-Merrill.

Troeltsch, Ernst. 1931. *The Social Teaching of the Christian Churches*. New York: Macmillan.

Triumph. June 1970: 25.

Turner, Ralph. 1970. "Determinants of Social Movement Strategies," pp. 145–155 in *Human Nature and Collective Behavior*, edited by Tamotsu Shibutani. Englewood Cliffs, New Jersey: Prentice-Hall.

Una Voce Newsletter. 42, 1974.

The Voice. February 3, 1973.

The Wanderer. December 26, 1967.

Whitehead, Kibby. 1979. "The New Protestantism," *Homiletic and Pastoral Review* 79: 18–28.

Wiltgen, Ralph. 1967. *The Rhine Flows into the Tiber*. New York: Hawthorn Books.

7.

Keepers of the Faith:

Lay Militants, Abortion,

and the Battle for Canadian Catholicism

Michael W. Cuneo

If they think we're going to just piss off into the wind, they're way off base. We've been fighting for the lives of innocent babies for years, and nothing they say or do will stop us. The abortion battle is the colosseum of the twentieth century, and there's no way we'll lose faith, even if it means martyrdom. It doesn't matter how much they persecute us or ridicule us. Christ is with us, even if they're not, and we're in this struggle to the finish.[1]

It is unlikely to evoke surprise that these words were spoken by a Canadian Catholic layperson who is a leading anti-abortion activist. What is noteworthy, however, is that these sentiments of anger and defiance were directed *not* at the political opponents of the Canadian anti-abortion movement, but rather at the Roman Catholic bishops of Canada. Perhaps no aspect of the ongoing Canadian abortion debate is more intriguing, and certainly none more ironic, than the bitterness which many Catholic pro-life activists have come to feel toward the institutional Catholic church. This paper examines how the abortion issue, famous enough for producing deep societal fissions, has also been a source of internal dissension for Canadian Catholicism.

---

1 This quotation is taken from an interview conducted by the author in 1985 while doing field research on the Canadian pro-life movement. It should be stressed that the movement is discussed here only in its *English*-Canadian dimension. The French-Canadian variant is quite different and would thus require a separate study. For a more extensive analysis of the Canadian pro-life movement, see Michael W. Cuneo, *Catholics Against the Church: Anti-Abortion Protest in Toronto, 1969–1985* (Unpublished Ph.D. dissertation, University of Toronto, 1988).

The Canadian Catholic Bishops and Abortion: An Overview

In the immediate years following the close of Vatican II, the Canadian bishops were forced to deal with several domestic political issues which would prove a testing ground for the *rapprochement* with the modern world which seemed to be mandated by the Council. The first two of these, which involved proposals to repeal the legal prohibition against contraceptives and to relax Canadian divorce law, provided an opportunity for the bishops to formulate a blueprint for a new *modus vivendi* between the church and Canadian political culture.[2]

In briefs addressed to the Parliamentary committees responsible for reviewing these proposed changes to the Criminal Code, the bishops acknowledged that there exists a clear and judicious distinction between civil law and sacred law. Especially in a pluralistic society such as Canada, they wrote, it would be ill-advised to abrogate this distinction by legally enshrining the moral preferences or misgivings of any particular religious group. Thus despite their opposition on *religious* grounds, the bishops stated, they would not stand in the way of the liberalization of Canadian laws governing contraception and divorce.

In any event, the bishops further said, Vatican II's teaching regarding the separate spheres of responsibility to be exercised by clergy and laity respectively was an additional reason which precluded their legitimate intervention in the Canadian political process. Matters pertaining to the civil or mundane domain, they advised, are properly the jurisdiction of the laity rather than the clergy. And lay Catholics who are legislators, they insisted, best fulfill their civic responsibilities by voting for laws which, in good conscience, they believe to be in the common public interest, regardless of whether such laws are in conformity to the moral teaching of the church.[3]

Affecting as they did sensitive areas of family and sexual life, areas traditionally close to the heart of Catholic ethical thinking, these proposed revisions to the Canadian Criminal Code had forced the bishops to show their political hand. They had been expected to make some kind of response, and at least some Canadians had awaited it as a litmus test of the bishops' Canadianism. Would the bishops place their religious beliefs above Canada's ideal of democratic pluralism, or would they give Catholic politicians free rein to make laws strictly on their presumed social merit? In acknowledging the inapplicability of Catholic moral principles to the political process, the bishops had passed this initial test. They had suitably recognized that the Canada of the 1960s was happy to grant Catholic bishops the right to pious

---

2 In December 1967, the federal Liberal government introduced an Omnibus bill to Parliament which included reform of Canadian laws regulating contraceptives, divorce, and abortion among its more than one hundred items.

3 The episcopal briefs on contraception and divorce are included in the booklet entitled *Contraception, Divorce, Abortion: Three Statements by Canadian Catholic Conference* (Ottawa: Canadian Catholic Conference, 1968), pp. 12–25.

opinion, but not political influence.

The principles rehearsed by the Catholic bishops in their briefs on contraception and divorce—that what is forbidden by the church should not necessarily be forbidden by civil law, that the Catholic legislator's primary responsibility is to serve the public good, and that politics is the proper purview of the laity—corresponded to a secularizing impulse in Canadian institutional life which had gathered momentum in the post-World War II years and which had finally won ascendency in the 1960s.[4] The new secular vision of Canada, to which the bishops had tacitly deferred, was given ceremonial expression on 15 December 1967 when Pierre Trudeau, then federal Minister of Justice, addressed Parliament at the second reading of the bill to widen grounds for divorce:

> We are now living in a social climate in which people are beginning to realize, perhaps for the first time in the history of this country, that we are not entitled to impose the concepts which belong to a sacred society upon a civil or profane society. The concepts of a civil society in which we live are pluralistic and I think . . . it would be a mistake for us to legislate into this society concepts which belong to a theological or sacred order.[5]

That the bishops accepted and, in a certain sense, anticipated the thrust of Mr. Trudeau's remarks regarding the separation of church and state is not surprising in light of Canadian Catholicism's well-adjusted denominational character. As Andrew Greeley has pointed out, Canada is one of only a few countries in the Western world to have a tradition of denominational pluralism.[6] Partly because it has never enjoyed the privilege of formal establishment, the English-speaking church in the post-confederation era has seldom been tempted to indulge a specifically Catholic theocratic vision for Canada. Moreover, with at most a sporadic tradition of anti-Catholicism, Canada has been a congenial territory for the church's expansion and regional consolidation. Despite occasional turbulence, usually generated by debates over the legal status of Catholic schools, the church has been confident that it shares a common language and sense of national purpose with other denominations and with Canadians generally.

---

4 See John Webster Grant, "Religion and the Quest for a National Identity: The Background in Canadian History," in Peter Slater (ed.), *Religion and Culture in Canada/Religion et Culture au Canada* (Canadian Corporation for Studies in Religion, 1977), p. 18; and Roger O'Toole, "Society, the Sacred and the Secular: Sociological Observations on the Changing Role of Religion in Canadian Culture," in W. Westfall *et al.* (eds.), *Religion/Culture: Comparative Canadian Studies* (Ottawa: Association for Canadian Studies, 1985), pp. 99–117.

5 Quoted in Reginald Whitaker, "Reason, Passion and Interest: Pierre Trudeau's Eternal Liberal Triangle," *Canadian Journal of Political and Social Theory* 4, 1 (1980): 5–31.

6 A. M. Greeley, *The Denominational Society* (Glenview, Ill.: Scott, Foresman, 1972), p. 1.

The 1950s and 60s was a time when English-speaking Catholics joined with most Canadians in celebrating the "good life" of Canadian democracy, civility, and ordered affluence.[7] Though they likely had reservations about the proposed changes to the laws concerning contraceptives and divorce, the bishops were understandably reluctant to drive a partisan wedge into this national spirit of optimism and progress. Moreover, the new era of secular emancipation proclaimed by Trudeau likely struck some bishops as a natural stage of Canada's evolution from a Protestant dominion to a multicultural nation.[8] The church had in the past been a beneficiary of this momentum toward greater pluralism and toleration, and there seemed little reason to greet the Trudeau manifesto with consternation.

The questions of contraception and divorce, however, were far easier to submit to the court of ethical pluralism than would be abortion. And yet reform of Canada's abortion law, then one of the most stringent in the English-speaking world, was next on the Parliamentary agenda. By calling into question the very meaning of humanity and sexuality, abortion cuts to the nerve of Catholic cosmology, and thus the proposed amendment to legalize *therapeutic* abortions posed a quandary for the Catholic bishops. Although they clearly found abortion abhorrent, they could not directly—*qua* Catholic bishops—oppose legalization without straining the political code of conduct they had set themselves in their briefs on contraception and divorce. Indeed, commentators in both the secular and liberal Protestant media were quick to point out that the distinction between civil and moral law, and the prudential separation of the two in a pluralistic society, was a formula which the bishops should also apply to the question of abortion.[9] The prevailing attitude of Canada's mainstream Protestant churches regarding the conflict between Catholic belief and abortion law reform was tersely summarized in the Anglican monthly *Canadian Churchman*:

> In the areas of abortion, contraception and homosexuality the choice is government by the individual's conscience. If his church is opposed then he has a moral obligation to obey his church's rules but he has no right to impose these rules on people of other faiths or no faith at all. There is a clear distinction between moral and civil law.[10]

On 5 March 1968 a delegation from the Canadian Catholic Conference (C. C. C.), led by Bishop Remi De Roo of Victoria, B. C., appeared before the Parliamentary committee responsible for reviewing the abortion law. In his opening remarks,

---

7 See John Webster Grant, *The Church in the Canadian Era* (Toronto: McGraw-Hill Ryerson, 1972), pp. 160–183.

8 See N. Keith Clifford, "His Dominion: A Vision in Crisis," in Slater (ed.), *op. cit.*, pp. 24–41.

9 See, for example, the *Globe and Mail* editorial of 21 December 1967, "Now the job is to be done, let it be done right."

10 Editorial, "A clear distinction" (April 1968).

Bishop De Roo stressed that the episcopal delegation had come "in a spirit of dialogue" and did not want "to impose a particular point of view" upon a "complex and difficult question." The bishops' profound concern with the proposed abortion legislation, explained the Rev. E. J. Sheridan, S. J., stemmed from their conviction that it was "a bad law . . . that introduces . . . a fundamental disrespect for life" and thus militates against "the common good." And far from intending to obfuscate the distinction between divine law and civil law, Fr. Sheridan concluded, the bishops respected the autonomy of the political sphere and did "not believe that our moral principle must be enshrined in criminal law."[11]

Despite its irenic, almost apologetic tone, this episcopal presentation of March 1968 was accorded a hostile reception by at least some influential segments of Canadian society. The *Globe and Mail*, for example, responded to it by denouncing the bishops for ecclesiastical meddling.

> The bishops are now opposing abortion reform not because it threatens public order or the common good. They oppose it on essentially moral and theological grounds. Their imposition of Catholic morality and dogma on the rest of Canada is incompatible with their own distinction between moral and civil law. . . . At stake here is . . . a certain high conception of liberal democracy. That means a tolerant respect for the conscience of all—not just the consciences of the most dogmatic.[12]

Perhaps feeling chastened by commentaries like the above, the bishops withdrew from direct political involvement in the abortion arena, an arena which they would not reenter until twenty years later.[13] In May 1969 the House of Commons approved an amendment to the Criminal Code's section on abortion which authorized that abortions could be performed for broadly therapeutic reasons in accredited Canadians hospitals after approval by a therapeutic abortion committee (TAC). According to the new law, abortion would be permitted if, in the opinion of a duly constituted TAC, "the continuation of the pregnancy" of the female seeking abortion "would or would be likely to endanger her life or health. . . "[14]

The deferential caution with which the bishops approached abortion reform is

---

11 See Alphonse de Valk, *Morality and Law in Canadian Politics: The Abortion Controversy* (Montreal: Palm Publishers, 1974), pp. 73–80.

12 Quoted in *ibid.*, p. 82.

13 The political interest of the bishops in the abortion issue would recrudesce in January 1988 when the Supreme Court of Canada struck down the 1969 abortion law and, effectively, made abortion a private matter between a woman and her physician. See, for example: G. Emmett Cardinal Carter (Archbishop of Toronto), *Statement by Cardinal Carter to the Right Hon. The Prime Minister of Canada and the Members of the Federal Parliament*, 29 February 1988; and James M. Hayes (Archbishop of Halifax, President of the CCCB), *Faithful to the Future: Pastoral Statement on Abortion*, April 1988.

14 *Criminal Code, Revised Statutes of Canada*, 1970, Chapter C–34, Sect. 251.

perhaps better understood in view of several factors. Firstly, they did not wish the abortion issue to jeopardize Canada's pattern of denominational coexistence. The nation's mainstream Protestant churches unanimously supported liberalization, and the bishops did not desire to convey an impression of moral superiority or of contempt toward attitudes on abortion at variance with their own. Nor did they wish to puncture the prevailing mood of ecumenical buoyancy in the wake of Vatican II by resurrecting the spectre of triumphalism.

Secondly, it is likely that the bishops wished to forestall any social discord which would potentially result from a strong Catholic campaign against abortion reform. The Catholic church in Canada has historically placed a great premium on national harmony and has, in fact, been a major force in both preserving and subtly shaping the Canadian social fabric.[15] Considering that most other cultural elites were strongly in favour of modifying the abortion law, an intransigent stance of opposition by the bishops would have produced precisely the element of social dissension which they had for generations been concerned to avoid.[16] In their March 1968 presentation and, indeed, in their subsequent pastoral statements on abortion, the bishops thus tried to strike a balance between their dual obligations as Catholic pastors and members of a pluralistic democracy. By speaking out, but not too vigorously, against abortion law reform, they gave public notice of their allegiance to the traditional Catholic teaching against abortion without overstepping assumed cultural limitations of civil discourse.

And, lastly, the circumspection of the bishops had much to do with the *nature* of the new abortion law. In broadening the legal grounds for abortion while retaining safeguards for the fetus, the 1969 legislation purported to be a *compromise* solution to the abortion controversy. It represented neither complete victory for the pro-choice side nor complete defeat for the pro-life. By making legal abortion contingent upon the ritual of approval by a TAC, the new law accorded ostensible recognition to the independent value of intrauterine life. In other words, implicit in the 1969 amendment was the assumption that "termination of pregnancy" should not be allowed without demonstration of a proportionately grave cause. Although the bishops clearly disapproved of the 1969 law, it seemed to reflect enough of the Catholic viewpoint on abortion to be at least palatable.

The Bishops and the Canadian Pro-Life Movement

The Canadian pro-life (or anti-abortion) movement arose in response to the 1969 abortion legislation. Although predominantly Roman Catholic in composition, the

---

15 See John H. Simpson and Henry MacLeod, "The Politics of Morality in Canada," in R. Stark (ed.), *Religious Movements: Genesis, Exodus, and Numbers* (New York: Paragon House, 1985), pp. 224–226.

16 For an overview of the public debate over abortion law reform, see Alphonse de Valk, *Morality and Law in Canadian Politics*, pp. 19–42.

movement was entirely lay-initiated and was, even in its fledgling stage, completely independent of the institutional Catholic church. Because the movement has frequently been depicted as a creature of the *official* church, its total autonomy from the Catholic hierarchy warrants special emphasis. The Canadian bishops believed, first of all, that the pro-life cause was a lay apostolate that could be managed quite well without their interference and, secondly, they feared that too close an identification of the movement with the institutional church would brand it as Catholic and thereby circumscribe its public appeal.

Just how far removed the Catholic bishops have been from the movement may be comparatively illustrated by observing the prominent activist role played by their American counterparts since the 1973 pro-abortion decision (Roe v. Wade) of the American Supreme Court. As James Kelly points out, the American bishops have inserted their own internal structures into the right-to-life movement, including the *Bishops' Prolife Action Committee* which sponsors educational material, and the separately incorporated *National Committee for a Human Life Amendment* which actively lobbies in support of various pro-life legislation.[17] Through these structures, and also with their *Respect Life* program, the American bishops have succeeded in giving the anti-abortion gospel a much higher profile at the parish level than has been the case in Canada. The Canadian bishops did not (nor have they yet to) develop structures remotely equivalent to these, and in the years ahead they would be accused by angry Catholic activists of crossing the line from arm's length support of the pro-life cause to actual desertion of it.

Virtually from the movement's inception, there arose among its Catholic participants two divergent ideological tendencies.[18] Some Catholic activists, many of whom were professionals in law, medicine, or academia, favoured a *reformist* approach to the abortion issue. By formulating the pro-life position in terms congenial to the prevailing secularist climate, without reference to either religious dogma or confessional morality, they hoped gradually to win greater cultural legitimation for the movement's goal of full legal protection for the fetus. Reformist Catholic pro-lifers sympathized with the predicament which the Canadian bishops had faced in their effort to oppose the 1969 abortion law without conveying an intention of hierocratic coercion. And far from resenting the free rein given the movement by the bishops, they preferred that the Catholic hierarchy minimize its involvement as a precaution against the *Catholicization* of the anti-abortion cause in the public mind.

---

17 James R. Kelly, "Towards Complexity: The Right to Life Movement," Unpublished paper, 1986, p. 25. On the response of the Catholic hierarchy in Ireland to the issue of abortion law reform, see John Hannigan's chapter in the present volume.

18 Although the Canadian pro-life movement is broadly ecumenical in composition, it is primarily Catholics who have shaped its ideological course and provided its mainstay of support. The present discussion is limited to the movement's specifically *Catholic* dimension.

In diametrical opposition to this reformist strain, however, were Catholics whose anti-abortionism was linked to a more extensive project of counter-modernization. Liberalized abortion represented to these more *militant* Catholic activists[19] a composite symbol of pervasive cultural decadence. In their view, the 1969 abortion law amendment reflected a deep-seated spiritual disorder in Canadian society, a disorder traceable to the rise to cultural ascendency of *secular humanism* and the corresponding demise of traditional Christianity as the guardian of the nation's virtue.

During the middle 1970s this ideological dichotomy among Catholic activists erupted into a bitter factionalism which drained the movement of much of its energy and creativity. By situating the anti-abortion cause within an encompassing theory of cultural decline and wedding it to a religious *Weltanschauung* of diminished significance for shaping the national consciousness, reformists contended, their more militant counterparts had condemned the movement to a zone of social irrelevance. Militant Catholics, for their part, mistrusted the strategy of accommodation to secularism and pluralism to which Catholic reformists were committed. As they saw it, the reformist faction had one foot planted in the enemy camp and was thus of doubtful pro-life credentials.

Of more enduring significance for the movement's evolving fortunes than this internecine conflict, however, was an hostility toward the Canadian bishops which by the mid-1970s had become commonplace within pro-life circles. As militant Catholic activists effectively assumed control of the movement during the late seventies, they angrily cast their attention back to the circumstances surrounding passage of the 1969 abortion law. By their policy of appeasement to secularism, as well as their misguided ecumenism, Catholic militants complained, the bishops had bungled a critical opportunity to restore moral decency to Canadian public life.

In this vein, the political sins of the Canadian bishops are retrospectively recounted in a 1982 essay by Fr. Alphonse de Valk, a leading militant and one of the very few Catholic clergymen active in the pro-life movement. The distinction articulated by the bishops in the late 1960s between moral and civil law, de Valk concedes, was motivated by sincere respect for Canadian democracy and the diversity of ethical views that inevitably exists in a heterogeneous society. But, he argues, the bishops misplayed this distinction into the hands of cultural elites who advocated the total secularization of Canadian society and, concomitantly, the total withdrawal of the Catholic church from the political forum. Thus, apologetic and

---

19 The anti-abortion activists described in this chapter as *militant* Catholics have been examined elsewhere by the author under the designation *Revivalist* Catholics. See Michael W. Cuneo, "Soldiers of Orthodoxy: Revivalist Catholicism in North America," *Studies in Religion/Sciences Religieuses* 17, 3 (1988): 347–363; and Michael W. Cuneo, "Conservative Catholicism in North America: Pro-Life Activism and the Pursuit of the Sacred," *Pro Mundi Vita* 36 (1987): 3–28. The term *militant* Catholics is adequate for present analytic purposes.

defensive at the hour of decision, the bishops offered "no prophetic stand," but instead stood by meekly as the "legalization of abortion was introduced, defended and pushed through by a heavily Catholic party, thereby making Canada the only country in the world where Catholics bear this responsibility."[20] The price paid by the bishops for their irenic approach to the Canadian political process, bemoans de Valk, has been the relegation of Catholic moral principles to a sectarian, culturally redundant backwater.

> Let us ask once more: why did the Bishops withdraw their opposition to legalizing contraceptives and widening the grounds for divorce, and why did many Catholics do the same to abortion? Answer: because they had come to accept, willingly or unwillingly, consciously or unconsciously, what was being hammered into their heads by the secular media and a wide variety of spokesmen and women for the new ethic, namely, that opposition in these matters was purely theological and denominational, in short, for Catholics only.[21]

To the thinking of Catholic militants, the tentativeness of the bishops on the questions of contraception and divorce was at least pardonable, if not an occasion for applause. But when it came to the issue of abortion, where "the supreme values of life are at stake,"[22] they expected from the hierarchy nothing less than an implacable campaign for truth. In a country where in 1969 almost half the population professed membership in the Catholic church and the governing Liberal party was composed predominantly of Catholics, they reasoned, the bishops should have been able to mount sufficient electoral pressure to prevent passage of the law. That they failed to do so, it was surmised, indicated the extent to which the Canadian hierarchy had capitulated to the secularizing agenda of pro-abortion supporters.

Just as exasperating to Catholic militants was the apparent aloofness of the bishops toward the abortion issue and the pro-life movement throughout the 1970s. The several pastoral statements on abortion issued by the bishops during the decade, intended primarily for consumption by Canadian Catholics, were seen by militants as pale, ineffectual discourses guaranteed to offend or to challenge no one.[23] By these statements, militants claimed, the bishops were merely engaging in an *ex post facto* damage control, trying to mitigate the consequences of the 1969 legislation without bringing embarrassment to themselves or divisiveness to the larger Cana-

---

20 Alphonse de Valk, "Understandable but Mistaken: Law, Morality and the Catholic Church in Canada, 1966–1969," *Canadian Catholic Historical Association, Study Sessions* 49 (1982): 107–108.

21 *Ibid.*, p. 108.

22 Alphonse de Valk, *Abortion: Christianity, Reason and Human Rights* (Edmonton: Life Ethics Centre, 1982), p. 2.

23 See, for example, Canadian Catholic Conference, *Statement on Abortion* (Ottawa: C.C.C., 1970).

dian community. Reformist Catholics within the movement appreciated the inherent difficulty of translating absolute moral disapprobation of abortion into language that would bear some credibility in a secular social environment, and were thus able to maintain cordial relations with the bishops. But by the close of the decade a pattern of mutual mistrust between the Canadian hierarchy and the movement as a whole was firmly established. Catholic militants, by this time a commanding force within the movement, were convinced that the bishops' anti-abortion commitment was limited to what the traffic would bear, and that the future of the pro-life cause belonged to lay Catholics who would be foolish to count on the support of the church hierarchy in moments of political crunch. Conversely, by seeming not to appreciate the sensitive nature of church-state relations in a country of pluralistic design, Catholic militants gained among the bishops a lasting reputation for obtuseness.

While the belief of Catholic militants that the Canadian hierarchy had forsaken the pro-life cause was exaggerated, it would not likely have achieved such secure standing within pro-life ranks without a *prima facie* plausibility. Indeed, the response of the bishops to the abortion issue throughout the 1970s was largely one of calculated reticence. And although individual prelates made episodic ventures into the abortion arena,[24] the hierarchy as a whole seemed intent upon cultivating a hygienic distance from the pro-life movement itself.

Like reformist activists within the movement, the bishops preferred a pragmatic, Fabian approach to the abortion question. By expanding dialogue on the issue with feminists, the major Protestant churches, and other sectors of mainstream Canadian society, and by promoting programs of economic support for underprivileged mothers, they hoped to arrest and eventually reduce the abortion rate. In stark contrast to this dialogic approach, the movement's Catholic militants were committed to a strategy of frontal assault against the purveyors of abortion freedom. Thus, they openly castigated feminists, "anti-life" politicians, and virtually anyone else deemed unsupportive of the cause as moral monsters who would place personal comfort or political expediency above nascent human life. When Catholic militants outwrestled the reformist camp for control of the movement in the mid-1970s, anti-abortion protest in general came to assume a rancorous and bellicose tone with which most bishops clearly did not wish to be associated.

There is an additional dimension to the escalating tension between the pro-life movement and the institutional church, one more closely related to the internal dynamic of Catholicism's contemporary transformation. The abortion issue attained

---

24 Perhaps the most visible gesture of public support for the cause from the church establishment during the decade occurred in March 1976 when Archbishop Pocock of Toronto protested the inclusion of Planned Parenthood, the leading abortion referral agency in the country, as a beneficiary of the annual United Way charity drive. Pocock subsequently withdrew Catholic support from the United Way and instituted Share Life as an independent Catholic charitable foundation.

celebrity status in Canada in the immediate aftermath of Vatican II, when upheaval and confusion stemming from the Council were at highest pitch. Many Catholic militants were initially attracted to anti-abortion protest precisely because it promised an absolute measure of Catholic commitment at a time when most parameters of Catholic distinctiveness were overtaken by doubt. If Catholics could be certain of anything in this tumultuous period, they thought, it was the inviolability of the church's teaching concerning the sanctity of life. The pro-life activism of these Catholics thus was invested with powerful religious incentive; it was a conveyance for a reconsecrated Catholic identity and an opportunity to demonstrate unabridged fidelity to the church. In their handling of the abortion issue, militants believed, the bishops were guilty not only of political negligence, but also of denying the faithful perhaps their last gasp of Catholic certitude.

Catholic Sectarianism in the Pro-Life Movement

In the 1970s the conflict between the Canadian bishops and the pro-life movement centred upon competing conceptions of the church's political role in a secular democracy. In their response to the abortion issue, the bishops were protective both of the interests of the fetus and the maintenance of Canada's pluralistic ideal. Accordingly, they attempted to publicize their opposition to abortion liberalization without communicating the impression that they aspired to impose their moral code upon the wider society. To militant pro-lifers, however, this represented acquiescence to moral relativism. Given Vatican II's condemnation of abortion as an "abominable crime,"[25] they reasoned, the bishops were morally compelled to fight the 1969 abortion law unstintingly, regardless of expense either to Canadian social equilibrium or to the church's ecumenical relations. That they failed to do so, either in 1969 or subsequently, Catholic militants concluded, meant that the bishops were willing to sacrifice the lives of preborn children for social tranquility or, perhaps worse, that they had secretly fallen away from the Catholic teaching on the sanctity of life.

Throughout the 1970s, then, militant Catholic pro-lifers were animated by a theocratic impulse. If the secular culture was too obdurate to realize the fundamental evil of abortion, their thinking went, the bishops were obliged to settle the issue in the name of divine justice. Millions of Canadian Catholics, they believed, stood waiting in the wings ready to answer their chief shepherds' cue for a massive demonstration of pro-life strength. Harbouring as they did an exaggerated estimation of the Catholic hierarchy's influence both within and outside the church, militants could only attribute the bishops' failure to act more decisively on the issue to a lack of moral resolve.

In the early 1980s this theocratic impulse of the movement's militant Catholics

---

25 See Alphonse de Valk, "Pluralism and Secularism in Canadian Law and Society, 1968–1982," *Canadian Catholic Historical Association, Study Session* 50 (1983): 631–654.

was replaced by a sectarian one. It was during this time that they fashioned the conviction that their most urgent mission of evangelization was not to the wider secular culture, but rather to Canadian Catholicism itself. Whereas in the previous decade they were concerned to convert, forcibly if necessary, the broader society to the Catholic position on abortion, in the 1980s they turned their attention to the even more challenging task of *deconverting* Catholicism from secularism and reconstituting the Canadian church as a culturally separatist enclave of the stalwart faithful. In other words, they came to the jarring conclusion that the mainstream Canadian church was itself an apostate institution, that an astonishing number of Catholics had themselves grown soft on abortion. And the chief cause of this, they believed, was the continuing complacency of the Canadian bishops.

The relationship between the Canadian hierarchy and militant pro-lifers soured completely in 1981 when the bishops seemed to pass up a golden opportunity to atone for their previous political sins on the anti-abortion front. The occasion for conflict this time was provided by the proposed Charter of Rights and Freedoms which the Trudeau government sought to entrench in Canada's new constitution. Because it did not include a clause explicitly protecting the right to life of the fetus, militant Catholics lobbied vigorously against the Charter, and expected their bishops to do likewise. Instead, Cardinal Carter of Toronto, Archbishop of English-Canada's largest diocese, accorded the Charter his personal *imprimatur*, advising that its silence on fetal rights should not obscure for Canadian Catholics its many other "positive values."[26] In May 1981, the Canadian bishops did, mildly and unsuccessfully, petition Prime Minister Trudeau to include a clause in the Charter which would guarantee its neutrality on abortion, but their detractors within the pro-life movement were unimpressed. In a letter of distress sent to the Vatican, Catholic militants advised Pope John Paul II that the "*precarious* situation regarding . . . the leadership of the Catholic Church in Canada merits your direct attention [emphasis added]." The Canadian pro-life movement, the Pope was further informed, could no longer withstand the dreadful irony of having its efforts sabotaged by Catholic bishops.

> The Archdiocese of Toronto needs an Archbishop who will truly stand up for the right to life of the unborn. Our country needs strong and courageous religious leaders who will speak out publicly on behalf of pro-life.[27]

Although the bishops drew heaviest fire, this appeal to the Pope was actually an open declaration of war against mainstream Canadian Catholicism as a whole. What

---

26 See Tom Sinclair-Faulkner, "Canadian Catholics: At Odds on Abortion," *The Christian Century* (9 September 1981), pp. 870–871.

27 Letter from Campaign Life (signed by members of the Toronto and national executives) to His Holiness John Paul II (Vatican City, Europe), 12 May 1981. Campaign Life is the principal organizational home for Catholic militants in the Canadian pro-life movement.

the Charter affair had vividly brought home to Catholic militants was the prospect that their cause enjoyed only marginal support among Canadian Catholics in general. By responding to the Charter with their customary circumspection, the bishops had behaved according to form, but why had there not been cries of outrage from elsewhere in the church? Why did so many Canadian Catholics, including priests and nuns, seem passively prepared to accept abortion as an inevitable component of contemporary existence?

The answer to these questions, militant Catholics believed, was already at hand. For several years prior to the Charter debate, militant pro-lifers had been preoccupied with understanding the cultural sources of changed attitudes toward abortion. What had impelled the rapid ascent to social respectability of the pro-choice ethic? The *contraceptive mentality* thesis, already popular by then in American pro-life circles, seemed to provide the most satisfying explanation. Since the popularization of artificial contraceptives in the 1960s, according to this thesis, pleasure has been separated from procreation in the sexual practice of Western society. This rupture between intercourse and procreation has become so culturally entrenched that couples believe that they have both the right and responsibility to prevent conception. And finally, this "contraceptive mentality" has engendered a social climate which condones abortion as a belated solution to contraceptive failure.[28]

The contraceptive mentality thesis held compelling appeal for Catholic militants in large part because it coincided with a crucial element of their own piety. Virtually without exception, they adhered reverentially to the papal encyclical *Humanae Vitae* and believed it to be an essential requirement of Catholic belonging.[29] The idea of artificial birth control being the cultural progenitor of liberalized abortion was in their view *Humanae Vitae*'s supreme vindication. Through *Humanae Vitae*, Pope Paul VI had attempted both to challenge the "contraceptive mentality" and to immunize Catholics against it.

The failure of Canadian Catholics generally to align themselves to the pro-life cause, militants reasoned, could be traced directly to the widespread neglect of *Humanae Vitae* within the Canadian church. And primary responsibility for this neglect they assigned to the Canadian bishops. Instead of giving *Humanae Vitae* their ringing endorsement upon its release in 1968, militants recalled, the bishops had presented it as an ideal rather than a binding requirement for Catholic sexual conduct. In so doing, they not only diluted the force of *Humanae Vitae*, but furthermore

---

28 See Donald DeMarco, *The Contraceptive Mentality* (Edmonton: Life Ethics Centre, 1982); and Paul Marx, "Explaining the contraceptive mentality," *The Interim* 6, 1 (April 1987), p. 27.

29 The encyclical letter *Humanae Vitae, On the Transmission of Human Life* was promulgated by Pope Paul VI on 25 July 1968. On the controversy engendered by *Humanae Vitae* within the Canadian Catholic church, see Anne Roche Muggeridge, *The Desolate City: The Catholic Church in Ruins* (Toronto: McClelland and Stewart, 1986), pp. 85–110.

provided a gateway for admittance of the "contraceptive mentality" into the Canadian church.[30] It seemed hardly accidental to Catholic militants that the most dedicated apostles of the pro-life gospel in Canada were lay Catholics who professed total conformity to *Humanae Vitae*. The vast majority of Canadian Catholics, those either indifferent to or contemptuous of the pro-life movement, had been led by their bishops into cultural captivity.

As the 1980s advanced, the value of the contraceptive mentality thesis for Catholic militants steadily accrued. It helped prepare them, for example, for public opinion polls reporting that Canadian Catholics show only a slightly lower tendency than the general population to favour abortion-on-demand.[31] Given the causal connection between contraceptive practice and acceptance of abortion, militants claimed, this was hardly a startling revelation. Was it not common knowledge, after all, that Canadian Catholics had massively defected from the church's teaching against artificial birth control? And when the great majority of Toronto-area Catholics greeted the opening of elective abortion clinics in their city with an apathetic resignation, the case as far as militant pro-lifers were concerned was clinched. The institutional Canadian church was proven, beyond doubt, apostate.

With the contraceptive mentality thesis, then, militant Catholic pro-lifers believed they had probed beyond epiphenomenal accounts of the abortion revolution and uncovered its ontological provenance. The movement for abortion freedom was founded upon a profound psychosexual pathology which had made alarming inroads even into Canadian Catholicism. The value of the thesis for Catholic militants, however, exceeded its presumed explanatory power; it served also as an ideological anchor for their evolving group identity. For by the mid-1980s they conceived themselves as a holy elect called to rescue the Canadian church from spiritual lassitude and, ultimately, from absorption in the melting pot of secular humanism. The battle against abortion had been converted by them into a battle for the soul of Canadian Catholicism.

---

30 See Alphonse de Valk, "Our Bishops on Humanae Vitae," *The Interim* 4, 6 (September 1986), p. 12.

31 A survey conducted for the *Globe and Mail* in 1985 found that forty-seven per cent of Canadian Catholics, and fifty-three per cent of all Canadians, favour abortion-on-request. See M. Adams, D. Dasko, and Y. Corbeil, "The Globe-CROP Poll: Slim majority of Canadians favors free choice, poll finds," *Globe and Mail* (June 15, 1985), pp. 1, 12. The Globe-Crop poll provoked the following editorial comments in the Canadian *Catholic Register* (June 29, 1985, p. 4), "Conclusion: our Church is in serious trouble. Only a very strong campaign by the responsible Church authorities, re-inforcing [Catholic teaching against abortion], can counter the influence of the world, the flesh and the devil. We do not see such a campaign developing."

Denominationalism and the Quandary of Abortion

By the mid-1980s, then, the Canadian pro-life movement, at least in its militant Catholic dimension, had been transformed from a project of political reform to one of religious crusade. And correspondingly, the totemic Catholic issue of abortion had become a fulcrum of disunity for the Canadian church. It had been turned into a battlefield for competing conceptions and ideals of episcopal leadership, the meaning and requirements of Catholic belonging in a secular age, and the relationship of the church both to Canada's pluralistic ideal and to Canadian political culture.

To lay Catholic militants, the scenario was strikingly simple. Where unborn human life was at stake, loyalty to both church and *saeculum* could not possibly be reconciled. Catholics could only legitimately remain Catholic by a stance of absolute opposition to abortion, one unconditioned by public norms of civil discourse, democratic convention, or political restraint. By pitching their dissent against abortion in the dominant cultural key, the bishops had diluted the pro-life message and blunted its urgency even for the majority of Canadian Catholics. They had, in short, treated abortion as a political issue to be negotiated like any other.

For lay militants, abortion was not merely a matter of political controversy; nor was their political intractability governed by a merely instrumental logic. While manifestly directed toward the defence of fetal life, the pro-life activism of militants was also, and just as profoundly, a medium for the crystallization of a heroic and contracultural piety. In an age of widespread moral and cognitive relativism, when even most criteria of Catholic separateness from profane culture seemed uncertain or to have dissolved altogether, it was an opportunity to demonstrate unqualified religious virtue.

Abortion thus has been the issue which best reflects the internal tensions faced by Catholicism in its continuing adjustment to Canadian patterns of liberal democracy, ecumenism, and secularism. In achieving compatible coexistence with both its social environment and neighbouring religious bodies, the Canadian church has come to resemble a denomination, perhaps *primus inter pares*, more than an exclusive, culturally remote hierocracy.[32] By their pragmatic and tolerant response to changes in Canadian laws governing contraceptives and divorce, the bishops confirmed this denominational development. For lay militants, however, abortion was a different matter altogether. It was the line of last retreat, the final opportunity for the church to reassert a claim to privileged moral insight and social influence. By failing to seize this opportunity, they concluded, the bishops and Canadian Catholics generally showed themselves to be more committed to Canadian pluralism and prevailing cultural reality than to the church herself. Accordingly, and as indicated by the

---

32 On the denominationalization of Canadian Catholicism, see Kenneth Westhues, "The Adaptation of the Roman Catholic Church in Canadian Society," in S. Crysdale and L. Wheatcroft (eds.), *Religion in Canadian Society* (Toronto: Macmillan, 1976), pp. 290–306.

following remarks by a prominent pro-life activist, lay militants believed that the fate of the Canadian church as an authentic vehicle of cultural transcendence was in their hands.

> The Bishops are concerned with public relations and being seen as nice guys. With contraception and abortion, they take the path of least resistance, trying not to offend, trying to come across as magnanimous. But Catholicism isn't supposed to be soft and easy. It's a religion of hard truths. The bishops have hidden the light of the faith under a bushel, just for the sake of social tranquility. They've made the Church a spiritual retail outlet of the secular culture. In fighting abortion, we're doing the job the Bishops don't have the fortitude to do themselves. We're saying "This is what it means to be Catholic. You've got to pay the price. Abortion is where you dig your trench and refuse to surrender." We're the keepers of the faith.

Conclusion

The Canadian pro-life movement is customarily, and stereotypically, assumed to be a puppet of the Catholic hierarchy.[33] From a superficial point of view, this assumption is justifiable. The movement, after all, is preponderantly Catholic in composition and is dedicated to a cause which, at least in principle, bears the blessing of the Canadian bishops. Closer scrutiny, however, reveals that the relationship of the movement to the hierarchy has been one more of defiance than of obeisance. It would be strange indeed for a mere puppet to have turned so angrily against its supposed master. Not only has the pro-life movement operated independently of the Catholic hierarchy, but many of its most dedicated members have regarded the Canadian bishops as moral inferiors incapable of taking an unequivocal stand against contraception and abortion. Indeed, for some of its Catholic participants the movement has become a conventicle of lay dissent against the adaptation of their national church to Canadian patterns of pluralism and denominationalism. Ironically, therefore, the very political cause which best conjures an image of Catholic concertedness has been a force of disruption rather than of unity for Canadian Catholicism.

---

33 On the stereotypical treatment of the pro-life movement in the Canadian news media, see Michael W. Cuneo, *Catholics Against the Church*, pp. 56–107.

8.

Liberation Theology as Social Science:
Contributions and Limitations

W. E. Hewitt

From the turmoil of Latin America in the middle decades of this century, Liberation Theology has emerged as an extremely important current in Catholic thought. On the one hand, it has contributed to an enhanced awareness of social conditions and exploitative class relations in Latin America generally. On the other hand, in countries such as Brazil, Chile, and Nicaragua, it has proven to be a powerful force justifying Catholic Church intervention in the alteration of the social, political, and economic *status quo*.

Though ostensibly a religious phenomenon, a central feature of Liberationism is its rootedness in 'this' as opposed to 'other-worldly' matters. The social and religious reality of Latin America, its adherents suggest, provides, in fact, the starting point for, and the rationale behind the development of an empirically grounded theology which expresses uniquely Third World concerns and aspirations.

To this point, the Liberationist worldview and analysis have been viewed relatively uncritically by interested observers of the Latin American scene. Even social scientists, for the most part, have failed to subject Liberationism's 'social-scientific' foundations to systematic evaluation. This chapter seeks to rectify this deficiency, through an examination of the central linkage between Liberationism and regional domination, using the same critical analysis which the model itself applies to Latin America. This is undertaken with specific reference to a wide body of empirical data, much of it drawn from Brazil—Latin America's largest country, and one where Liberationism has gained considerable respectability in recent years.

What the investigation reveals is a model much less tightly bound to the regional reality than Liberationists would care to admit. Indeed, summary investigation of its origins suggests that Liberationism's fundamental concerns are rooted less in material than in intellectual processes. The chapter concerns itself primarily, however, with the exposure of more serious irregularities in the interpretation of Latin American society upon which Liberationist 'theology' is ostensibly built. In their examination of the secular world, it is argued, Liberationists have tended to employ social-scientific tools of investigation selectively, while failing to make adequate use of available empirical evidence. This has given rise to an unduly circumscribed and often self-serving portrait of the region which not only misinforms, but seriously undercuts Liberationism's own credibility as a genuinely 'grounded' theology.

Basic Postulates of the Liberationist Perspective

Before proceeding with a critique of Liberationism and its relationship to the Latin American experience, it is important to outline some of the basic postulates of this brand of theology. This is no easy task, given that Liberation Theology comprises a number of diverse tendencies. The content of Liberationist writing often tends to reflect the varied origins of its prinicipal contributors in an array of social and geographical settings located throughout the length and breadth of Latin America. Indeed, some of its best known exponents, including Reubem Alves and José Míguez Bonino, are not even Catholic.

Such diversity in the Liberationist literature tends, for the most part, to be overlooked;[1] especially so with respect to political orientation. Many observers tend to assume that Liberationism is, in essence, Marxist—both in its interpretation of Latin American reality, and in its call for fundamental restructuring of the social order. But while some Liberationists, such as Miranda, rely heavily upon Marxian formulations, others do not. Sobrino, for example, makes few references to Marx, while Bonino, Comblin, Assman, and Boff, tend to be somewhat critical of Marxian thinking. Moreover, while most Liberationists affirm the need for revolutionary transformation in Latin America, by no means all of them accept solutions rooted in Marxism. While Gutiérrez and Dussel show a certain affection for the socialist model of the state and society, others such as Bonino are marginally sympathetic to a more humane form of capitalism. There are also differences with respect to the

---

1 The following discussion is based upon an overview provided by Deane William Ferm, *Third World Liberation Theologies* (Maryknoll: Orbis, 1986), Chapter 2. See also the major works of Liberationists as follows: Rubem Alves, *A Theology of Human Hope* (Maryknoll: Orbis, 1969); Hugo Assman, *Theology for a Nomad Church* (Maryknoll: Orbis, 1976); Leonardo Boff, *Jesus Christ Liberator* (Maryknoll: Orbis, 1978) and *Church: Charism and Power* (New York: Crossroads, 1985); José Comblin, *The Meaning of Mission: Jesus, Christians, and the Wayfaring Church* (Maryknoll: Orbis, 1977); Enrique Dussel, *Ethics and the Theology of Liberation* (Maryknoll: Orbis, 1978); Gustavo Gutiérrez, *A Theology of Liberation* (Maryknoll: Orbis, 1973); José Míguez Bonino, *Doing Theology in a Revolutionary Situation* (Philadelphia: Fortress, 1975); José Miranda, *Being and the Messiah* (Maryknoll: Orbis, 1977); Juan Luis Segundo, *The Liberation of Theology* (Maryknoll: Orbis, 1976); Jon Sobrino, *Christology at the Crossroads* (Maryknoll: Orbis, 1978). Additional sources cited throughout the text.

potential role of ideology in societal transformation. Some, such as Segundo and Assman, insist that ideology is a useful tool which must be employed actively in an effort to transform reality, while Gutiérrez and Alves adopt a more passive stance in this regard.

Within Liberationism, there is also great variation in attitudes toward traditional forms of Catholic teaching and practice. First, with respect to theology, some, including Sobrino, Boff, and Dussel, appear to reject European influence outright. Others, such as Gutiérrez and Alves, adopt a more conciliatory stance, arguing that traditional theology can at least provide a starting point for Liberationism. Secondly, disagreement abounds regarding the organization and activities of the traditional institutional Church. Segundo, for his part, is a virulent critic of traditional Catholic practices, especially the use of the sacraments, while Gutiérrez, Boff, and Comblin have been more subdued in their opposition. Thirdly, Liberationists are divided in their interpretation of the symbolic role of Christ in the Liberation process. For some, such as Gutiérrez, Sobrino, and especially Boff, Christ is a revolutionary on the side of the poor and oppressed, providing a salient example of leadership for the Church and its members in the political arena. For others, such as Alves and Segundo, this vision of Christ is less acceptable, although God *per se* may be seen as essentially liberating.

Despite their differences, there does, of course, exist a considerable measure of consensus among these various authors. With respect to basic *procedure*, first of all, there is a uniform commitment to a 'see-judge-act' methodology, involving: a) the recognition of empirical reality, b) biblical reflection, and c) proposals for ameliorative action. As regards the *content* of Liberationist writing, observers such as Cleary[2] have noted a number of themes running through the literature which contribute to a 'central core' of Liberationist thought. To begin with, Cleary notes, there is virtual unanimity among Liberationists regarding the utility of social-scientific analysis as the principal means for uncovering the essence of Latin American reality. Secondly, Liberationists essentially agree on a 'unified' vision of the world which questions the dichotomized, artificial religious/secular conception of history held by traditional Catholicism. Thirdly, they accept the inevitability of conflictual class relations, and fourthly, within the context of this conflict, actively support the political involvement of the institutional Church on the side of the poor. Fifthly, they assert that the prinicpal driving force behind such involvement is the now famous 'preferential option for the poor' which has been adopted and implemented in the various national Churches of Latin America. Finally, he suggests, there is a common abiding hope among Liberationists that the efforts of the poor and their supporters will result in a better world to come; one which expresses the values of the Biblical Kingdom of Heaven.

---

2 Edward L. Cleary, *Crisis and Change: The Church in Latin America Today* (Maryknoll: Orbis, 1985), pp. 83–97.

Origins of Latin American Liberationism

For Liberationists and others attracted to the model, the principal factor conditioning the development of these core concerns is the changing social reality of postwar Latin America.[3] In essence, they insist, Liberation Theology emerged as part of a coherent attempt to describe and understand the emergence of class-based consciousness and action among a predominantly Catholic lower class in response to three interrelated processes: rapid and uneven industrialization; the rationalization of agriculture; and the rise of bureaucratic-authoritarian regimes in a number of countries throughout the region. Consequently, it is *not*, Liberationists stress, a product of *institutional* initiative. Documents released in the progressive wake of Vatican II and the 1968 Medellín CELAM meetings, they assert, merely endorsed a process of theological renewal which was *already* underway in Latin America.

Not all those sympathetic to Liberation Theology, however, fully accept this account of its material roots. In his interpretation of the phenomenon, Cleary, for instance, assigns a much more central role to long-gestating changes in the political orientation of Church teaching which came to be incorporated into the curricula of Europe's major Catholic universities and schools of theology after 1960. It was within the walls of such institutions, he reminds us, that many aspiring Liberationists received their theological training. In addition, Cleary suggests, the current was further influenced by growing contact between Liberationists and Latin American social scientists. The latter, Cleary suggests, have historically maintained a more 'critical' (Marxist) perception of Third World reality than their counterparts elsewhere.[4]

Overt critics of Liberation Theology have similarly tended to emphasize intellectual influences over unique sociohistorical factors in accounting for the development of Liberationist thought. McCann,[5] for example, has tended to view the Latin American Liberation Theologian as the penultimate middle-class ideologue. Most Liberationists, he notes, are from well-established *criollo* families. Consequently, unlike the vast majority of their countrymen, they were uniquely positioned to take advantage of superior post-secondary training in the Catholic learning centres of Europe. Here, McCann suggests, concurring with Cleary, they came into close contact with the new social teaching of the Church. It was not their educational experience alone, however, McCann insists, which induced them to adopt the cause of the poor. If anything, they experienced a certain dissatisfaction with the instruction they had received in Europe, insofar as it left them less than prepared for their day-to-day pastoral work in Latin America. What eventually radicalized these individuals, Mc-

---

3 See, for example, Ferm, *Third World Liberation Theologies*, pp. 11–12.

4 Cleary, *Crisis and Change*, pp. 67–70.

5 Dennis McCann, *Christian Realism and Liberation Theology* (Maryknoll: Orbis, 1981), pp. 144–148.

Cann claims, was the first-hand knowledge of popular concerns which they gained through direct involvement with lower-class basic Christian communities and other lay groups. The glaring injustice which they saw present in these concrete situations, McCann concludes, induced them, with the aid of critical insight offered by their peers in social-scientific academic disciplines, to develop Liberation Theology as a new, more socially relevant alternative to traditional European theological expression.

Cleary and McCann thus introduce at least some measure of doubt into the Liberationist contention that their theology is a mere reflection of recent events occurring within Latin American society. Far more important for these authors is the way in which the career paths of an intellectual and social elite unfolded during a time of great changes in ecclesiastical teaching and action.

Liberationism and Social Science

In and of itself, however, the issue of whether Liberationism ultimately springs from a unique moment in history as opposed to a unique moment in the personal biography of its proponents is of relatively minor consequence. Far more important, and indeed potentially fatal to Liberation Theology, is the gap which exists between fact and fancy in the Liberationist conception of what precisely constitutes the current Latin American reality.

Problems with the Liberationist use or misuse of social science to reveal this reality can be identified in a number of areas. Here, discussion will focus upon distortions contained in the Liberationist interpretation of general postwar transformations in Latin American society, and with respect to specific developments within the Roman Catholic Church, namely, the rise of the 'preferential option for the poor,' and the phenomenon of the basic Christian communities or CEBs.

The Liberationist Interpretation of Recent History

In their analysis of recent Latin American social, political, and economic history, Liberationists have relied upon two of the standard diagnostic tools of Marxist sociology: dependency theory and class analysis. Their utilization of both, however, has been far from unproblematic.

For its part, the dependency approach of Baran, Frank, Wallerstein, and others[6]

---

6 For a general overview of the dependency model, and a sample of original writing in this field, see Hamza Alavi and Teodor Shanin, eds., *Introduction to the Sociology of Developing Societies* (New York: Monthly Review Press, 1982). The most recent critique of the literature on development and underdevelopment is Robert G. Gilpin, "Development and Underdevelopment: Conflicting Perspectives on the Third World," in Sidney Hook, William L. O'Neill and Roger O'Toole, eds., *Philosophy, History and Social Action* (Dordrecht, Boston and London: Kluwer Academic Publishers, 1988), pp. 173–208.

is used by Liberationists such as Gutiérrez, Assman and Dussel[7] to explain overall trends in Latin American society since the end of the Second World War. Since that time, the Liberationist version of the model holds, the profound disruptions which the region has experienced—involving sporadic industrialization, rapid urbanization, and the rationalization of agriculture—have been conditioned primarily by Latin America's dependent position within a world trading system dominated by a handful of wealthy, industrialized nations. The world's developed countries, it is argued, have an abiding interest in maintaining relations of international exchange favourable to them. To a considerable extent, this has meant preserving and encouraging colonialist relations with Latin America, primarily through the importation of low-priced materials, and the subsequent exportation of finished goods back to the region. Some development, Liberationists admit, has occurred, but the pace and extent of growth has been tightly controlled by a select group of multinational companies with head offices in New York or London. Moreover, the benefits of any and all domestic growth have accrued, for the most part, to foreign elites and their local 'comprador' agents. For the poor, development of this sort has meant nothing but misery. Many more rural workers have been drawn to city factories than are needed, resulting in poor wages, overcrowding and inadequate services. Those who remain on the land have been forced from their subsistence plots into employment by agricultural conglomerates in the production, at starvation wages, of cash crops for export. International programmes, designed at face value to facilitate more balanced growth in the region, Liberationists add, have actually assisted the exploitation process. The IMF, the World Bank, and programmes like the ill-fated Alliance for Progress, are simply tools used by foreign capitalists and their agents in Latin America to maintain trade relations favourable to their interests.

The trends in migration, income distribution, and so forth which the Liberationist literature describes cannot be refuted. There is little question that industry-led growth has largely failed to meet the rising aspirations of the poor, that urban areas have grown at a rate far exceeding that for the provision of basic services, and that rural wages and working conditions have worsened in response to the 'capitalization' of agriculture in recent years. As an analytical tool for explaining these facts, however, the utility of the dependency model which Liberationists have espoused may be seriously questioned.

For one thing, the dependency approach tends to overemphasize economic factors and transnational class interests in its interpretation of the development process, at the expense of indigenous cultural variables. Certainly, there has been no attempt to account for the role of regionalism and regional interests in the development of

---

7 For an example of how the model has been applied by these and other authors, see Enrique Dussel, "Current Events in Latin America," in Sergio Torres and John Eagleson, eds., *The Challenge of Basic Christian Communities*, trans. John Drury (Maryknoll: Orbis, 1981), pp. 77–102; and Cleary, *Crisis and Change*, pp. 69–73.

Brazil,[8] or the 'ethnic' character of early industrialization in São Paulo[9] or Buenos Aires.[10] Secondly, the dependency model overestimates the degree of foreign economic ownership and control in Latin America. On the one hand, trade between Latin America and the developed world—ostensibly a key mechanism of economic subservience—is not nearly as extensive as many would believe. Latin America, in fact, currently accounts for less than six percent of all world exchange in commodities.[11] On the other hand, foreign investment in the region is far from pervasive. Between 1950 and 1965, for example, the United States—the world's principal 'core' nation—invested about $US 3.8 billion in Latin America, or about $US 253 million per year. As Novak[12] has observed, this amount would hardly seem sufficient to ensure the submission of the entire region. Moreover, there is evidence that the level of U.S. involvement is falling dramatically. In 1950, Latin America accounted for 39 percent of U.S. investment outflows. By 1968, this figure had dropped to 20 percent.[13] In many countries, it might also be noted, private offshore sources have been surpassed by Latin American governments as major investors—if anything, it is now the state sector which is the dominant force in the local development process. In Brazil, for instance, federal and state companies control 75 percent of the assets of the country's hundred largest enterprises.[14] A final criticism of the dependency approach is that it fails to account for the meteoric rise of Latin America's industrial capacity in recent years. Between 1945 and 1975, the average annual GNP growth rate for Latin America was in excess of five percent, twice that recorded for the developed world.[15] Brazil, in particular, between 1950 and 1987, experienced an industrial boom which elevated it from the world's 48th to the 7th largest economy.[16]

---

8 See Hélio Jaguaribe, "Political Strategies of National Development in Brazil," in Irving Louis Horowitz, et al., eds., *Latin American Radicalism* (New York: Vintage, 1969), pp. 390–439.

9 See Warren Dean, *The Industrialization of São Paulo, 1880–1945* (Austin: University of Texas Press, 1969).

10 See Gino Germani, "Mass Immigration and Modernization in Argentina," in Horowitz, *Latin American Radicalism,* pp. 314–355.

11 Fernando Cardoso, "Dependency and Development in Latin America," in Alavi and Shanin, *Sociology of Developing Societies,* p. 125.

12 Michael Novak, "Why Latin America is Poor," *Atlantic Monthly* (March 1982), p. 70.

13 Michael Dodson, "Liberation Theology and Christian Radicalism in Contemporary Latin America," *Journal of Latin American Studies* 11 (1979), p. 213.

14 Peter Evans, *Dependent Development: The Alliance of Multinational, State, and Local Capital in Brazil* (Princeton: Princeton University Press, 1979), p. 224.

15 See Novak, "Why Latin America is Poor," p. 74.

16 See Brazil-Canada Chamber of Commerce, *Background on Brazil* (Toronto: BCCC, 1986).

Aside from problems with the model *per se*, there also exist a number of difficulties with the way in which Liberationists have adapted the dependency approach for their own use. First, they have tended to apply the model as if it were a coherent theoretical framework. In fact, it is not a unified theory at all, but rather a collection of approaches for understanding underdevelopment. These, furthermore, vary greatly in terms of scope and quality. Cruder forms of the model, such as as that offered by Frank,[17] dwell almost exclusively on patterns of trade, while Cardoso,[18] by contrast, offers a much more sophisticated account focusing on domestic and international class linkages. Secondly, Liberationists have tended to apply their brand of dependency theory in blanket form to the countries of Latin America. As is well known, however, there are considerable differences in national development levels. Paraguay could hardly be compared to Argentina, or Bolivia to Brazil, in terms of GNP per capita, value of industrial output, provision of education or social services, and so on.[19]

Class analysis, the other social-scientific tool which Liberationists employ to interpret the ebb and flow of recent Latin American history—often hand in glove with dependency theory—falls prey to another whole set of deficiencies. For the most part, these can be traced to the way in which Liberationists have utilized this Marxist analytical device. In rather simplistic fashion, they tend to see Latin American society as defined primarily by struggle between two social classes. On the one side are the externally supported agents of oppression—foreign and comprador elites, and landholders—and on the other, the great mass of the subjugated poor.

Considered in its static sense, first of all, the black and white conception of class situation which Liberationism has developed is never established empirically. Nor can it be. To begin with, between the extremes posited by Liberationist class theory, a small but identifiable middle class of professionals, government and white-collar workers has existed in Latin America since at least the 1930s.[20] Moreover, it is an error to assume the existence of homogenous strata at the extremes of the class spectrum. On the one hand, the so-called dominant classes of countries like Brazil or Mexico do not constitute anything approaching a unified bloc, and, in fact, are often extremely divided in terms of economic and life interests. As McDonough[21]

---

17 See, for example, Andre Gunder Frank, *Latin America: Underdevelopment and Revolution* (New York: Monthly Review Press, 1969).

18 See Fernando Henrique Cardoso and Enzo Faletto, *Development and Dependency in Latin America* (Berkeley: University of California Press, 1979).

19 See Dodson, "Liberation Theology," p. 211.

20 See, for example, Luis Ratinoff, "The New Urban Groups: The Middle Classes," in S. M. Lipset and Aldo Solari, eds., *Elites in Latin America* (New York: Oxford University Press, 1967), pp. 61–93.

21 Peter McDonough, *Power and Ideology in Brazil* (Princeton: Princeton University Press, 1981).

has shown in the case of Brazil, commonalities in terms of attitudes and behaviour among elites are frequently superseded by divisive regional, religious, ethnic, and other concerns. On the other hand, it is equally inappropriate to speak of the 'poor' as an undifferentiated category. Factory or blue-collar workers in urban areas earn far more and have adopted a lifestyle significantly different from underemployed slum dwellers. Similarly, small landholders may be poor by contrast with farmers in developed countries, but share little in common with landless peasants.

Table 1

Class Differences in Attitudes and Behaviour in Brazil (in percentages)

Attitude or Behaviour	Social Class		
	Lower (n=2433)	Middle (n=1670)	Tau B
Interested in politics	42	47	.044*
Have participated in political rallies	15	15	.001
Support strikes	49	52	.030*
Party identification			
PT	7	5	−.013
PMDB	35	35	
PTB	4	3	
PDT	6	6	
PDS	19	26	
Military should leave	28	30	.015
Support Church involvement in politics	32	29	−.028*
Support moral teaching of Church	66	62	−.046*

* Indicates that differences between categories are significant at or below the .05 level.

Nor are social classes in Latin America dynamic in the Marxist sense that they are locked in struggle. Despite differences in income and quality of life, there is often, in fact, as much consensus as conflict between dominant and subordinate strata. This observation may be demonstrated effectively through an examination of surveys recently conducted in Brazil on politico-religious attitudes and behaviour. One such study, which polled some 4200 urban respondents located in all parts of the country in 1982, revealed middle/upper and lower-class attitudinal and behavioural similarities in a number of key respects.[22] These are summarized in Table 1.

---

22 This survey was conducted prior to the 1982 Brazilian general election by the Rio de Janeiro-based *Grupo de Estudos sobre Partidos, Eleições, e Problemas Institucionais* of the *Associação Nacional de Programas de Pequisa e Pós—Graduação em Ciências*

Differences between classes on most items, as can be seen, are minimal. On some items, it is true, lower-class respondents do appear slightly more politically progressive than their more affluent counterparts, insofar as they are more likely to support left of centre parties such as the PT (Workers' Party), and the PTB (Party of the Brazilian Worker). Nevertheless, certain conservative tendencies among the poor are also clearly in evidence. Note, for example, that lower-class respondents are actually less likely to call for an end to the military dictatorship of the time, less interested in politics, and less supportive of workers' strikes than informants from more elevated class groups. In addition, though slightly more approving of Church involvement in political action, they are more likely to accept the traditional moral teaching of Catholicism.

Table 2

Class Differences in Attitudes and Behaviour of CEB Members
in the Archdiocese of São Paulo (in percentages)

Attitude or behaviour	Social Class		
	Lower (n=151)	Middle (n=124)	Tau B
Believed to defend interests:			
Unions	62	56	−.060
Armed Forces	34	38	.042
Catholic Church	82	83	.010
Government	18	29	.132*
Politicians	19	15	−.050
Support the PT	39	18	−.232*

* Indicates that differences between categories are significant at or below the .05 level.

Still another survey of participants of Roman Catholic basic Christian communities (CEBs) conducted in 1984 confirms these findings (see Table 2).[23] As expected, lower-class group members are less supportive of the government, and somewhat more confident in unions and working-class parties (such as the PT) than their middle-class counterparts. Nevertheless, they also express a degree of confidence in both the armed forces and the Church roughly equal to that of more affluent CEB participants.

Sociais.

23 See W. E. Hewitt, *The Structure and Orientation of Comunidades Eclesiais de Base (CEBs) in the Archdiocese of São Paulo* (Ph.D. dissertation, McMaster University, 1985).

Such evidence is not intended to negate the existence of serious inequality between social groups in Latin America generally, nor to deny the presence of class polarization, especially where economic interests are concerned. Certainly there are numerous instances of overt class conflict in Latin America, and much evidence of what Gutiérrez refers to as the 'irruption of the poor.'[24] The peasant unions and uprisings in Brazil and Peru of the late 1950s, as well as the Cuban and Central American 'liberation' movements, might be cited here as proof of a restless lower-class hungry for social justice. The question remains, however, as to whether or not such specific instances are necessarily indicative of a newly emergent general revolutionary class consciousness among the poor.

Lower-class involvement in Central American national 'liberation' movements does, most certainly, support the case for incipient popular revolutionary sentiment and action in Latin America. Nevertheless, as Levine has pointed out, "the situation [in this area] is so extreme as to be unrepresentative."[25] When the region as a whole is taken into account, many have argued, instances of popular revolt might more appropriately be interpreted within the context of the 'patron-client' pattern of class relations which has pervaded Latin American political culture since the Discovery.[26]

The peasant league activity of late 1950s and early 1960s Brazil provides a case in point. These organizations, it has frequently been argued, were as much oriented to reestablishing customary landholder-peasant relations in the face of agricultural rationalization, as to furthering land reform as a political cause. As Adriance[27] points out, the Agricultural Society of Planters and Cattlemen of Pernambuco, one of the earliest peasant movements of the era, was stimulated not by revolutionary conviction, but from a concrete threat to the *status quo*, that is, "eviction from the land in order to make way for capital-based cane production." In keeping with the patron-client pattern, moreover, many of these rural labour organizations relied heavily upon the organizational and political expertise of middle-class leaders. Among the most notable of these were Francisco Julião, an activist lawyer from the city of Recife, and Pernambuco state governor Miguel Arrães, who negotiated with large landholders in defence of peasant interests. Other peasant associations were organized and led by activists from groups as diverse as the Brazilian Communist

---

24 Gustavo Gutiérrez, "The Irruption of the Poor in Latin America and the Christian Communities of the Common People," in Torres and Eagleson, *Basic Christian Communities*, pp. 107–123.

25 Daniel Levine, "Holiness, Faith, Power, Politics," *Journal for the Scientific Study of Religion* 26 (1987), p. 557.

26 See, for example, Irving Louis Horowitz, "Electoral Politics, Urbanization, and Social Development in Latin America," in Horowitz, *Latin American Radicalism*, pp. 140–176; and in the same volume, Merle King, "Violence and Politics in Latin America," pp. 191–206.

27 Madeleine Adriance, *Opting for the Poor* (Kansas City: Sheed and Ward, 1986), p. 34.

Party and the Roman Catholic Church. Some were even stimulated and encouraged by the federal government, in an effort to capture and channel rural dissent.[28]

Even in present-day Latin America, in advanced industrial sectors of the economy, patron-client relations continue to structure the pattern of conflict between classes. In many countries, trade unions have long operated under the paternal supervision of the state.[29] Where conflict between workers and management has erupted, furthermore, the state has frequently assumed the role of 'super-patron,' mediating between opposing parties in an effort to restore harmonious relations.[30]

The Liberationist View of the Changing Role of the Church

As part of their more general deliberations concerning the path of recent Latin American history, Liberationists have made considerable efforts to describe and interpret two crucial developments within the Roman Catholic Church itself: the rise of the Church's 'preferential option for the poor,' and the phenomenon of the basic Christian communities or CEBs. Here again, however, Liberationist analysis has been undertaken with less than vigorous adherence to the norms of social science.

1) The Preferential Option for the Poor

For its part, the development of the Church's 'preferential option for the poor' tends to be interpreted by Liberationists as part of a process directly paralleling events unfolding within Latin American society generally. Thus, rather than considering institutional exigencies, the role of leadership, or official doctrine—such as that emerging from Vatican II or Medellín—in the development of the 'option,' they focus instead upon the role of the emergently conscious subordinate classes in effecting religious transformation.[31]

---

28 See Emmanuel de Kadt, *Catholic Radicals in Brazil* (London: Oxford University Press, 1970), pp. 25, 48, 60, 195.

29 See Emilio Maspero, "Trade Unionism as an Instrument of the Latin American Revolution," in Horowitz, *Latin American Radicalism*, pp. 207–231.

30 For an excellent overview of state-worker relations in Brazil, see Kenneth Erickson, *The Brazilian Corporative State and Working-Class Politics* (Berkeley: University of California Press, 1977).

31 See, among others, Alvaro Barreiro, *Basic Ecclesial Communities*, translated by Barbara Campbell (Maryknoll: Orbis, 1982); Frei Betto, *O Que É Comunidade Eclesial de Base?* (São Paulo: Brasiliense, 1981) and "As Comunidades Eclesiais de Base como Potencial de Transformação da Sociedade Brasileira," *Revista Eclesiástica Brasileira* 43 (1983); Leonardo Boff, "Theological Characteristics of a Grassroots Church," in Torres and Eagleson, *Basic Christian Communities*, pp. 124-144, and "CEBs: A Igreja inteira na base," *REB* 43 (1983).

The 'option for the poor' arose, authors such as Dussel[32] and Gutiérrez[33] explain, as the secular struggles of an inherently Christian population for justice and equality came to permeate the structure of the institutional Church. There, as in society generally, asserts Gutiérrez, "the poor [have] increasingly [gotten] across their right to live their faith." The Church was able to respond to this pressure, adds Leonardo Boff,[34] since it is a relatively autonomous institution, and consequently not condemned to a conservative function, as orthodox Marxism might claim.

Similarly, Maduro[35] sees the change occurring within the Latin American Church as the result of class conflict coinciding with the rise of the 'national security state' during the 1960's and early 1970's. In response to economic and political repression, the poor, he argues, have turned to the Church as the one available space where they could freely direct their opposition to the State. Thus, they have moved to 'take over' the Latin American Church, breaking the chains which have traditionally bound it to the dominant classes.

Certainly, there is no question that the hierarchy's adoption of a 'preferential option for the poor' was *conditioned* by the suffering of the least privileged classes in Latin America. Nevertheless, one must seriously question the notion that this change has resulted from a 'takeover' orchestrated by the lower classes themselves. As Bruneau,[36] for example, points out, the Church (or any religious movement, for that matter), is not defined primarily by economic relations of domination and subordination. Rather, it might more appropriately be described as a community of believers. In addition, he asserts, the Church is not *all* of society, nor does it embrace within it—even metaphorically speaking—all productive means. It is difficult to see, consequently, how the dynamics of class could permeate it as thoroughly as the Liberationist perspective suggests.

Aside from the question of theoretical plausibility, Liberationists have failed to provide empirical evidence for the existence of any large-scale social movement of or for the poor and oppressed within the Church. They have merely *assumed* its presence—often as not citing the large numbers of politically active basic Christian communities operating in Latin America. The CEBs, however, do not necessarily provide evidence of a widespread popular desire for social change. While these groups do possess very real sociopolitical implications, even the most generous estimates put their numerical strength at fewer than 200 thousand. Thus, allowing some 50 members per group, the total number of Latin Americans participating in this innovative phenomenon would number 10 million—an impressive figure, to be

---

32 Dussel, "Current Events in Latin America."

33 Gutiérrez, "The Irruption of the Poor in Latin America."

34 Boff, "Theological Characteristics of a Grassroots Church."

35 Otto Maduro, *Religion and Social Conflicts* (Maryknoll: Orbis, 1982).

36 Thomas C. Bruneau, "Church and Politics in Brazil: The Genesis of Change," *Journal of Latin American Studies* 17 (May 1985), p. 289.

sure, but one which represents only about 4 percent of the entire population of the region.

Table 3

Rates of Agreement with Church Action Among Lower and
Middle-Class Practising Catholics (in percentages)

Type of action	Social Class		
	Lower (n=1012)	Middle (n=748)	Tau B
Recent changes in Church	55	64	.088*
Political participation of Church personnel	30	26	−.018
Church involvement in agrarian reform	57	50	−.054*
Church support for strikes	52	45	−.041*
Church teaching on family education	82	75	−.083*
Church teaching on family life	54	53	−.008
Church teaching on morality	68	68	.008

* Indicates that differences between categories on item are significant
at or below the .05 level.

The results of the 1982 Brazilian survey mentioned previously, conducted at the very height of Church activity in the political arena, further demonstrate the difficulty of locating any well defined, activist lower-class constituency with strong ties to the Church. The survey findings—a select portion of which are summarized in Table 3—illustrate that among those of the poor who identify themselves as practising Catholics, support for Church action in the social justice sphere is both uneven and ambiguous. For example, the table shows lower-class approval of post-Vatican II changes in the Church to be relatively high; yet this support drops considerably where Church participation in politics is concerned. Further, where the poor within the Church show strong support for involvement in agrarian matters and workers' strikes, they are equally likely to approve of more traditional Church teaching such as that on family life. Perhaps most surprisingly, the highest approval ratings among lower-class respondents are reserved for Church teaching on religious education and morality. It might be noted as well, that on many of the items presented in the table, the poor do not distinguish themselves from their middle-class counterparts in any meaningful way. Though generally somewhat more supportive of Church teaching and action (with the exception of approval for post-Vatican II changes), lower-class informants view the Church and Church activities in much the same light as do their more affluent counterparts.

The relative weakness of any 'grassroots' social movement backing Church in-

Table 4

Approval of Core Items of Church's Option for the Poor among
Lower- and Middle-Class Practising Catholics (in percentages)

	Social Class	
	Lower	Middle
	(n=1012)	(n=748)
Approve all forms of political	19	18
action (items 2 to 4 in Table 1)		
Do not uniformly approve	81	82

p=0.1994;   tau b=−.020.

volvement in social justice issues may be similarly revealed in the limited proportion of respondents agreeing in whole or part with all of the three critical variables associated with the social justice current. As we see from Table 4, only about 21 percent of all lower-class Catholics agree in some measure with Church action in politics, agrarian reform, *and* workers' strikes. This figure, it is true, is marginally higher than for the middle class, and shows, in and of itself, a significant base of lower-class support for Church involvement in political matters. Nevertheless, here again, it is more than apparent that there exists in Latin America's largest country no exclusive movement of the believing and faithful poor and oppressed of the intensity or size envisioned by Liberationists such as Dussel, Gutiérrez or Maduro.

2) *The Role of the CEBs in Societal Transformation*

Liberationists have been less than thorough, also in their description and interpretation of the recently emergent basic Christian community (CEB) phenomenon. These small, faith-inspired and politically active lay circles have been assigned a key role in the social transformation process as Liberationists have interpreted it. In effect, they are seen as evidence that the long-gestating radicalism of the masses, operating within a religious context, has finally risen to the surface of Latin American society. As the principal carriers of this revolutionary fervour, the CEBs, Liberation Theologians claim, will ultimately bring about the people's total emancipation from centuries-old social, economic, political, and even religious oppression.

Recent social scientific research in Brazil, where at least 70,000 CEBs are located, paints a somewhat different portrait of the CEBs and their societal role. One such study was conducted by the author in 1984 in the southeastern Archdiocese of São Paulo. On the one hand, this research, which involved some 22 groups located in a variety of social and geographical locations, demonstrates the existence of far more CEB heterogeneity—in terms of structure and orientation—than previously revealed by the Liberationist literature. On the other hand, the study points to the importance of non-material factors in determining the shape of CEB activation. Rather than a product of grassroots innovation, as Liberationists would suggest, the CEBs are shown to be largely a product of institutional initiative.

Heterogeneity of the CEB Phenomenon: Within the 22 CEB sample, heterogeneity of form and action, first of all, is clearly evident in a number of respects, beginning with the most basic background characteristics. Group ages, for instance, as presented in Table 5, range anywhere from 1 to 17 years, while the number of group participants varies from 5 to 50. Moreover, though females and older people are dominant within many groups, different CEBs nevertheless attract different proportions of the two constituencies. Finally, the data reveal a relatively high level of fluidity within CEBs. This is evidenced by the turnover apparent within more mature groups. Though Table 5 shows at least 8 groups aged 9 to 17 years, very few (1 or 2) CEB members indicated on questionnaires that they had been affiliated with their group for more than 7 years.

Table 5

Basic Features of Sample CEBs

Characteristic	Number of CEBs (n=22)
Group age:	
0–3 years	8
4–8	6
9–17	8
Group size:	
5–15 members	9
16–30	8
31–50	5
Sex ratio:	
Predominantly female (over 60%)	14
Even	6
Predominantly male (over 60%)	2
Members' mean age:	
Under 40	6
Over 40	16

Perhaps most importantly, a good deal of diversity was uncovered as well in the class background of group members. Quite clearly, the CEBs are not exclusively lower-class, as Liberationism would seem to suggest. In fact, as Table 6 shows, the social location of the sample communities is extremely diverse, with groups located in every possible type of setting, from well-manicured middle-class neighbourhoods to *favelas* (slums) on the outskirts of the city. These findings confirm the results of previous research conducted by both the National Conference of Brazilian Bishops[37] and Afonso Gregory.[38] While these sources affirm that the bulk of Brazilian CEBs are formed among the rural and semi-urban poor, both also indicate that a sizable minority can be found in strictly urban areas, the preserve of the middle classes. In the bishops' study, 17 percent of CEBs polled were situated in urban residential areas, while the figure for the Gregory report is about 9 percent. Bruneau also, in his 1982 study of Catholic lay groups in Brazil, concludes that the CEBs are not exclusively communities of the poor and oppressed. As a strategy, claims Bruneau, the CEBs relate to all social classes.[39]

Table 6

Social Location of Sample CEBs

Area	Number of CEBs (n=22)
Upper Middle Class	3
Middle Class	8
Working Class	8
Favela or Cortiço	3

Such diversity of background features is also apparent in the variety of activities which the sample CEBs from São Paulo undertake and in the organizational forms which they have developed in support of these. Instead of pursuing a limited range of societally transforming activities, as the Liberationist literature argues, the CEBs, in actuality, engage in a limitless array of religious and political functions operationalized through a variety of means.

The main activities in which the sample CEBs are engaged can be grouped into two broad categories. The first group consists of the more traditional functions of a kind which have been historically practised in Catholic lay groups. These include: i) bible study (in the strict interpretive sense); ii) charity work; and iii) the planning of festive occasions to mark holy days. Secondly, there are the more innovative

---

37 Conferência Nacional dos Bispos do Brasil, *Comunidades: Igreja na base* (São Paulo: Paulinas, 1977), pp. 20–21.

38 Afonso Gregory, "Dados Preliminares sobre Experiências de Comunidades Eclesiais de Base no Brasil," in *Comunidades Eclesiais de Base: Utopia ou Realidade?* ed. Afonso Gregory (Petrópolis: Vozes, 1973).

39 Thomas C. Bruneau, *The Church in Brazil* (Austin: University of Texas Press, 1982), p. 140.

activities which have largely appeared in the wake of Vatican II and have come to be synonymous with the CEB phenomenon in Brazil. Such functions, which possess significant political implications for both the Church and Brazilian society generally, include: i) the preparation and offering (often by lay ministers) of local religious services known as *celebrações*; ii) preparation for, and offering of certain other sacraments (baptism in particular); iii) reflection and discussion (where CEB members critically discuss biblical teaching in light of the existing social reality); iv) political consciousness-raising (designed to awaken the local citizenry to the reality of social, economic and political oppression); and finally v) community action projects. This last activity is perhaps the most explicitly political function which the CEBs practise. In lower-class semi-urban or rural areas, community projects are normally designed to secure basic services, infrastructural improvements, land or legal land title for residents. In more affluent urban neighbourhoods, where local needs are obviously somewhat different, community action usually takes a less drastic form, involving perhaps *mutirões* (joint-labour initiatives), neighbourhood crime watches, food cooperatives, or CEB promotion in adjacent slum areas.

The organizational structures which the CEBs have adopted are equally varied. With regard to group leadership, first of all, a number of options exist. Some CEBs are directed by individual lay leaders or *pastoral agents* dispatched by the Church. Others possess lay-run *conselhos* (councils) which are either elected or volunteer-based. Moreover, depending upon the complexity, type, and the number of activities undertaken, CEBs may sometimes maintain auxiliary sub-groups or teams which are given responsiblity for coordinating specific functions or facilitating these functions in a more intimate setting. Groups which emphasize religious functions also often possess their own locally trained lay ministers. Even the range of CEB meeting times and places is quite varied. Some CEBs meet once a week, others less frequently; some meet in members' homes, some in Church basements, and still others in their own locally constructed community centres.

Factors Influencing CEB Activation: Based upon the various combinations of activities and organizational forms present within the sample groups, one may, for purposes of analysis, construct a number of CEB types or categories. All in all,[40] some 6 types present themselves, ranging from simple devotional groups (Type I) which engage in basic religious functions such as Bible reading and charity work, to ideal-typical CEBs (Type VI) which possess their own community centres, are run by elected *conselhos* and are regularly involved in an intricately organized web of complex religious and advanced political activities. A summary of these types

---

40 See W. E. Hewitt, "Basic Christian Communities (CEBs): Structure, Orientation and Sociopolitical Thrust," *Thought*, 63 (June 1988), pp. 162–175; in a similar manner, Welsh has developed a number of CEB types based upon his experience with basic communities in São Paulo state. See, John R. Welsh, "Comunidades Eclesiais de Base: A New Way to be Church," *America* 8 (1986), pp. 85–88.

and their basic attributes is presented in Table 7 (on the next page).

Such a codification helps to simplify the very complex portrait of CEB heterogeneity presented earlier. It is a useful tool, moreover, for assessing Liberationist assumptions with respect to the relationship between the material conditions of existence which the CEBs endure and group activation—in particular, the supposed link between social class, CEB maturity and the tendency towards political progressiveness.

Further analysis of these CEB types reveals, in fact, little relationship between these variables. There is simply no evidence provided by the data to suggest, for example, that the ranks of the most advanced CEBs are open only to groups of lower-class origin. Nor is it evident that the CEBs move through a kind of staging process, where, seasoned by the hardships of confronting their social and political reality, they eventually reach advanced levels of political engagement.

Table 8

Social Location and Age of CEB Types

| | CEB Types | | | | | |
Features	I (n=5)	II (n=1)	III (n=4)	IV (n=5)	V (n=1)	VI (n=6)
Social location:						
Lower class	3	1	1	–	–	6
Middle class	2	–	3	5	1	–
Group age:						
Under 5 years	3	–	1	1	–	4
Over 5 years	2	1	3	4	1	2

These assertions can be substantiated by breaking down each of the CEB types by social location and age, as has been done in Table 8. With respect to social location, first of all, the table reveals that both lower- and middle-class groups are capable of adopting a variety of forms. Certainly, it *is* true that some CEB types tend to occur more frequently in certain settings. For example, CEBs of types III, IV, and V tend to be more popular within middle-class areas, while the most advanced CEBs of Type VI are exclusively lower-class. Nevertheless, the table shows that within the more politically advanced types *generally* (IV to VI), lower- and middle-class groups are almost equally represented.

As in the case of social class, group age, which reflects the length of time which a CEB has had to interact with the environment, also has no strong effect on politicization and organizational development. Newer CEBs, Table 8 shows, are just as likely as older ones to adopt more advanced, or conversely, more elementary

Table 7

Typology of CEBs

Feature	CEB Category**					
	I (n=5)	II (n=1)	III (n=4)	IV (n=5)	V (n=1)	VI (n=6)
Traditional activities:						
Charity work	*	*	*	*		*
Bible study	*	*	*	*		*
Festive days	*	*	*	*		*
Innovative activities:						
Preparation and offering of celebrações		*		*		*
Preparation for and offering of other sacraments		*		*		*
Reflection and discussion		*		*		*
Political consciousness-raising			*	*	*	*
Basic community action				*		
Advanced community action					*	*
Organizational features:						
Functional subgroups		*		*	*	*
Conselho		*		*	*	*
Lay ministers		*		*	*	*
Meet in community centre		*		*	*	*

* Indicates presence of feature in question
** Designated names of CEB types are as follows:

Type I:	Simple Devotional
Type II:	Devotional Mini-Parish
Type III:	Elementary Devotional and Political
Type IV:	Politically Oriented Mini-Parish
Type V:	Politically Oriented Missionary
Type VI:	Classical or Ideal-Typical

forms.

One factor which does consistently appear as an independent variable explaining CEB activation is the quality of leadership in the groups which, as we saw, varies significantly from CEB to CEB. Liberationists, for their part, tend to downplay this aspect of CEB life. The groups, in their view, are born not of institutional initiative, but of a popular desire for liberation. In them, the people work in unison for total emancipation. External activists, be they the bishops or their designated agents (who are most often recruited from within the ranks of the middle classes), act as mere advisors, helping only to guide the people's own emergent political consciousness. Borrowing a term from the Italian neo-Marxist Antonio Gramsci, Clodovis Boff[41] has described such individuals as 'organic intellectuals' who aid— but do not directly excite—the revolutionary potential of the popular will in specific sociohistorical contexts.

Table 9

Effect of Leadership on CEB Type

	CEB Type					
	I	II	III	IV	V	VI
Quality of leadership	(n=5)	(n=1)	(n=4)	(n=5)	(n=1)	(n=6)
Pastoral agent directly present and politically oriented	1	–	–	–	1	4
Pastoral agent not present and/or not politically oriented	4	1	4	5	–	2

The sample data reveal, however, a much more direct association between the presence of pastoral agents and various aspects of group life. The precise nature of this relationship is represented in Table 9. Here we have broken down the CEB types delimited previously by the quality of pastoral agents' presence. The political orientation of religious personnel and the degree to which they spent time in individual CEBs were determinined through interviews and participant observation. Priests and nuns designated as progressive were those who generally upheld the Church's 'option for the poor' and the political role of the CEBs, while those deemed traditional tended to avoid political or class-related themes. To be designated directly present, religious personnel had actively to serve their CEB in a leadership capacity.

What Table 9 indicates is that *group type complexity is directly and positively linked to the presence of Church representatives active in a leadership capacity.*

---

41 Clodovis Boff, "Agente de Pastoral e Povo," *REB* 40 (1980): 216–241.

Among the more basic group types (I to III), first of all, politically active pastoral agents are all but nonexistent. At the other end of the scale, where the more advanced group types (IV to VI) are concerned, the situation is slightly more complex, yet consistent with the general pattern. Pastoral agents, while not present in Type IV groups—which in any case tend to undertake more basic forms of political activity— are rarely absent in Types V and VI which engage in the most explicit forms of community action.

Contrary to Liberationist assumptions, then, it is the institutional Church, rather than extant material conditions, which exerts the greater influence over when, where, and how the groups will emerge. Moreover, the Church has a good deal of influence—through the manner in which pastoral agents are selected, trained, and dispatched—in the determination of the organizational structure and activity profile of individual CEBs.

Conclusion

This examination in no way seeks to challenge the theological validity of Liberation Theology or to assess its utility as a force for badly needed socioeconomic and political change in Latin America. It does, however, take issue with Liberationism's self-proclaimed grounding in Latin American reality. Not only can Liberationism's materialist roots be questioned—insofar as biographical factors outweigh sociohistorical influences in its generation—but there also exist serious gaps in the 'social scientific' understanding of Latin America upon which Liberation Theology is built. As has been shown, its interpretation of recent secular and Church history, including the nature and role of CEBs, often displays a questionable use of diagnostic tools and a measurable disregard for readily available empirical data. In essence, then, Liberationism—which claims to be anchored in social scientific analysis—has failed to meet the standards of social science to which, as Dodson quite correctly points out, it is accountable.[42]

Lakeland[43] suggests in a recent review essay that there may well be, at present, a move on the part of Gutiérrez and other Liberationists to address these criticisms and to correct their past errors with respect to economic and political analysis. Obviously, however, there are very real constraints on the extent to which the Liberationist conception of Latin American reality may be altered to remove misleading distortions and to provide a more solid basis for Liberationist 'theology.' In the final analysis, as authors such as Dodson and Bruneau have pointed out, Liberationism is more ideological than objectively analytical. Liberationists, after all, are men of faith. Their fundamental interest lies not in describing reality for the sake of knowledge, but in promoting profound change designed to make the world a more

---

42 Dodson, "Liberation Theology and Christian Radicalism," p. 211.

43 Paul Lakeland, "Will it Liberate? Questions about Democratic Capitalism," *Cross Currents* 37 (Summer/Fall 1987), pp. 339–341.

'Christian' place. It is unlikely, consequently, that Liberationists will allow the free and vigorous inquiry which the social scientific enterprise demands to undermine those present and future visions of Latin American society which they hold to be sacred.

INDEX

STUDIES IN RELIGION AND SOCIETY

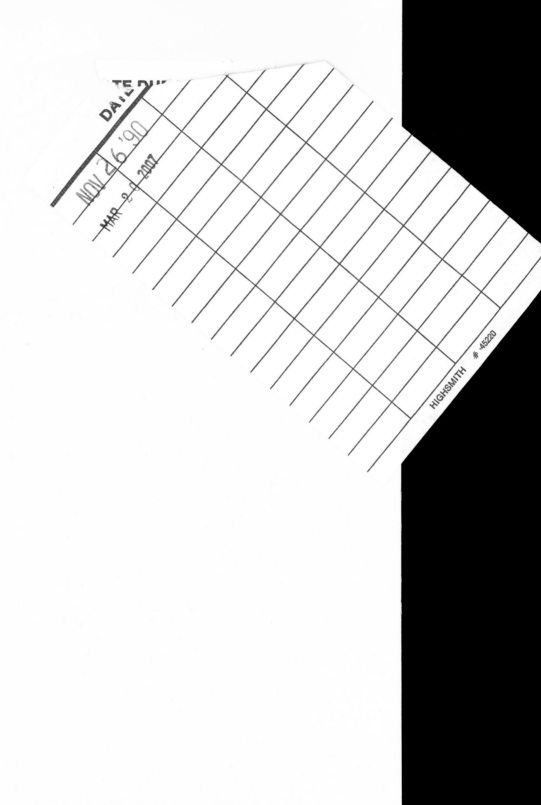